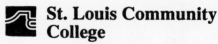 **St. Louis Community College**

Forest Park
Florissant Valley
Meramec

Instructional Resources
St. Louis, Missouri

GAYLORD

THE AMERICAN
JOURNALIST

THE AMERICAN JOURNALIST

A Portrait of U.S. News People and Their Work

SECOND EDITION

David H. Weaver and G. Cleveland Wilhoit

WITH CONTRIBUTIONS BY
LORI A. BERGEN, DAN G. DREW, AND SUE A. LAFKY

Indiana University Press

BLOOMINGTON   INDIANAPOLIS

The paper used in this publication meets the minimum requirements of
American National Standard for Information Sciences — Permanence of
Paper for Printed Library Materials, ANSI Z39.48-1984.
⊗ ™

MANUFACTURED IN THE UNITED STATES OF AMERICA

Library of Congress Cataloging-in-Publication Data
Weaver, David H. (David Hugh), 1946–.
   The American journalist : a portrait of U.S. news people and their
work. — 2nd ed. / David H. Weaver and G. Cleveland Wilhoit, with
contributions by Lori A. Bergen, Dan G. Drew, and Sue A. Lafky.
      p.   cm.
   Includes bibliographical references and index.
   ISBN 0-253-36364-0 (alk. paper), — ISBN 0-253-20668-5 (pbk. :
alk paper)
   1. Journalists — United States.   I. Wilhoit, G. Cleveland.
II. Title.
PN4871.W4   1991
070'.92'273—dc20   91-62

1 2 3 4 5   95 94 93 92 91

To Richard G. Gray, 1932–1984:
Colleague, friend, supporter

CONTENTS

PREFACE TO THE
SECOND EDITION

Half a decade has passed since the publication of the first edition of *The American Journalist*. In that time, many changes have occurred in U.S. journalism and in the society at large. In journalism, the proportion of women in daily newspapers and television remained fairly constant throughout the 1980s (about 35 percent), whereas the percentage of minorities has increased considerably in television and radio (to about 17 percent and 9 percent, respectively, from 10 percent and 4 percent in the early 1980s), but not as much in newspapers (from 3.5 percent to 7 percent). In addition, more women (50 percent) are represented in the ranks of minority newspaper journalists than among all such journalists, suggesting that as more minorities are hired, the ratio of men to women will become more balanced.

These figures come from a 1987–88 national survey of 1,200 daily newspaper journalists conducted by the American Society of Newspaper Editors (ASNE), and a mid-1989 mail survey of 493 U.S. commercial TV and 352 commercial radio stations sponsored by the Radio-Television News Directors Association (RTNDA). While such surveys of separate media industries are valuable, another large-scale survey of journalists working for all major news media is needed for the 1990s so that comparisons can be made with the early 1970s and 1980s.

That survey is still to be done, but what we have provided in this revised edition is three new chapters that pull together detailed information on the role of women in journalism; that provide a thorough comparison of television, radio, and newspaper journalists; and that analyze carefully the samples of "best work" sent to us by journalists in our original study.

Chapter 7 on women in journalism was written by Sue A. Lafky, who earned her Ph.D. in mass communication here at Indiana University and is now an assistant professor of journalism at the University of Iowa. This chapter is based on her dissertation, which drew not only upon our data from the 1982–83 national survey of journalists, but also upon many other sources of information.

Chapter 8 on television, radio and newspaper journalists was written by David Weaver, Dan Drew and Cleve Wilhoit after completion of the original *American Journalist* book. An earlier version of this chapter was published in *Journalism Quarterly* in the Winter 1986 issue. Dan Drew is professor of journalism at Indiana University, where he earned his Ph.D. in mass communication in 1973. In addition to working as a broadcast journalist in Baltimore, Washington D.C. and Los Angeles, he taught on the faculties of Stanford and the University of Wisconsin before returning to Indiana in 1984.

Chapter 9 on journalists' best work was written by Lori A. Bergen, also a former doctoral student here at Indiana and now an assistant professor of journalism at Wichita State University in Wichita, Kansas. This chapter is based upon her dissertation, which goes beyond describing the best work of journalists to linking the kinds of reporting journalists do to their personal and organizational characteristics.

We are grateful to Sue Lafky, Dan Drew and Lori Bergen for mining our original data more deeply than before, and for permitting us to include their new discoveries in this revised edition. We also appreciate very much the interest of John Gallman, director of the Indiana University Press, in publishing this new edition, especially since the original 1986 edition is now out of print.

PREFACE

This book deals with the backgrounds, education, career patterns, professional values and ethics, and job conditions of U.S. journalists working for daily and weekly newspapers, news magazines, news services, and radio and television stations during the early 1980s. Telephone interviews with 1,001 full-time journalists throughout the country in late 1982 and early 1983 were the basis for most of the findings and conclusions discussed here. The book also compares our findings with those of a 1971 national survey of journalists conducted by sociologists from the University of Illinois at Chicago. We appreciate the cooperation of Professor John Johnstone, the principal author of the earlier study, in furnishing the questionnaire and sampling plan from that survey.

Our chief concerns here are with the ways the role of the journalist in this country has changed over time; changes in the backgrounds and education of those entering journalism; the professional attitudes, beliefs, and values of journalists; effects of new technology on journalists' work; and the problem of retaining the best and brightest people in journalism. Our primary goal was systematic inquiry, but we do not claim to be value-free in our choice of questions or in our interpretations of the patterns of answers to these questions. There is no denying that we have a deep interest in improving journalism and making journalistic careers more fulfilling and rewarding. This bias undoubtedly shines through many of our interpretations and conclusions.

The writing of this book originally was to be divided fairly equally among David Weaver, Cleveland Wilhoit, and Richard Gray. But the death of Dr. Gray on November 20, 1984 necessitated a change of plans. Before his death, Dr. Gray helped write the grant proposal and helped outline and supervise some of the library research for the introductory chapter and the chapter on the education and training of journalists. His research assistant, Robert L. Baker, finished the research, wrote the first draft of the chapter on the historical view of the journalist, and assisted with some of the research on the education and training chapter. We are grateful for his assistance at a critical time and for Dean Gray's help in writing the proposal for The Gannett Foundation's grant for this study. Without his encouragement and support, our research would not have been possible. We regret that he was not able to complete his part of the book, but we are pleased to dedicate it to him.

We are indebted to many people for the opportunity to conduct this study and to complete this book. To begin with, the generosity and patience of The Gannett Foundation made it all possible. Without the interest and support of Eugene C. Dorsey, president and chief executive officer, and Gerald M. Sass, vice president/education, there would have been no study. Their support came with no strings attached. We proposed the idea for the study, and they supported it. Never was there a single request to include a question, to see a draft of the questionnaire, to look at the preliminary findings, or to influence the analysis or interpretation in any way. It was, in short, the ideal situation for an independent researcher. We are deeply grateful for their support of this study.

We are also very grateful to the journalists throughout the country who agreed to extensive interviews about their backgrounds, education, job conditions, attitudes, values, and beliefs. Their cooperation is reflected in the 80 percent response rate for completed interviews that makes this study's findings representative of the entire country's journalists.

And we are indebted to the many persons at Indiana University's School of Journalism who worked on coding, keypunching, data cleaning, data analysis, and other tasks. Graduate students Sue Lafky, Jo Ellen Fair, and Hemant Shah played key roles in supervising the coding and carrying out numerous complicated computer runs with the nearly 200,000 pieces of information generated from this study. Mary Alice Sentman, now assistant professor of journalism at the University of North Carolina, helped in drawing the sample and in persuading various news organizations to supply lists of editorial employees. Others who helped with coding and keypunching were Michael McClellan, Kathleen Ristow-Harriman, Timothy Gallimore, Dawn Kuhns, and Mary O'Doherty. Cathi Norton made it possible to meet our deadline to Indiana University Press with incredibly fast and accurate processing of the manuscript.

Frances Goins Wilhoit, head of the Weil Journalism Library, did reference work and kept us informed about books and studies related to our survey. Also helpful were Joanne Bailey, Keith Buckley, and Michael Parrish, all librarians at Indiana University.

David Nord, associate professor of journalism at Indiana University and a specialist in journalism history, made helpful suggestions on the introductory chapter. We also appreciate the suggestions of other colleagues at Indiana, especially those of Trevor Brown, Eric Fredin, Edmund Lambeth, and Dan Drew. And we thank the many journalists who have reacted to our findings, thereby helping us to validate our interpretations. Of course, those interpretations and the conclusions of this book are ours, as are any errors or shortcomings, and none of those cited above bear responsibility for them.

—1—

A Historical View of the Journalist

Late in his life, Joseph Pulitzer, considered by many to have been America's greatest nineteenth-century editor, worried deeply about the vocation he had done so much to shape.[1] "We need a class feeling among journalists," he wrote in 1904; "one based not upon money, but upon morals, education and character."[2]

At the time Pulitzer was articulating these high goals, a move was underway in his home state of Missouri to establish a separate school of journalism at the University of Missouri, which had offered courses in journalism since 1878.[3] Opening its doors in 1908, the Missouri journalism school would be the first such program in the world.[4] At his death, Pulitzer bequeathed an endowment to Columbia University that led to the establishment of a graduate school of journalism.[5] Thus began what some saw as a crucial pillar in the building of a journalism profession in America — formal centers for the education of journalists at major universities. Talcott Williams, a former newspaperman and the first director of the Columbia school in 1912, even predicted that the "State" eventually would require journalists to have minimal education and professional training that would culminate in a certifying examination.[6]

The dream of a profession of journalism that began in early twentieth-century America was painted on a canvas of very earthy origins. Less

1

than a century earlier, Alexis de Tocqueville, the French writer-politician, in his travels throughout the America of 1831, was impressed that almost every hamlet had a newspaper. But the printers who produced them were "generally in very humble position with a scanty education and vulgar turn of mind." Furthermore, the newspapers shocked de Tocqueville with their "open and coarse appeals to the passions of their readers."[7]

The concept of the American journalist changed greatly from the late seventeenth through the mid-nineteenth centuries, when the role of the journalist was fulfilled largely by the town printer and correspondent. But by the mid-nineteenth century, as American society became more complex and many of its journalistic operations resembled more a corporate enterprise, the term *journalist* came to describe all full-time reporters, writers, correspondents, columnists, newsmen (and women) and editors. In the twentieth century, this term also includes radio and television editorial personnel in news and public-affairs programming.

During the first half of the eighteenth century, seventy-three newspapers were begun in the U.S. colonies.[8] These early newspapers and the people who produced them established some enduring images, both positive and negative, that helped to define the craft of the journalist in the United States. Colonial printer-journalists, like copy editors and many supervisory editors of news organizations today, generally wrote very little. Instead, they relied on other papers, letters, travelers, ship crews, and official sources for their news. But they also relied on a second kind of journalist — the correspondent who then, as now, reported on what was going on in the hinterlands. The work of these usually unpaid correspondents was largely a combination of the functions of today's reporter, editorial writer, and town booster.[9] Their services were in great demand, because of the irregularity of intercolonial and transoceanic communication.

Being a printer-journalist was strenuous work in the colonial period, especially if one had no apprentice to operate the crude wooden hand-operated press. When Benjamin Franklin bought the *Pennsylvania Gazette* in 1729, he noted that "to publish a good News-Paper is not so easy an Undertaking as many People imagine it to be."[10] One of the drawbacks, he observed, was that early printer-journalists seemed to be known more for their mechanical ability than for their intellect. Even Richard Draper of the Boston *News-Letter*, who earned the reputation of being "the best compiler of news in his day," was disparaged by a

Harvard College student as "a meer mechanic in the art of setting and blacking types."[11] This condescending attitude is explained at least partly by the fact that colonial printer-journalists generally landed their jobs after serving as apprentices, and not as a result of formal education.

During the colonial period, the chances for employment as a journalist must have been slim. The number of weekly newspapers grew from one in 1690 to three in 1720, and to only eighteen by 1760. Of the twelve magazines that were begun between 1741 and 1760, only one lasted more than three years, and it was edited by a lawyer.[12] Information about the wages of colonial printer-journalists is scarce, but one historian has found evidence that "the ratio between the wages of the day laborer of 1754 and the journeyman printer was about as one to four."[13]

Although apprentice training continued to be the primary route into journalism even into much of the nineteenth century, such college-trained persons as Alexander Hamilton, Noah Webster, and Phillip Freneau not only gained respect from the intellectual community but also began to see new possibilities for molding public opinion.[14] The 1 daily and 34 weekly papers operating in 1783 had grown to 65 dailies and more than 1,100 weeklies in 1832, giving the United States a newspaper growth rate greater than that anywhere else in the world.[15] As the population centers shifted from the seaport towns and capital cities of the colonial period, so did media opportunities. Daily newspapers grew from 65 in 1832 to 138 by 1840, and nondailies grew from more than 1,100 in 1832 to 1,266 by 1840. Magazines increased from 1 in 1780 to 12 in 1800, and to 500 by 1840.[16]

Thus, when de Tocqueville traveled throughout the country in 1831, he stood on the very threshold of socioeconomic and technological changes that would make possible the development of news reporting and editing as an occupation separate from printing in the United States.

THE CRADLE OF THE MODERN JOURNALIST: THE PENNY PRESS

In 1833, when a twenty-three-year-old job printer by the name of Benjamin Day began the *Sun* in New York by selling copies on the street for a penny while most other newspapers were six cents by subscription only, news indeed had changed. Day's dream was "to lay before the public, at a price within the means of every one, all the news of the day, and at the same time afford an advantageous medium for advertising."[17] News in the *Sun* was not tied to the typical fare of political speeches and congressional activities which had characterized papers for half a century, or to the reprinted foreign news that likewise had consumed colonial papers. Instead, Day focused on local stories of human interest by relying largely "on police reports and the coarse humor of the police courts for interesting material for his columns."[18] Day's hiring of veteran London police reporter George Wisner for four dollars a week and a share of the profits proved a wise investment.[19] It also saw the task of journalist as reporter emerge as a full-time occupation.

Sociologist Michael Schudson has written that the idea of paying reporters "was not only novel, but to some, shocking. Until the late 1820s, New York coverage of Washington politics relied mainly on members of Congress writing occasionally to their home papers."[20] But by 1834, two of New York's eleven papers each employed four reporters, "exclusively to obtain the earliest, fullest, and most correct intelligence on every local incident."[21] The occupation of "hired" reporting was not accorded instant respect, however.

At the one-cent *Philadelphia Public Ledger* in 1836, the "reporter was not considered essential to the success of the journal giving him employment, but was rather looked upon as a hunter-up of 'unconsidered trifles' of no great value, but still well enough to have."[22] Yet, by 1854, the work of reporters was vital to Horace Greeley's *New York Tribune*, which employed fourteen of them in a rudimentary beat system: one of them kept "an eye on the Police" to chronicle arrests, then walked to the hospital "in search of dreadful accidents." Three others reported lectures and speeches going on in the city. Another reported on Jersey City, Newark, "and parts adjacent." One "gentleman" spent his time reporting fires and the "movements of the military." Two staffers translated items published in the city's ethnic papers in German, French, Italian, and Spanish. Rounding out the reporting staff of Greeley's innovative paper were the law reporter, a police-court reporter, and a collector of Marine intelligence.[23]

While the penny papers in America's large cities were establishing journalistic conventions that still exist, most of the newspapers in the country were still relatively small operations in the mid-nineteenth century. Papers in the West, especially, relied heavily on the mail for their news, just as colonial papers had relied on exchanges. However, mail service was not very reliable, prompting one Western editor to write,

"This is taxing genius as well as patience. Uncle Sam must have a very queer notion of Western editors to suppose they can make up a newspaper without news."[24]

Newspapers indeed needed news, and the telegraph — invented by Samuel F. B. Morse in 1847 — eventually did more to get the news to and from more places than any invention since the printing press. British writer Anthony Smith argues that the telegraph forged the news value of timeliness. Rapid electronic transmission of news "made possible the idea that a daily newspaper should encompass the events of a 'day.' " That introduced a "new tense" to news, that of the "instantaneous present."[25]

When the Civil War (1861-1865) became the first long-run news event to challenge the reliability of the telegraph in getting the latest battle news to all parts of the country, the reporter emerged as a more vital part of American journalism. Several hundred reporters from the North and more than one hundred correspondents from the South literally went out on the battle fronts looking for news.[26] Some of these "special" correspondents would produce truly great stories of battle, but many of them were little more than "news scavengers."[27]

While attempting to provide the "eyewitness" accounts demanded by their editors, many Civil War journalists ran into the issue of censorship, raised first by Union General William T. Sherman, who insisted that the confederacy could anticipate his strategies by reading the newspapers.[28] Although Sherman would have preferred more stringent controls on the journalists in the field, the best he could get was to require press passes as a means of accrediting reporters in the field, and "by" lines as a means of identifying reporters' names after articles containing military information.[29] For Civil War reporters making twenty-five dollars a week, the top wage of the period, by-lines became a way for some of them also to become famous.[30]

Pay Rates for Early Journalists. At mid-nineteenth century, many journalists were being hired by the month, and their wages, with board and washing, ran from twelve to twenty dollars. In America's premier newspaper position, Horace Greeley, editor of the *New York Tribune*, in 1848 allowed himself fifty dollars weekly, while his city editor got twenty dollars. By 1884, the New York *Journalist*, the first trade journal in the field, claimed that reporters averaged "fifteen to twenty-five dollars a week." Many reporters were paid on a space rate, and moonlighting was not uncommon as a means of supplementing low wages. Some journalists wrote advertisements, while others were stenographers in city courts. The standard rate of pay for magazine writers of the "quality magazines" in the period after the Civil War was ten dollars a page or three-fourths of a cent per word.[31]

By the time Joseph Pulitzer had moved east to purchase the New York *World* in 1883, the reporter had "come into his own." Historian Frank Luther Mott notes that reporters were getting frequent by-lines, especially in Sunday editions, and that those in the larger cities tended to be educated.[32] Salaries had doubled since the Civil War, with city editors getting $3,000 to $5,000 a year. The most talented reporters in the cities were earning about as much as the city editors. "But these were in the top brackets," Mott said, "and $15-a-week police-court reporters and $25-a-week general assignment men were common." Payment by space rates was also common. Pulitzer, by paying "liberal" salaries, fought the abuses of the space-rate system that still were occurring at the time.[33]

Women began to make inroads into journalism during the 1880s. The *New York Journalist*, one of the first professional journals in the field, estimated that some 500 women worked on the editorial side of American newspapers during this period, and that 200 of them were on New York papers. Women's press clubs were organized at the local level, and a Women's International Press Association was founded in 1885, with Mrs. E. I. Nicholson, of the New Orleans *Picayune*, as president.[34]

Early Professional Debate. By the late 1800s, already some journalists were characterizing their field as something more than a mere occupation. Whitelaw Reid, who had come up through the ranks as a reporter to become managing editor of Greeley's New York *Tribune*, told a meeting of the newly formed Ohio Press Association in 1879 that journalism was now a profession.[35] Some quickly disagreed with Reid's argument, as did the *Nation*, an elite journal of commentary, in an article that noted that journalism was a commercial field that required no special education.[36] And a decade later, Harvard University President Charles William Eliot was quoted as saying reporters were "drunkards, deadbeats, and bummers."[37]

Thus, we see the beginnings of the profound contradictions in both the public and self-images of the American journalist. One minute the hero, the next the rogue — the "curious existence" of the journalist, as Michael Kirkhorn has labeled it, seems harder to pin down than for other occupations.[38]

Influence of the Muckrakers. It was probably the "muckraking" journalists of the 1890s who did more to effect the self-concept of twentieth-century journalists than any other source. Lincoln Steffens' magazine exposés of government in America's "despoiled" cities had an impact far beyond their subject matter.[39] Journalism historian David Nord writes, "The work of Steffens and of his less talented imitators was appealing then and now because it took the form of objective, empirical, even scientific description."[40] Furthermore, Nord says that themes of democracy in crisis and political bosses ruling for private gain were "rooted in an essentially moral understanding of man and an optimistic faith in democracy."[41] And the spirit of reform that dominates Steffens' magazine work was also evident on the news pages of major newspapers. In Chicago, for example, Nord found the newspapers to be more than the "mere tools" of 1890s reformers. Often they were the "progenitors" of the reform political movement of the period. In St. Louis, on the other hand, of the three leading papers, only Pulitzer's *Post-Dispatch* supported public utility regulation, the focus of reform in that city during the period.[42]

The importance of the reformist tradition to the mindset of the American journalist is suggested by a number of sources. Talcott Williams, writing in 1922 as Columbia University emeritus professor of journalism, observed that interviews with "scores of journalists" and experiences with university students over a decade convinced him that a "zeal for the advance, this deep-rooted desire to see all schools, streets, homes, trade, politics grow better, burns like a flame, consuming and unconsumed, in the soul of the American journalist."[43] Williams added that he never had known a working journalist who did not have some share of that zeal.[44]

Other voices from outside the major journalism centers of the Northeast were not so sure of the twentieth-century journalist's direction. Henry Watterson, the brilliant and eloquent Southerner who edited the Louisville *Courier and Journal* for fifty years,[45] saw journalism as having "no sure standards of either work or duty." Watterson, who was said to be very popular with his fellow editors, added that the field's "intellectual landscapes are anonymous, its moral destination confused." Unlike the village lawyer or the country doctor who knew his place and kept it, Watterson said the journalist had "few, if any mental perspectives to fix his horizon — neither chart of precedent nor map of discovery upon which his sailing lines and travel lines have been marked."[46]

Watterson's characterization of journalists as victims of a confused moral destination would turn out to be the mildest of criticisms when compared to what was to come. When the muckrakers turned their pens on journalists in the 1920s, even the picture of reporters as "drunkards, deadbeats, and bummers" would suggest socially redeeming qualities. Upton Sinclair, already famed for *The Jungle*, a brutally graphic novel about the Chicago stockyards and meat-packing plants, wrote in 1919 that the price of shame was being paid by the journalists of the day. *The Brass Check* derided the journalistic "betrayal of mankind into the loathesome brothel of Big Business." The "Brass Check" found in the journalist's pay envelope each week from the forerunners of today's large media corporations was the payoff for selling the "fair body of truth" in the marketplace.[47] Sinclair would not be the last to compare journalists to prostitutes, but even he must have been surprised at the wide public acceptance of the materialistic indictment.[48]

Tools of capitalism was not a label many journalists were willing to accept, but some lamented that the businesslike organization of newsrooms in large cities was robbing them of their individuality.[49] As one retired journalist put it, "Cyclonic attics with desks geremandered into disorderly clusters by sulphurous editors were supplanted by modern city rooms as regimented as a real estate office."[50]

It was Walter Lippmann, who as a young magazine writer for the muckrakers had grown impatient with the "intellectual laziness" of Lincoln Steffens, their leading light, who would put a considerable intelligence to work on the role of the modern journalist. Lippmann, Harvard graduate and student of the emerging behavioral sciences, would conduct one of the first truly systematic analyses of journalistic performance.[51] In a special supplement to the *New Republic* in 1920, Lippmann, and his friend Charles Merz, claimed that improper training, gullibility, and a "downright lack of common sense" plagued the news coverage of the Bolshevik Revolution, the event they studied in detail. Furthermore, the news had been affected by "what men wished to see," rather than what was.[52]

That same year, Lippmann would publish *Liberty and the News*, in which he argued that a free press was not enough. It also had to be *intelligent*. Unfortunately, Lippmann observed, reporting was "not a dignified profession for which men will invest the time and cost of an education, but an underpaid, insecure, anonymous form of drudgery, conducted on catch-as-catch-can principles.'' Still, journalists were writers of the "bible of democracy, the book out of which a people determines its conduct.'' That bible, the press, had to be filled with unbiased, reliable, and accurate information that only properly trained journalists could provide.[53]

The young Lippmann, who joined the editorial-page staff of the renowned Pulitzer paper the New York *World*, very soon had grave doubts whether journalists ever could perform the critical information role of "disinterested reporting" that American democracy needed so desperately. Instead, he said in *Public Opinion*, a classic work published in 1922, the job would have to go to a class of experts, a "specialized class" working in a "national university." Those who produced the news could do little more than "signalize events."[54]

JOURNALISTS AS "COMMON CARRIERS" OF INFORMATION

Lippmann's contention never has been fully resolved. One thing that is certain, though, is that the news and the journalists who produce it — "common carriers," Lippmann had called them — increasingly have become center-stage in American life.[55] The critical importance of journalists that was articulated so well early by Lippmann was underscored at mid-century by the most prestigious blue-ribbon panel ever to aim a critical eye at the press, the Hutchins Commission on Freedom of the Press. Chaired by Robert M. Hutchins, chancellor of the University of Chicago, and working under a grant of $200,000 supplied by Henry R. Luce, publisher of *Time*, the commission of thirteen distinguished professors and cultural leaders called for press responsibility.[56]

Journalists needed to be better educated, said the commission's 1947 report, but just as important, they must extend their reporting skills to place facts in a context that gave them meaning. This call for interpretive reporting was accompanied by the implicit acknowledgment that journalists were now a leading social institution in America, a nation in which other traditional institutions, such as the church and the educational system, had been diminished, by what Lippmann had called "the acids of modernity." More important, though, was the commission's view that the journalist was fully accountable to the society, with very heavy obligations to democracy.[57]

The immensity of the burden levied on journalists by the Hutchins

Commission's conception of press responsibility — which has been widely accepted by the society at large, if not by the press — has become apparent in the growing tensions between the mass media and other major social institutions in America. But the true burden is not understood fully until one grasps just how *few* persons make up the press corps in America and, more important, how *little* we have known about them. Johnstone, Slawski, and Bowman, in a major landmark study of modern journalists in the United States in 1971, estimated that there were only about 70,000 journalists.[58] Thus, something equivalent to the population of a small American city was responsible for the lifeblood of a huge nation's public information flow. No previous inquiry had included the entire journalistic workforce as a universe, so the Johnstone findings provide the first important baseline information on the demography, education, job situations, and professional attitudes of American journalists.

The final chapter in Frank Luther Mott's classic history of American journalism was titled "The Professional Spirit." The distinguished historian said that the mid-twentieth century had seen professional attitudes in journalism gain in importance. He attributed that growth largely to higher educational levels and the emergence of professional organizations in the field.[59]

The Johnstone research, conducted ten years after the publication of Mott's final work, found some evidence to support the view of a professional spirit among the American press corps. The Johnstone team also found some serious stresses and divisions. They were impressed by the quality of talent entering the field in 1971, but they saw signs that the news media were to have trouble retaining their most promising stars. They concluded that retention of that talent would require a reassessment of how newswork was controlled, and they predicted that greater editorial autonomy would have to be granted to journalists.[60]

The main objective of our book is to compare the backgrounds, work situations, and professional attitudes of contemporary journalists with those found in this earlier study. In addition, we attempt to assess important new problems. Journalists' responses to new technology, their attitudes about key reporting practices, and their ideas about important ethical matters are covered here. Most of all, we hope the work will say something about news in America, on the assumption that, as the Johnstone group concluded, news is "ultimately what newsmen make it."[61]

Survey research is the primary source of the information compiled here, although postsurvey interviews and historical documents also are used. Lengthy telephone interviews conducted by Market Interviews — a subsidiary of the Market Opinion Research organization of Detroit — were completed with journalists across the United States. The representative random sample of 1,001 journalists — persons in news-editorial positions in the public media of newspapers, television, radio, news magazines, and news agencies — were interviewed between December 1982 and February 1983. After preliminary results were compiled from this response of 80 percent of the original sample of 1,250, the authors conducted personal interviews and group presentations with journalists to obtain their interpretations of the findings. Thus, the book attempts to provide a comprehensive portrait of the American journalist. (See Appendix I for a detailed description of the methodology.)

Organization of the Book. The following chapter provides detailed information on the employment opportunities in U.S. journalism during the dozen years between 1971 and 1983, as well as the geographic distribution of journalists and their demographics. This chapter is followed by others concentrating on education and training of U.S. journalists, job conditions and satisfactions (including earnings), professional values and ethics, and the impact of new technology on journalists' work.

These chapters document the remarkable change and growth in the occupation known as "journalist" during the late twentieth century in the United States. The findings they present stand in sharp contrast to those reported in this chapter for the colonial press, partisan press, penny press, and early-twentieth-century periods. These findings also suggest, however, that the ideas of Pulitzer and the founders of the first school of journalism about professionalization of journalists have not been forgotten, but never have been heeded fully, in this century.

—2—

Basic Characteristics
of U.S. Journalists

It is difficult to write in general terms about the characteristics of modern U.S. journalists, because they are such a diverse group. Although it may be said from our 1982-83 national telephone survey of 1,001 journalists in all news media that the "typical" U.S. journalist is a white Protestant male who has a bachelor's degree, is married and has children, is middle-of-the-road politically, is thirty-two years old, and earns about $19,000 a year, such a picture is inadequate, as this chapter will show. (See Appendix I for details of the survey methodology.) There are substantial proportions of women, non-Protestant, single, politically left and right, young and old, and relatively rich and poor journalists working in this country for a variety of news media, including daily and weekly newspapers, radio and television stations, news magazines, and news services. This chapter attempts to paint a more detailed and richer portrait of these men and women who provide the raw material for U.S. citizens' mental pictures of the world.

First, estimates of the size of the journalistic workforce are presented and compared with the estimates of Johnstone and his colleagues from their 1971 national survey of 1,328 journalists. Next, the geographic dispersion of journalists is described, followed by data on the age and sex of U.S. journalists, their ethnic and religious origins, their political views, and their media use patterns. The chapter concludes with a discussion of how U.S. journalists have changed and remained stable in the dozen years from 1971 to 1983.

SIZE OF THE JOURNALISTIC WORKFORCE

In 1971, Johnstone and his colleagues estimated the total full-time editorial workforce in English-language news media in the United States to be 69,500, with more than half of these journalists employed by daily newspapers alone. In late 1982, we estimate this editorial workforce to be 112,072, an increase of 61 percent in nearly a dozen years, with slightly less than half of these journalists employed by daily newspapers. Table 2.1 shows that the growth in raw number of journalistic jobs from 1971 to 1982 is slightly greater within the print media than within the broadcast, but the percentage of increase in jobs is substantially greater in the broadcast media than in the print media. In fact, there is a small decrease in the percentage of journalistic jobs available in daily newspapers and news magazines, as well as in the news services such as the Associated Press and United Press International.

As in the 1971 study by Johnstone and his colleagues, these estimates are for salaried editorial staff employed full-time by news organizations.

Table 2.1 Estimated Full-Time Editorial Workforce
in U.S. News Media

News Medium	April 1971[a]		November 1982	
	Number	Percentage	Number	Percentage
Daily newspapers	38,800	55.8	51,650	46.1
Weekly newspapers	11,500	16.5	22,942	20.5
News magazines	1,900	2.7	1,284	1.1
Total print media	52,200	75.1	75,876	67.1
Television (and combined radio and TV stations)	7,000	10.1	15,212	13.6
Radio	7,000	10.1	19,583	17.5
Total broadcast media	14,000	20.2	34,795	31.1
News services	3,300	4.7	1,401	1.2
Total workforce	69,500	100.0	112,072	100.0

[a]From John Johnstone, Edward Slawski and William Bowman, *The News People*. Urbana: University of Illinois Press, 1976, p.195.

They do not include the part-time correspondents, freelancers, and stringers working on an occasional basis.[2] These estimates are also subject to varying amounts of sampling error, because they are based on different-sized random samples of news organizations. The most reliable estimates are those for daily and weekly newspapers, followed by those for radio and television stations. The least reliable estimates are those for news services (based on 47 organizations) and for news magazines (based on 21 organizations). For more details on how these estimates were calculated and how the sample of journalists was drawn, see Appendix I.

The increase in the size of the *editorial* workforce since 1971 appears to have exceeded the overall growth in the number of news media employees. For example, the growth in the total workforce of U.S. newspapers — including those employed in advertising, circulation, production, and the business side — was only 13 percent from 1970 to 1983, compared to 48 percent growth in the editorial workforce. That suggests that the consolidation and concentration of news media ownership that have continued during the past dozen years have not resulted in a reduction of the resources devoted to editorial departments, contrary to what some observers have claimed.[3] In spite of the significant growth of the editorial workforce in the United States during the 1970s, it is still apparent that editorial personnel are a minority in the overall news media workforce. They are a small "profession" within a huge industry. They are also a small group when compared to the size of established professions such as law, accounting, or medicine.

Although the total number of persons who report and disseminate news is considerably larger than the number employed full-time by the various news media, it is clear from our estimates in table 2.1 that the bulk of full-time journalists are still concentrated within the print media, and especially within daily newspapers, although this concentration is less pronounced than it was in 1971, because of the growth in numbers employed in weekly newspapers, television, and radio. This concentration of journalists in the print media is not peculiar to the United States. Figures from West Germany, for example, show about three-fourths of all journalists working for print media.[4]

When we speak of "journalists" in this study — full-time or otherwise — we are using the same definition employed in the 1971 Johnstone study: those who have editorial responsibility for the preparation or transmission of news stories or other information, including full-time reporters, writers, correspondents, columnists, newsmen, and editors. In broadcast organizations, only editorial staff in news and public affairs are included. Our definition of journalist, like Johnstone's, includes editorial cartoonists, but *not* comic-strip cartoonists, and does *not* include photographers who are not also reporters. We also excluded librarians, and camera and audio technicians, as did Johnstone, on the assumption that most of them usually are directed by reporters and editors (or assist them in carrying out their work) and therefore do not have direct editorial responsibility for the information they communicate.[5]

In the 1971 study, Johnstone and his colleagues concluded that because some research had shown that television was relied upon more than print media for news about world happenings, and because television was rated the most credible information source among the major media, the public's primary information source was staffed by a relatively small cadre of journalists — some 7,000 or so.[6] This conclusion must be tempered, however, by the evidence that newspapers and television are about equal as suppliers of news if one measures actual audience exposure to the news pages and television news broadcasts. Also, several studies of media organizations and content suggest that much of what television presents as news actually originates with the large daily newspapers and news services such as the Associated Press.[7] When the findings of these studies are taken into account, it is evident that many more journalists contribute to the public's supply of national and international news than just those working for television stations.

GEOGRAPHIC DISTRIBUTION OF JOURNALISTS

Johnstone and his colleagues argue that from its beginnings, the American news industry has been concentrated in the Northeast, largely because that region was the center of population and of trade and commerce.[8] In 1971, the Johnstone study found journalists overrepresented by 12.2 percent in the Northeast as compared with the total population, and underrepresented in all other major regions of the country.[9] (See table 2.2.) A dozen years later, we find a dramatic decline in the percentage of journalists working in the Northeast, significant increases in the percentages employed in the North Central and South regions, and almost no change in the proportion located in the West. (See table 2.2.)

Table 2.2 Regional Distribution of Journalists
Compared with Total U.S. Population
(Percentage in Each Region)

Region	Journalists (1971)[a]	Journalists (1982–83)	Total Population (1970)[b]	Total Population (1981)[c]
New England	7.5	9.7	5.8	5.4
Middle Atlantic	28.8	11.2	18.3	16.1
East North Central	15.3	19.2	19.8	18.2
West North Central	7.4	11.5	8.0	7.5
South Atlantic	11.0	12.8	15.1	16.5
East South Central	4.6	6.8	6.3	6.4
West South Central	9.1	13.3	9.5	10.7
Mountain	6.4	4.5	4.1	5.1
Pacific	9.9	11.1	13.1	14.1
TOTAL	100.0	100.1[d]	100.0	100.0
Total Northeast	36.3	20.9	24.1	21.5
Total North Central	22.7	30.7	27.8	25.7
Total South	24.7	32.9	30.9	33.5
Total West	16.3	15.6	17.2	19.3

[a]From Johnstone, Slawski, and Bowman, *The News People*, p. 195. N equals 1,328, compared with 1,001 for the 1982–83 sample.
[b]U.S. Bureau of the Census, 1971, table 11, p. 12.
[c]U.S. Bureau of the Census, *Statistical Abstract of the United States, 1982–1983*, 103d edition. Washington, D.C.: U.S. Government Printing Office, 1982, p. 30.
[d]Does not total to 100.0 percent because of rounding.

The decline of more than 15 percentage points in journalists working in the Northeast from 1971 to 1983 far outstrips the 2.6 percentage point decrease in total population in that region. The 8.2 point increase in journalists employed in the South significantly exceeds the 2.6 point increase in total population in the South, as table 2.2 indicates. In general, however, the proportions of journalists working in different regions of the country in 1982-83 more closely match the proportions of total population living in these regions than in 1971, because the rapid growth of broadcast journalists (especially radio journalists) has occurred largely in the North Central and South.

Even though the percentages in table 2.2 indicate a lower concentration of full-time journalists in the Northeast than in 1971, it is still true that the major broadcast networks, news magazines, and wire services tend to be heavily concentrated in the New York area. In terms of national prominence and influence, then, the regional imbalances are much greater than table 2.2 indicates, as was true in the 1971 Johnstone study. This point is reinforced by our data on journalists' media exposure patterns, discussed later in this chapter.

Even in terms of sheer numbers, our data indicate that 71 percent of the journalists in our sample working for news magazines are located in the Northeast, as are nearly one-third of those working for news services such as the Associated Press and United Press International. (See table 2.3.) On the other hand, we find about four-fifths of the radio and TV journalists working in the North Central and South, suggesting that the increase in broadcast journalism jobs during the past decade has not been primarily in the Northeast. In addition, 70 percent of the weekly-newspaper journalists work in the North Central or South, whereas the daily-newspaper journalists are distributed fairly evenly across the four major regions of the country. In short, with the rapid growth of broadcast journalism jobs, the U.S. news industry seems to be becoming less concentrated in the Northeast, at least in terms of numbers of jobs if not in influence and prestige.

AGE AND SEX

It is clear from tables 2.4 and 2.5 that U.S. journalists are younger and more likely to be female in 1982-83 than they were in 1971, but compared to the total U.S. labor force, they are disproportionately clustered in the 25-to-34-year-old age bracket, and they are a decade behind in the proportion of women employed. (See tables 2.4 and 2.5.) In fact, the proportion of women employed as journalists in 1982-83 almost exactly matches the proportion of women in the total U.S. labor force in 1971.[10] It should be noted, however, that the proportion of women in journalism has increased at a faster rate from 1971 to 1983 than it has in the total U.S. labor force, so that the difference between the percentages of women journalists and all women employees is not as great in 1982-83 (8.7 percent) as it was in 1971 (13.3 percent). More significantly, it appears that women have made greater progress in gaining employment in journalism than they have in some of the more established professions. For example, a survey of practicing attorneys in 1980 found that only 9 percent of them were women.[11]

With regard to age, there is dramatic growth in the percentage of

Table 2.3 Distribution of Journalists by Region and News Medium (Percentage in Each Region in 1982–83)

			News Medium			
Region	*Daily Newspaper* (n=463)	*Weekly Newspaper* (n=183)	*News Magazine* (n=63)	*News Service* (n=47)	*Radio Station* (n=119)	*Television Station* (n=121)	*TOTAL* (n=996)
Northeast	23.5	12.0	71.4	29.8	9.2	5.8	20.9
North Central	26.8	44.3	4.8	27.7	40.3	30.6	30.7
South	30.2	26.2	15.9	25.5	41.2	55.4	32.7
West	19.4	17.5	7.9	17.0	9.2	8.3	15.7
TOTAL	99.9[a]	100.0	100.0	100.0	99.9[a]	100.1[a]	100.0

[a]Does not total to 100.0 percent because of rounding.

Table 2.4 Age Distribution of U.S. Journalistic Workforce
(Percentage in Each Age Group)

Age Group	Journalists (1971)[a]	Journalists (1982–83)	U.S. Civilian Labor Force 18 and Older	
			(1971)[b]	(1981)[c]
Under 20	.7	.1	5.1	8.3
20–24	11.3	11.7	13.9	14.8
25–34	33.3	44.9	22.2	28.0
35–44	22.2	21.0	20.0	19.5
45–54	18.8	10.9	21.0	15.6
55–64	11.3	8.9	14.1	11.0
65 and older	2.3	1.6	3.9	2.8
TOTAL	99.9[d]	99.1[d]	100.2[d]	100.0
Median age	36.5	32.4	39.2	33.6

[a]From Johnstone, Slawski, and Bowman, *The News People*, p. 197.
[b]U.S. Department of Labor, 1971, table A–3, p. 29.
[c]U.S. Bureau of the Census, *Statistical Abstract of the United States, 1982–1983*, 103d edition, p. 379.
[d]Does not total to 100.0 percent because of rounding.

Table 2.5 Sex of U.S. Journalists
(Percentage)

Sex	Journalists (1971)[a]	Journalists (1982–83)	Total Full-Time U.S. Labor Force 20 and Older	
			(1971)[b]	(1981)[c]
Male	79.7	66.2	66.4	57.5
Female	20.3	33.8	33.6	42.5
TOTAL	100.0	100.0	100.0	100.0

[a]From Johnstone, Slawski, and Bowman, *The News People*, p. 197.
[b]U.S. Department of Labor, 1971, table A–2, p. 28.
[c]U.S. Bureau of the Census, *Statistical Abstract of the United States, 1982–1983*, 103d edition, p. 379.

journalists from twenty-five to thirty-four years old from 1971 to 1983 (more than an 11 percentage points increase). This age category also showed the most rapid growth among all employed U.S. civilians, but the increase was only 6 percentage points. (See table 2.4.) The largest decrease for both journalists and the total U.S. labor force occurred among those forty-five to fifty-four, followed by those fifty-five to sixty-four years old.[12] In both time periods, the median age of journalists is a bit below the median age for all U.S. workers, offering some support for the oft-cited observation that journalism tends to be a younger person's occupation, because of the stresses produced by deadlines, uncooperative news sources, difficult reporting assignments, etc.

Another source of support for the idea that journalism is a younger person's occupation comes from the percentages in the top three age categories in table 2.4, which show considerably lower proportions of journalists forty-five years old and older than all civilian workers, especially in 1982-83. These percentages suggest that many journalists leave the field in their forties to pursue other occupations, and other data from our survey point to low pay as one of the primary reasons for leaving journalism.[13] (See chapter 4 on job conditions for more details.)

In addition, we find that minority journalists (blacks, Hispanics, and Orientals) are significantly younger (about 29 years old on the average) than majority white journalists (about 36 years old on the average), and that male journalists are slightly older on the average (36.5 years) than are females (34 years), suggesting that minorities and women are likely to be lower in seniority and hold less-prestigious and lower-paying journalistic jobs than white males, probably because they entered the workforce more recently. We also find that radio and television journalists are significantly younger (about 31 years old on the average) than are print journalists (about 37 years old on the average), which perhaps reflects an increased interest in broadcast journalism jobs by recent graduates of journalism schools and departments.[14]

Sex of U.S. journalists is related to their marital status and family situation. Females are less likely to be married (42 percent versus 62 percent) and are less likely to have children (65 percent versus 75 percent). But men and women journalists do not differ much with respect to education, race, religious background, political party preferences, or employment in group-owned versus independently owned media.

The proportion of women employed by different news media in 1982-83 does vary, as table 2.6 indicates, but not as much as in 1971. Fewer women journalists are employed by the wire services and by radio stations than by the other media, and the highest proportions of women work in daily and weekly newspapers and for television stations. There have been larger increases in the percentage of women employed in the

Table 2.6 Representation of Women Journalists
in Different Kinds of U.S. News Media

News Medium	Percentage Women (1971)[a]	Percentage Women (1982–83)	Case Base (1971)[a]	Case Base (1982–83)
Radio	4.8	26.3	89	118
Television	10.7	33.1	162	121
Wire Services	13.0	19.1	46	47
Daily Newspapers	22.4	34.4	920	462
Weekly Newspapers	27.1	42.1	78	183
News Magazines	30.4	31.7	33	63
			1,328	994

[a]From Johnstone, Slawski, and Bowman, *The News People*, p. 198.

broadcast media from 1971 to 1982-83 than in the print media, but radio and TV lagged far behind newspapers and news magazines in 1971. The proportions of women working for news magazines and wire services have changed very little during this time period. (See table 2.6.)

The largest increases in the percentage of women journalists from 1971 to 1982-83 have occurred among the youngest and oldest persons, although there have been notable increases in all age categories except fifty-five to sixty-four years. (See table 2.7.) The proportion of women journalists under twenty-five years old in 1982-83 does not lag much behind the proportion of women in the total labor force in 1981, and it is clear that real gains have been made in the employment of younger women as journalists in U.S. news media during the years since Johnstone's 1971 study.[15] If the news media are able to retain these younger women as employees, the percentages in the older age brackets will become closer to the percentages of women in the total labor force in the next two or three decades. As it stands now, the differences between the proportions of women journalists and the proportions of women in the total labor force in the early 1980s are substantially less than in the early 1970s.

In short, U.S. journalists are younger on the average in 1982-83 than are other U.S. workers, but less likely to be female. It appears that those in their forties and older leave journalism for other occupations in larger numbers than do U.S. workers in general, apparently because of low pay. Minority journalists are significantly younger than others, as are

Table 2.7 Representation of Women Journalists in U.S. Media
and in U.S. Labor Force by Age
(Percentage of Women)

Age Group	Journalists (1971)[a]	Journalists (1982–83)	Total Labor Force (1970)[b]	Total Labor Force (1981)[c]
Under 25	25.5	42.0	40.9	46.5
25–34	17.9	35.1	32.3	42.5
35–44	15.5	28.6	35.6	42.6
45–54	22.5	33.0	38.4	41.8
55–64	25.5	24.7	36.8	40.1
65 and older	9.1	31.2	32.8	38.7

[a]From Johnstone, Slawski, and Bowman, *The News People*, p. 198.
[b]From U.S. Bureau of the Census, 1971, table 328, p. 211.
[c]From U.S. Bureau of the Census, *Statistical Abstract of the U.S., 1982–1983*, 103d Edition, p. 379.

those working for radio and television, which suggests that minorities are more likely to be attracted to the faster-growing broadcast media than to the more traditional print media of newspapers, news magazines, and news services. This conclusion is supported by a recent national survey of journalism students which shows that significantly more black students are interested primarily in working in radio or television (nearly 35 percent) than for daily newspapers (5.4 percent), magazines (4.8 percent), or wire services (.2 percent).[16] This 1980 survey of 25,290 students from fifty-four schools of journalism also found that about 60 percent of all journalism majors were women, 7.6 percent were black, 2.3 percent were Hispanic, and nearly 2 percent were Oriental or other minority.[17]

Thus, while the proportions of women and minorities are likely to increase in U.S. journalism, especially in the broadcast media, the challenge will be to retain these people beyond their forties, if present employment patterns continue.

ETHNIC AND RELIGIOUS ORIGINS

In their 1971 study of U.S. journalists, Johnstone and his colleagues concluded that journalists come predominantly from the established and dominant cultural groups in the society. Table 2.8 indicates that that is

Table 2.8 Ethnic Origins of U.S. Journalists
Compared with Total U.S. Population
(Percentage in Each Group)

Ethnicity	Journalists (1971)[a]	Journalists (1982–83)	Total U.S. Population (1970)[b]	Total U.S. Population (1980)[c]
Black	3.9	2.9	11.1	11.8
Hispanic	1.1	0.6	4.4	6.5
Oriental (Japanese and Chinese)	—[d]	0.4	0.5	0.7
Jewish	6.4	5.8	2.6	2.6
Other (includes Caucasian)	89.7	90.3	81.4	78.4
	100.0	100.0	100.0	100.0

[a]From Johnstone, Slawski, and Bowman, *The News People*, pp. 26 and 198.
[b]From U.S. Bureau of the Census, *Statistical Abstract of the United States, 1972*, 93d edition, pp. 29, 33, 45.
[c]From *Statistical Abstract of the United States, 1982–1983*, 103d edition, pp. 32, 33, 54, 55.
[d]Not reported by Johnstone, Slawski, and Bowman, in *The News People*.

still very much the case in 1982-83. In our sample there are no gains in percentages of journalists identifying themselves as of black or Hispanic or Jewish origin from those Johnstone, Slawski, and Bowman found in 1971. That is disappointing, given the efforts to recruit minorities by U.S. news media, the increased enrollments of minorities in U.S. journalism schools, and increases in the proportions of blacks and Spanish-Americans from 1970 to 1980 as reported by the Census Bureau. Orientals (Japanese and Chinese) are the only ethnic group that appears to be represented in U.S. journalism in about the same proportion as in the overall society. Whether that was also true in 1971 is not clear, because the percentage of journalists with an Oriental background is not reported in the Johnstone study.

Johnstone and his colleagues conclude from their 1971 study that their findings support the generalization that in any society those in charge of mass communications tend to come from the same social strata as those in control of the economic and political systems, and that journalism is a "historic occupation" which has a strong sense of identity and continuity and is therefore resistant to the assimilation of minorities.[18] Given the changes in U.S. society in the past decade in the political and economic power of minorities, especially blacks, and the demographic changes in the overall society, it is disappointing that the proportions of U.S. minority journalists have not increased (and in some cases actually have decreased) since the time of the Johnstone study. This finding certainly casts doubt on the effectiveness of the efforts of many U.S. news media to recruit and retain minority journalists.

The conclusion that journalists represent the dominant and established groups in society is also supported by the figures in table 2.9, which show that U.S. journalists almost perfectly match the overall society in general religious background, and that the proportions of journalists and general public have not changed much in the past decade or so. Of the three major religious classifications in U.S. society, only Jewish persons are slightly overrepresented as journalists. Certainly with regard to ethnic and religious backgrounds, U.S. journalists represent the dominant groups in U.S. society.

This finding puts the findings of Lichter and Rothman's study of media elites in a wider perspective.[19] In their interviews with 240 journalists and broadcasters at the *New York Times*, the *Washington Post*, the *Wall Street Journal*, the three weekly news magazines, the three TV networks, and the Public Broadcasting Service, Lichter and Rothman found that half claimed no religious affiliation, 14 percent were Jewish,

Table 2.9 Religious Backgrounds of U.S. Journalists
Compared with U.S. Adult Population
(Percentage in Each Group)

Religion	Journalists (1971)[a]	Journalists (1982–83)	U.S. Adult Population (1974)[b]	U.S. Adult Population (1981)[c]
Protestant	61.5	60.5	60	59
Catholic	24.5	26.9	27	28
Jewish	6.4	5.8	2	2
Other or none	7.7	6.8	11	11
	100.1[d]	100.0	100	100

[a]From Johnstone, Slawski, and Bowman, *The News People*, pp. 90 and 225. Figures calculated from table 5.9.
[b]From George H. Gallup, *The Gallup Poll: Public Opinion, 1972–1977*, vol. 1. Wilmington, Del.: Scholarly Resources, 1973, p. 393.
[c]From *The Gallup Poll: Public Opinion, 1982*, p. 37.
[d]Does not total to 100.0 percent because of rounding.

and 23 percent were raised in a Jewish household. Only 20 percent identified themselves as Protestant, and about 12 percent said they were Catholic.[20] Ninety-five percent were white, and 79 percent were male. Our national percentages indicate far more U.S. journalists with Protestant and Catholic backgrounds than Lichter and Rothman found, far fewer journalists with Jewish heritage, and considerably more women working as journalists.

Even though the journalists included in Lichter and Rothman's study were identified as "elites" who work for the most prestigious and influential media in this country, our findings suggest that it is not accurate to think of all U.S. journalists as being as demographically unrepresentative of U.S. society as those studied by Lichter and Rothman. And, even though the "elite" journalists may be more secular, more Jewish, more white, and more male than the general U.S. society, it is questionable how much influence they exert over the hundreds of smaller news organizations throughout the country. Certainly with regard to local and regional news, the influence of these media "elites" is likely to be minimal or nonexistent. It is also questionable how much demographics affect news values. There is evidence from several studies to suggest that organizational constraints and routines are powerful shapers of news values.[21]

POLITICAL VIEWS

Journalists often have been characterized as social reformers who are likely to be more left than right on the political scale.[22] Lichter and Rothman's study of elite journalists found 54 percent placing themselves to the left of center, compared to only 19 percent who chose the right side of the spectrum. The elite journalists' voting records strongly supported their affinity for the Democratic party in presidential elections from 1964 to 1976. Over the entire period, less than one-fifth of the elite journalists studied by Lichter and Rothman voted for any Republican candidate.[23]

We also find a slight left-leaning tendency among our national sample of U.S. journalists, but it is much less pronounced than that found in Lichter and Rothman's sample of Northeastern elite journalists. Table 2.10 shows a rather dramatic tendency for journalists in 1982-83 to place themselves in the middle fifth of the political scale, as compared to journalists studied in 1971 by Johnstone and his colleagues. Table 2 10

Table 2.10 Political Leanings of U.S. Journalists
Compared with U.S. Adult Population
(Percentage in Each Group)

Political Leanings	Journalists (1971)[a]	Journalists (1982–83)	U.S. Adult Population (1982)[b]
Pretty far to left	7.5	3.8	
A little to left	30.5	18.3	21
Middle of the road	38.5	57.5	37
A little to right	15.6	16.3	32
Pretty far to right	3.4	1.6	
Don't know/Refused	4.5	2.5	10
	100.0	100.0	100

[a]From Johnstone, Slawski, and Bowman, *The News People*, p. 93.
[b]From George H. Gallup, *The Gallup Poll: Public Opinion, 1983*. Wilmington, Del.: Scholarly Resources, 1984, p. 82.

also shows that in 1982-83, about the same proportion of journalists claimed to lean left as did the U.S. adult population in a 1982 Gallup poll (21 percent), but considerably fewer journalists said they leaned to the right than did the general public, and substantially more journalists claimed to be middle-of-the-road than did the general public.

In general, then, our study suggests that U.S. journalists as a whole are less likely to claim to be conservative and more likely to claim to be middle-of-the-road than are U.S. adults; but we do not find that substantially more journalists claim to be left-of-center than do U.S. adults in general, in sharp contrast to Lichter and Rothman's finding of 54 percent of elite journalists claiming to be left-of-center politically.[24] And, in contrast to Rothman and Lichter's prediction that the next generation of journalists is likely to be somewhat more to the left than is the current generation,[25] we find substantially fewer journalists in 1982-83 than in 1971 claiming to be left-of-center politically (table 2.10), although we also find slightly more journalists in 1983 than in 1971 claiming to be Democrats (table 2.12).

When the political leanings of U.S. journalists are analyzed separately for executives (those who supervise editorial employees) and staffers of prominent and nonprominent news organizations,[26] we find more journalists (both executives and staffers) from prominent organizations claiming to be left-of-center than from nonprominent ones. (See table

2.11.) This finding is consistent with what Johnstone, Slawski, and Bowman found in 1971, and with Lichter and Rothman's 1979-80 study of elite journalists, but the differences between prominent and nonprominent organizations in 1982-83 are less pronounced than they were in 1971.

Nevertheless, there is no denying that journalists working in the prominent news organizations (almost all of which are located in the Northeast) are more likely to identify themselves as left-of-center politically than those working for less prominent organizations throughout the country, and considerably fewer journalists from the prominent organizations claim to lean to the right. (See table 2.11.) But whereas the proportions of journalists who lean right do not differ much from 1971 to 1982-83, the proportions who claim to be left-of-center are dramatically lower in 1982-83, especially within the more prominent organizations. And the proportions claiming to be in the middle of the political spectrum are dramatically higher in 1982-83, especially in the more prominent news media.

Thus, there is some support in our study for the notion that more journalists working in the prominent, or elite, media see themselves as left-of-center than do those working in less-well-known organizations, but our percentages are considerably lower (by 20 points or so) than those reported in Lichter and Rothman's 1979-80 study of elite journalists and by Johnstone and his colleagues in their 1971 study. This difference could be partially a result of the fact that we allowed our respondents to place themselves along a left-right political scale from 0 to 100 and then divided this scale into five categories, whereas Johnstone, Slawski, and Bowman asked journalists to choose from five statements describing political leanings, and Lichter and Rothman used a seven-point scale from conservative to radical. These differences in measures cannot account for the similarities in percentages of journalists in all three studies claiming to be right-of-center, however, which suggests that there have been some real changes in the political self-perceptions of U.S. journalists from 1971 to 1982-83.

Like Johnstone, we find that the managers in nonprominent news organizations are the most likely to claim to be conservative politically, but more than half of executives and staffers in both prominent and nonprominent organizations in our study place themselves in the middle of the political spectrum, whereas in the 1971 Johnstone study less than 30 percent of executives and staffers in the prominent organizations claimed to be middle-of-the-road politically.

Table 2.11 Political Leanings of U.S. Journalists in Prominent and Nonprominent Organizations (Percentage in Each Group)

	Prominent Organizations				Nonprominent Organizations			
	Executives		Staffers		Executives		Staffers	
	(1971)[a]	(1982–83) (n=58)	(1971)[a]	(1982–83) (n=78)	(1971)[a]	(1982–83) (n=413)	(1971)[a]	(1982–83) (n=450)
Left	6.8	6.9	12.4	9.0	4.1	5.6	9.5	6.4
Leaning left	56.1	24.1	40.4	24.4	24.4	16.2	31.0	18.4
Middle of the road	27.1	56.9	29.9	55.1	46.7	56.9	41.0	58.7
Leaning right	8.7	12.1	15.1	11.5	19.7	19.1	15.3	14.9
Right	1.4	0.0	2.2	0.0	5.1	2.2	3.2	1.6
	100.1[b]	100.0	100.0	100.0	100.0	100.0	100.0	100.0

[a]From Johnstone, Slawski, and Bowman, *The News People*, p. 226. Ns are not reported for 1971 because they are weighted and therefore not directly comparable to those in 1982–83. See Johnstone et al., p. 225.
[b]Does not total to 100.0 percent because of rounding.

In short, with regard to general political leanings, we find much less difference between prominent and nonprominent news organizations than did Johnstone in 1971, and we find a dramatic shift from the left to the center, especially among journalists working for the more prominent news media. And we find almost no evidence to support Rothman and Lichter's prediction that the next generation of journalists is likely to be more to the left than is the current generation.[27]

Another indicator of the political views of U.S. journalists is party identification. In 1971, Johnstone and his colleagues found that U.S. journalists were predominantly Democrats or Independents. We find the same to be true in 1982-83, but to a greater degree, because of a shift of about 7 percent from Republican to Independent. (See table 2.12.) We also find fewer journalists than the general public claiming to be either Democrats or Republicans (about 7 percent fewer in both cases), and more claiming to be Independents. These shifts are in line with the increases in proportions of journalists claiming to be middle-of-the-road politically, and they suggest that U.S. journalists are not becoming more leftist politically, but instead more likely to say they are politically independent.

Table 2.12 Political Party Identification of U.S. Journalists
Compared with U.S. Adult Population
(Percentage in Each Group)

Party	*Journalists* (1971)[a]	*Journalists* (1982–83)	*U.S. Adult Population* (1972)[b]	*U.S. Adult Population* (1982–83)[c]
Democrat	35.5	38.5	43	45
Republican	25.7	18.8	28	25
Independent	32.5	39.1	29	30
Other	5.8	1.6	—[d]	—
Don't know/Refused	.5	2.1	—	—
	100.0	100.1[e]	100	100

[a]From Johnstone, Slawski, and Bowman, *The News People*, p. 92.
[b]From George H. Gallup, *The Gallup Poll: Public Opinion, 1983*. Wilmington, Del.: Scholarly Resources, 1984, p. 43.
[c]From *The Gallup Poll: Public Opinion, 1983*, p. 42.
[d]Not reported by Gallup.
[e]Does not total to 100.0 percent because of rounding.

Furthermore, the decrease in the proportion of journalists claiming to be Republicans and the slight increase in the proportion claiming to be Democrats parallel similar trends in the overall U.S. adult population as measured by Gallup polls during the years between 1971 and 1982-83. (See table 2.12.) The chief difference between journalists and the general public is that substantially more journalists are now likely to claim to be Independents than was true in 1971. When compared to the overall population or to other professionals such as university faculty members (56 percent of whom claim to be Democrats),[28] U.S. journalists as a whole do not appear to be the "new liberals" that Lichter and Rothman term their sample of elite journalists.[29]

This conclusion is supported mostly by the percentages in table 2.13, which indicate the proportions of executives and staffers in prominent and nonprominent news media who identify with each political party. In 1982-83, the only group claiming to be Democrats in greater proportion than the overall public is staffers working in prominent organizations. All other groups in 1982-83 identify with the Democratic party in lower proportions than does the U.S. public. On the other hand, the proportions of journalists claiming to be Republicans has declined substantially in all groups except prominent media executives, with increases in those now claiming to be Independents. Among journalists working for nonprominent organizations, we do not find much difference in political party preference between executives and staffers, but among those working for prominent organizations we find the staffers significantly more likely to be Democrats than the managers, and significantly less likely to be Independents than their bosses. That suggests that perhaps Lichter and Rothman's prediction that the next generation of journalists is likely to be more liberal applies only to staffers in the prominent news media.

In short, with regard to political attitudes of U.S. journalists, we find a left-leaning tendency, but it is much less pronounced than what Johnstone found in 1971 or what Lichter and Rothman found in their study of media elites in 1979-80. We find substantially more U.S. journalists claiming to be middle-of-the-road and Independents than Johnstone found in 1971, and we generally find no substantial increases in the proportions claiming to be Democrats. When compared to the U.S. adult population, the only journalists who are more likely to be Democrats are staff workers at prominent Northeastern media, and even they are only 6 percent more likely to identify with Democrats than is the U.S. public.

Thus, our national study of U.S. journalists suggests a trend toward

Table 2.13 Political Party Identification of U.S. Journalists in Prominent and Nonprominent Organizations (Percentage in Each Group)

| | Prominent Organizations | | | | Nonprominent Organizations | | | |
| | Executives | | Staffers | | Executives | | Staffers | |
Party	(1971)[a]	(1982–83) (n=58)	(1971)[a]	(1982–83) (n=78)	(1971)[a]	(1982–83) (n=413)	(1971)[a]	(1982–83) (n=450)
Democrat	44.0	33.3	43.2	50.7	31.1	37.7	35.3	39.8
Republican	8.5	8.8	15.6	4.0	31.8	22.4	27.8	19.8
Independent	44.7	57.9	33.7	44.0	30.6	37.7	31.8	39.1
Other	2.7	0.0	7.4	1.3	6.5	2.2	5.2	1.4
	99.9[b]	100.0	99.9[b]	100.0	100.0	100.0	100.1[b]	100.1[b]

[a]From Johnstone, Slawski, and Bowman, *The News People*, p. 226. Ns are not reported for 1971 because they are weighted and therefore not directly comparable to those in 1982–83. See Johnstone et al., p. 225.
[b]Does not total to 100.0 percent because of rounding.

the center of the political spectrum and away from the right and the Republican party, but no visible swing to the left. This conclusion holds regardless of kind of ownership of the news organization or sex and age of the journalist, although journalists working in the West and the Northeast rate themselves as somewhat more liberal than do others, as do those working for larger organizations, news magazines, daily newspapers, and the wire services. Overall, though, we do not find differences in political views between journalists in the top news media and others that are as great as Johnstone found in 1971.

MEDIA USE

As might be expected, U.S. journalists are heavy consumers of not only their own media but also the news produced by journalists in other media. Our journalists reported reading an average of 3.5 different newspapers each week, watching an average of 3.3 TV network news shows and 4.2 local TV news shows per week, and reading an average of 3.7 magazines regularly. (See table 2.14.) These figures indicate that

Table 2.14 Frequency of General Media
Use by U.S. Journalists
(Percentage in Each Category)

Frequency	Number of Different Newspapers Read per Week	Number of TV Network News Shows per Week	Number of Local TV News Shows per Week	Number of Magazines Read Regularly
0	.7	21.6	13.0	6.1
1	7.3	9.6	6.6	10.1
2	21.2	10.4	7.1	19.2
3	28.8	12.9	11.6	21.6
4	19.0	10.8	8.4	14.4
5	12.5	12.2	15.6	11.1
6	5.7	2.9	6.6	7.4
7	2.0	19.4	31.1	3.9
More than 7	2.8	—	—	6.2
	100.0	99.8[a]	100.0	100.0
Average:	3.5	3.3	4.2	3.7

[a]Does not total to 100.0 percent because of rounding.

journalists are much more exposed to newspapers than are nonjournalists. Less than 25 percent of the public reads two or more newspapers,[30] whereas 92 percent of our journalists report reading two or more different newspapers each week. These figures are very close to those found by the Burgoons in the 1981-82 studies of journalists working in ninety-one daily newspapers and seven television stations, and they confirm the Burgoons' conclusion that "information suppliers are information addicts."[31]

The number of different newspapers read each week is significantly higher (4.0) for those who majored in journalism in graduate school and for those with any college education than for other journalists. Membership in a journalistic organization, being male, working in a larger print organization, working in the Northeast, and being a supervisor or editor are all associated with reading more newspapers each week. The Burgoons also found that editors generally read a greater range of newspapers and magazines than do reporters.[32]

Table 2.15 shows that the most frequently read newspapers by U.S. journalists are the *New York Times*, the *Wall Street Journal*, and the *Washington Post*. Although Johnstone did not ask U.S. journalists in 1971 about frequency of reading, he did ask them to name what they considered to be the fairest and most reliable news organizations, and those most often relied upon in their work. In both of Johnstone's lists, the same three newspapers that we found most often read appeared at the top, along with the Associated Press and United Press International wire services.[33] As with Johnstone's study, our figures indicate that only a small number of newspapers have nationwide visibility among substantial proportions of journalists, and these newspapers tend to be located in the Northeast or in the Washington-Baltimore area.[34] This is true even for the most notable newcomer on the list, *USA Today*.

Although our list of newspapers most often read by U.S. journalists is similar to the lists of the fairest and most relied upon compiled by Johnstone and his colleagues from their 1971 study, there are some newcomers in addition to *USA Today*, including the Boston *Herald-American*, the Dallas *Times-Herald*, the Houston *Chronicle*, the New York *Post*, the Dallas *News*, the Indianapolis *Star*, the Atlanta *Constitution*, and the Des Moines *Register*. It should be noted, however, that all of these newcomers are read regularly by 5 percent or less of the journalists in our sample, whereas the leading papers (the *New York Times* and the *Wall Street Journal*) are read by one-fourth or more of

Table 2.15 Newspapers Most Often Read by U.S. Journalists
(Percentage Reading Once a Week or More)

Newspaper	Percentage of Journalists Mentioning (n = 994)[a]
New York Times	33.3
Wall Street Journal	25.3
Washington Post	15.3
USA Today	9.3
Boston Globe	9.2
Chicago Tribune	9.0
Los Angeles Times	8.7
Boston Herald-American	5.2
San Francisco Chronicle	4.3
Dallas Times-Herald	4.0
Houston Chronicle	3.9
Chicago Sun-Times	3.8
New York Post	3.7
New York News	3.6
Dallas News	3.4
Christian Science Monitor	3.3
Houston Post	3.3
Indianapolis Star	3.1
Atlanta Constitution	2.9
Des Moines Register	2.4
Minneapolis Tribune and Star	2.4
Philadelphia Inquirer	2.4
Louisville Courier-Journal	2.3
Miami Herald	2.3

[a]Percentages total to more than 100.0 because each journalist could name up to seven different newspapers. Only those newspapers mentioned by 2.0 percent or more of all responding journalists are listed here.

the journalists in our sample and the Gannett journalists studied by the Burgoons in 1981-82.[35] Since the Johnstone study in 1971, the *Wall Street Journal* has significantly overtaken the *Washington Post* as the second-most-read or relied-upon newspaper by U.S. journalists.

Not surprisingly, readership of these elite newspapers varies by region of the country, and size and type of news organization. There is a strong tendency for more journalists working in the Northeast and in the largest organizations to read the *New York Times,* and for those working in the West to read the *Los Angeles Times*. Journalists working for news magazines are much more likely to read the *New York Times* regularly (73 percent do) than are those working for other kinds of news media, and those journalists working for the wire services and news magazines are more likely to read the *Wall Street Journal* regularly than are other journalists.

Journalists' television network news viewing frequency is about the same as the general public's (34 percent of journalists view each weekday, compared to about 32 percent of the public).[36] The same is true for local TV news viewing (53 percent of the journalists view each weekday, compared to about 50 percent of the public).[37] The average number of days that journalists view network and local TV news shows (3.3 and 4.2) is very similar to the averages found by the Burgoons in their 1981-82 studies of daily-newspaper and television journalists.[38] Like the Burgoons, we find that those journalists with less formal education report watching network TV news more often than those with more education.[39]

We also find that those with a graduate education in journalism, those working for larger organizations, and those who are male watch TV news less often than others. But frequency of viewing does not vary significantly by undergraduate major or by type of job (reporter, editor, supervisor). It does vary by type of media organization, however, with television journalists (but not radio) viewing significantly more often than journalists working for other media, a finding replicated in the Burgoon study of Gannett newspapers and television stations.[40]

Our journalists reported reading an average of 3.7 different magazines regularly (almost every issue), as indicated in table 2.14. This figure is considerably lower than the average of 6.0 different magazines a month found by the Burgoons in their study of eight daily newspapers,[41] which suggests that journalists working for news organizations other than daily newspapers read fewer magazines on the average than do those working for daily papers. A check of our data shows that the number of magazines read regularly does vary by type of media organization, with radio and weekly newspaper journalists reading considerably fewer (about 3) magazines regularly than news magazine, television, and daily-newspaper journalists. Not surprisingly, news magazine journalists report reading the most (nearly 8) different magazines regularly. Although no direct comparable figures could be located for the U.S. public, the research director of the Magazine Publishers Association reports that the average U.S. adult reads 1.13 magazines a day, and between 8 and 10 different magazine *copies* (not different magazine titles) each month.[42]

While it is not possible to tell from the Magazine Publishers Association data whether journalists read fewer or more different magazines than do Americans in general, our data indicate that U.S. journalists are far more likely to read one of the three weekly news magazines than is the U.S. public. Table 2.16 shows that about half of the journalists in our sample report reading *Time* and *Newsweek* regularly, and about one-sixth read *U.S. News and World Report*. These percentages stand in sharp contrast to a 1977 national sample study of 3,000 adults that shows that 21 percent read one or more of the three weekly news magazines.[43] Other magazines read by more than 10 percent of U.S. journalists include regional or city publications, *Sports Illustrated*, and *Atlantic Monthly*. (See table 2.16.) In general, the list of magazines most often read by U.S. journalists in table 2.16 is focused on the leading information and opinion publications, rather than on the more mass-circulation entertainment ones. This emphasis on information and opinion magazines is also apparent in the 1981-82 studies of daily-newspaper and television journalists conducted by the Burgoons, where the most frequently read magazines were *Time*, *Newsweek*, *National Geographic*, the *New Yorker*, *Reader's Digest*, *Esquire*, *People*, and *U.S. News and World Report*.[44]

In short, the findings of our data on U.S. journalists' media consumption show that these journalists pay far more attention to newspapers than do average Americans, although no single paper commands a majority of readers. Journalists are also far more likely to read one of the three weekly news magazines (especially *Time* or *Newsweek*) than is the public, and *Time* magazine is read regularly by slightly more than half of all U.S. journalists.

In all, though, only three newspapers and five general-interest magazines are read regularly by more than 10 percent of U.S. journalists, and all of these publications are based on the East Coast, reinforcing Johnstone, Slawski, and Bowman's conclusions regarding the pyramidal shape of the prestige hierarchy within the news industry and the dominance of the eastern seaboard.[45] Our results also support the Burgoons' finding that U.S. journalists are especially exposed to the print media and have ample opportunity to keep up with the major developments in society as reported in these media.[46] (For a discussion of journalists' exposure to specialized professional publications, see chapter 4 on professionalism.)

Table 2.16 Magazines Most Often Read by U.S. Journalists
(Percentage Reading Almost Every Issue)

Magazine	*Percentage of Journalists Mentioning* $(n = 939)$[a]
Time	51.9
Newsweek	47.6
U.S. News and World Report	16.0
Regional or city magazines	15.9
Sports Illustrated	15.5
Atlantic Monthly	10.1
National Geographic	9.4
The New Yorker	9.5
Esquire	8.7
Reader's Digest	8.5
Rolling Stone	7.3
Broadcasting	6.1
People	5.6
Playboy	5.2
Harpers	4.4
Life	4.4
Smithsonian	4.2
Sporting News	3.9
Business Week	3.1
Consumer Reports	2.7
The New Republic	2.7
Fortune	2.3
Better Homes and Gardens	2.2
Mother Jones	2.2
Redbook	2.2
Money	2.1

[a]Percentages total to more than 100.0 because each journalist could mention up to 13 different magazines. Only those magazines mentioned by 2.0 percent or more of all responding journalists are listed here.

In addition, we find that those journalists most exposed to newspapers and news magazines work for the larger print organizations in the Northeast, belong to a professional journalistic organization, have studied journalism in graduate school, tend to be male, and are editors or supervisors. Mostly the opposite is true for those journalists who say they watch television news most frequently, except that journalists in group-owned organizations watch TV network news more and read local and regional newspapers less than those in independently owned media. In sum, our results suggest that those journalists who work for the most widely read and prestigious media are also those who read other newspapers and news magazines the most frequently.

CONCLUSIONS

This analysis of the basic characteristics of U.S. journalists in 1982-83 finds more differences from than similarities to such characteristics in 1971. Among the most striking differences are these:

1. The size of the journalistic workforce has increased 61 percent during the 1970s, with the greatest percentage of growth in radio and television.

2. There appears to be a dramatic decline in the percentage (not necessarily the actual numbers) of journalists working in the Northeast, and significant increases in the percentages working in the North Central and South.

3. The proportions of journalists working in different regions of the country more closely match the population percentages in those regions than in 1971, largely because of the growth of the number of broadcast journalists in the North Central and South.

4. U.S. journalists in 1982-83 are younger and more often female than in 1971. Broadcast journalists are significantly younger than those working for the print media, and minority journalists are younger on the average than nonminorities.

5. More journalists are leaving the field after age forty-five than in 1971, primarily because of low salaries.

6. There has been a significant gain in the proportion of women journalists employed in U.S. media during the 1970s. Overall, the proportion of women journalists has increased from about one-fifth in 1971 to about one-third in 1982-83, and this proportion is likely to increase further, given the 60 percent enrollment of women in U.S. journalism schools.

7. The largest increases in the percentages of women journalists have occurred in the broadcast media. The proportions of women employed as journalists in the various U.S. media are more consistent in 1982-83 than in 1971.

8. There are proportionately fewer blacks, Hispanics, and Jews in U.S. journalism in 1982-83 than in 1971, although the actual numbers are up somewhat. This finding suggests that although efforts to recruit and retain women journalists in U.S. news media have been successful, such efforts with regard to minorities have not been effective.

9. Politically, many more journalists place themselves in the middle of the scale than in 1971, and significantly fewer put themselves on the right. That suggests that U.S. journalists as a whole are becoming more centrist, not more leftist as some researchers have argued.

10. We find much less difference overall in the political leanings of journalists working for prominent and nonprominent organizations than Johnstone found in 1971, although we do find managers in the nonprominent organizations to be the most conservative, and staffers in the prominent media to be the most inclined to say they are Democrats. We do not find the managers in the prominent organizations to be left of the staffers, as was found in 1971.

These are the chief differences in basic characteristics of U.S. journalists from 1971 to 1982-83. Although the number of similarities is smaller, there are several notable ones, including:

1. The bulk of full-time U.S. journalists are still concentrated in the print media, especially in daily newspapers.

2. It is still true that the most prominent and most widely read news media by other journalists are concentrated on the eastern seaboard.

3. U.S. journalists come overwhelmingly from the established and dominant ethnic, racial, and religious groups in the society. The proportions of journalists from different religious backgrounds are almost identical to those in 1971 and to the population at large, in contrast to the findings of a recent study of elite journalists in the Northeast.

4. Journalists working for the more prominent media organizations are more likely to be left-of-center politically, as was true in 1971, but the difference between them and other journalists is not as great as it was in 1971, contradicting Rothman and Lichter's prediction that the next generation of U.S. journalists is likely to be more to the left than is the current generation.

Although Johnstone and his colleagues asked U.S. journalists in 1971 which news organizations were the most reliable and the most relied-upon in their own work, no questions were asked about general media use by journalists. We did ask about media use and found the following:

1. U.S. journalists, not surprisingly, are much heavier users of newspapers than the general public, but journalists are not more frequent viewers of television news, either local or network.

2. The most avid readers of newspapers are journalists with college educations who are members of a professional journalistic organization, and who are editors or supervisors in large print media organizations in the Northeast.

3. Only three newspapers, all on the East Coast (the *New York Times*, the *Wall Street Journal*, and the *Washington Post*), are read regularly by more than 10 percent of all U.S. journalists.

4. The number of magazines read regularly by U.S. journalists varies by type of media organization, with radio and weekly-newspaper journalists reading fewest, and news magazine journalists reading the most. Only five magazines are read regularly by more than 10 percent of all U.S. journalists, and all of these magazines are based on the East Coast.

5. Journalists are far more likely than the general public to read one of the three weekly news magazines regularly, especially *Time* and *Newsweek*. Most magazines read often by journalists are information and opinion publications, rather than mass-circulation entertainment ones.

These, then, are the main findings with regard to basic characteristics of U.S. journalists working for both print and broadcast media. They suggest both progress and problems — progress in matching journalists to population distribution, in recruiting women, in becoming more balanced politically, in reflecting the country in terms of religious backgrounds, and in keeping in touch with current events. But there are problems in retaining journalists beyond their mid-forties (primarily because of low salaries), in recruiting and retaining minorities, and in relying primarily on a very few East Coast newspapers and magazines as national and international information sources.

The next chapter discusses the education and training of U.S. journalists, followed by chapters on professional values and ethics, work conditions, and the impact of new technology.

—3—

Education and Training

In 1971, nearly three-fifths of all U.S. journalists were college graduates, and 34 percent of them had majored in journalism.[1] In 1983, nearly three-fourths of all U.S. journalists had completed a college degree, and 40 percent of them had majored in journalism. Thus, in a dozen years the proportion of U.S. journalists with a journalism degree jumped from slightly more than one-fifth to nearly one-third. This chapter discusses the educational backgrounds and preferences of U.S. journalists in light of the rapidly increasing numbers of journalism school graduates entering daily and weekly newspapers, radio and television news departments, and news magazines and news services. Whenever possible, comparisons are made with the 1971 Johnstone study of U.S. journalists, and also with U.S. Census figures for the population in general. But first, a brief historical look at journalism education in the United States is provided as a backdrop for the survey findings.

PAST DEVELOPMENTS IN JOURNALISM EDUCATION

The history of journalism education in the United States can be organized roughly into four periods. The first, loosely defined, extends from the 1700s to the 1860s. During this time, American journalism, as is still the case in much of the rest of the world, was basically an apprenticeship system.[2] Benjamin Franklin, for example, learned the trade as an apprentice in his brother's Boston printing shop and later refined his skills in one of London's leading printing houses. Subsequent early American journalists usually followed this apprenticeship path or perfected their writing skills in colleges on the eastern seaboard or abroad. Some of the early "journalists," such as John Peter Zenger, were really printers and little else — they set other persons' work into type. Other participants in early American journalism, such as Thomas Paine, were mainly writers without formal training whose knowledge of people and affairs came largely from the "school of life." This early emphasis on the school of life reinforced the idea that a journalist should be a "gifted amateur" rather than a more narrow specialist, and that a journalist should be broadly and liberally educated.[3]

The second period of U.S. journalism education, which extends from the 1860s to the 1920s, brought more formal journalism instruction in higher education. General Robert E. Lee, president of what is now Washington and Lee University, started training in printing after the Civil War. Other universities followed suit. Kansas State College began instruction in printing in 1873, the University of Missouri in 1878, and the University of Pennsylvania in 1893. Usually these classes were taught by former newspapermen. For example, Joseph French Johnson, a former financial editor of the Chicago *Tribune*, taught courses at Pennsylvania, and newspaperman Walter Williams headed the first separate school of journalism, founded in 1908 at the University of Missouri.

Most of these early journalism education programs stressed training in writing and editing at the undergraduate level, first within English departments, then in independent departments and schools of journalism. This undergraduate training later developed into master's-level instruction in writing and editing at Columbia and other schools.

The third period, roughly from the 1920s to the 1940s, saw journalism programs in the United States established on a much firmer basis. A number followed the pattern set by Missouri in 1908 and Columbia in 1912 of becoming independent professional schools. Others became separate departments within colleges of liberal arts. This pattern was followed at the University of Wisconsin, where Willard G. Bleyer started teaching journalism classes in 1904, and at the University of Minnesota, where Ralph Casey, a Bleyer student, took over the journalism program in 1930.

In 1927, Bleyer created the Ph.D. minor in journalism in Wisconsin's doctoral programs in political science and sociology. Although his own background was in English, Bleyer located journalism in the social sciences rather than in the humanities — a decision that had a far-reaching impact on the kind of journalism research and education carried out in many U.S. colleges and universities in the years to come.

Many founders of the major journalism programs around the country came out of the journalism minor Ph.D. program at Wisconsin, including Chilton Bush, Ralph Nafziger, Curtis MacDougall, and Ralph Casey. They carried empirical social-science assumptions with them to such schools as Stanford, Northwestern, and Minnesota.[4] The main thrust at this time was to follow the Bleyer school of thought by integrating journalism with the social sciences. As a result, journalism schools began hiring Ph.D.s primarily from political science, sociology, and psychology. Some came from the humanities, especially history, but often even they took a social-science viewpoint.

Largely because of this shift toward the social sciences in many leading U.S. journalism schools, more emphasis began to be put on ways of observing the world and systematically recording and analyzing such observations. More emphasis was placed on generalizing from specific observations, especially in journalism and mass-communication research.

The final period of U.S. journalism education, which extends from the 1940s to the present, began with the establishment of a journalism research division at the University of Minnesota in 1944. Other institutions — particularly in the Big Ten — also established doctoral programs of their own. Stanford on the West Coast and North Carolina on the East Coast extended this tradition beyond the Midwest. Typically, these Ph.D. programs were run by faculty members who had gained their terminal degrees in sociology, psychology, or political science. As a result, their protégés tended to be more closely attuned to social-science perspectives and methods than to humanistic ones.

Schools and departments of journalism have grown steadily in number, and in numbers of students, since the turn of the century. As Lindley notes, journalism's emergence in the academic world was part of a great surge in education for the professions and the so-called "emerging professions," which now dominates undergraduate education.[5] A tabulation of the number of schools with four-year journalism programs by the *Journalism Bulletin* showed an increase from 4 in 1910 to 28 in 1920, and 54 in 1927.[6] These programs produced fewer than 25 graduates a year in 1910, and 931 in 1927. Fifty years later, in 1977, Paul

Peterson reported 266 colleges and universities offering a major in journalism and/or mass communications, with a total of 64,502 declared journalism majors.[7] In 1971, when the Johnstone survey of U.S. journalists was conducted, Peterson reported 36,697 students who claimed journalism as a major and "slightly more than 200 colleges and universities offering majors in journalism."[8] By the fall of 1982, just before this present study was conducted, 304 schools reported programs in journalism.[9] Of these, 216 participated in Peterson's annual enrollment survey and reported total enrollments of 91,016 journalism or mass communication majors.[10]

RECENT DEVELOPMENTS IN JOURNALISM EDUCATION

Thus, it is obvious that tremendous growth in both the numbers of journalism programs and the numbers of journalism students has occurred in this country since the beginning of the century, especially during the 1970s. The early programs were concerned mostly with reporting, copy reading, feature writing, editorial writing, criticism, history, comparative journalism, and ethics, according to a survey of about 40 institutions in 1924 reported by Lindley.[11] More modern programs of journalism and mass-communication education also offer many of these same "news-editorial" subjects, but in addition include courses in photojournalism, public relations, advertising, and radio and television. Peterson's 1982 survey of 216 journalism schools shows that of 17,316 journalism baccalaureate degrees identified by sequence, 26 percent were in news-editorial, 21 percent in radio-TV, 13 percent in public relations, 19 percent in advertising, and 21 percent in other areas.[12]

In autumn 1980, Peterson conducted a study of 25,290 students from fifty-four schools and departments of journalism to determine journalism students' career expectations.[13] This study, funded by the Gannett Foundation, was largely in response to Ben Bagdikian's charge in the *Atlantic* in 1977 that more than enough journalism students were enrolled in journalism courses to replace every professional journalist employed on an American newspaper.[14] Peterson found, however, that only 11 percent of all journalism majors were interested in newspaper positions upon completion of college.[15] In contrast, nearly 18 percent wanted to work in public relations, and nearly 16 percent in advertising.

Even though newspapers were ranked third (behind public relations and advertising) in Peterson's 1980 survey of career preferences of journalism majors, the annual Dow Jones Newspaper Fund/Gallup survey of journalism/communications *graduates* indicated that daily newspapers continued to hire more college journalism graduates (about 14 percent in 1980 and 12 percent in 1982) than any other media-related field.[16] Of about 18,600 journalism/communications graduates who received bachelor's degrees in 1982, slightly more than one-half (53.2 percent) found media jobs, with 11.8 percent going to daily newspapers, 10.4 percent to public relations, 8.2 percent to advertising agencies, and 5.9 percent to television stations. The remaining graduates who found media jobs went to weekly newspapers, radio stations, magazines, and news services. Those who didn't find media jobs went to graduate and law schools (about 9 percent) or to nonmedia jobs (nearly 23 percent). Nearly 12 percent were unemployed after graduation, and 3 percent said they were not looking for work.[17]

Thus, at the same time that journalism education in the United States has expanded greatly in numbers of programs and in numbers of students, the recent surveys cited above indicate that the scope of journalism education also has expanded dramatically from its original emphasis on newspapers to include public relations, advertising, radio-television, and magazines. And the interests and career patterns of journalism students have both reflected and spurred this expansion of the original definition of journalism and journalism education.

But what are the educational backgrounds of working journalists in this country? How many have graduated from college? From a graduate school? What fields of study did they pursue in college and graduate school? Where did they attend university classes? Is attending college in a certain region of the country linked to working in that region? How many journalists would like additional education? In what subjects? To answer these and other questions, we turn to our survey findings from interviews with 1,001 U.S. journalists from throughout the country during December 1982 and January-February 1983.

EDUCATIONAL BACKGROUNDS OF U.S. JOURNALISTS

As Johnstone and his colleagues pointed out in the book based on their 1971 national survey of U.S. journalists, it would be redundant to ask most professional persons about their educational backgrounds, because their professional standing is based on certain programs of studies.[18] Although that is certainly true for medical doctors, lawyers, licensed nurses, and certified public accountants, it is not true for journalists. There is no single set of requirements for becoming a journalist — in fact, it is not absolutely necessary for one to have graduated from college to become a journalist, although that is more and more the basic requirement. There is no specific credential, license, or certificate necessary to enter the field of journalism, and there is still considerable disagreement among those currently in the field as to how one should go about becoming a journalist, as was true in 1971.

Years of Schooling. Yet, most journalists do graduate from college, and nearly half of them major in journalism, as noted at the beginning of this chapter. The figures in table 3.1 indicate a dramatic increase in the proportions of journalists who are college graduates, especially those below thirty-five years of age. Overall, slightly more than one-half of the journalists in our study claimed to have graduated from college, compared to about 40 percent who made this claim in 1971. When the percentages who have graduate training and degrees are included, the figures rise to 70.1 percent in 1982-83 and 58.2 percent in 1971.[19] But among those thirty-four and younger, the percentage of four-year college graduates jumped from 41 to more than 60. In fact, for those journalists younger than twenty-five years of age, the percentage of four-year college graduates was nearly 70, practically double what it was in 1971! Thus, there is no doubt that younger journalists in the United States are predominantly college graduates now, which was not the case only a dozen years ago. That is especially true if the percentages of those with graduate training and degrees are added to the percentages of four-year college graduates.

The percentage of U.S. journalists with graduate degrees also has increased from 1971 to 1982-83. Overall, this increase is small, even negligible (from 8 percent to 11 percent). But among journalists thirty-five to forty-four years old, there is a more substantial increase in the proportion holding graduate degrees (from 11 percent in 1971 to 18 percent in 1982-83).

When journalists are compared to the overall U.S. population, it is clear that journalists are significantly more likely to be college graduates than are members of the general population. That was true in 1971, as

Table 3.1 Amount of Formal Schooling by Age
(Percentage of U.S. Journalists with Different Amounts of Schooling)

Highest Educational Attainment	Under 25		25–34		35–44		45–54		55 +		TOTAL	
	1971[a]	1982-83	1971	1982-83	1971	1982-83	1971	1982-83	1971	1982-83	1971	1982-83
Some high school	1.7	.9	.8	0.0	1.8	0.0	1.8	.9	3.9	1.9	1.8	.6
Graduated from high school	3.8	8.6	8.6	3.3	11.4	5.2	12.3	16.5	28.8	20.2	12.2	9.4
Some college	44.4	16.4	26.6	14.0	22.7	21.4	29.9	26.6	21.8	20.2	27.9	19.7
Graduated from college	41.4	69.8	41.4	63.3	42.7	45.7	37.8	34.9	31.5	43.3	39.6	50.3
Some graduate training	6.0	1.7	13.9	10.2	9.9	9.5	10.6	8.3	7.4	6.7	10.5	8.7
Graduate degree(s)	2.7	2.6	8.7	9.1	11.4	18.1	7.6	12.8	6.6	7.7	8.1	11.1
TOTAL	100.0	100.0	100.0	99.9	99.9	99.8	100.0	100.0	100.0	99.1	100.1	99.8
N	130	116	409	449	310	210	274	109	180	104	1,303	988

[a]From John Johnstone, Edward Slawski, and William Bowman, *The News People*. Urbana: University of Illinois Press, 1976, p. 200.

well as in 1982, but the difference between the percentages of college-graduate journalists and college graduates in general has increased during the 1970s. That is because the percentage of journalists with college degrees has increased about 12 points, whereas the percentage of the general population with college degrees has increased by about 6 points.

Johnstone and his colleagues argued in 1971 that the most important feature of these figures on years of schooling was the heterogeneity of educational backgrounds they revealed, for while graduation from college was the modal educational achievement in 1971, there were sizable minorities who never had been to college and who had earned advanced degrees.[20] In 1982-83, we find less of this heterogeneity of educational achievement. The proportion of full-time journalists without college degrees has dropped considerably (from nearly 42 percent in 1971 to not quite 30 percent in 1983), and the proportion earning advanced degrees has not increased much. That means, then, that the basic undergraduate college degree is much more the standard educational background of U.S. journalists than was the case twelve years ago. It is also obvious from table 3.1 that far fewer young persons are becoming journalists without having completed a college degree than was true in 1971.

Variation among Media. In 1971, Johnstone found that different kinds of news organizations varied markedly in the percentages of college graduates they employed. Table 3.2 indicates that that is still true

Table 3.2 Number of U.S. Journalists Who Are College
Graduates by Media Type
(Percentage who Graduated from College)

Media Type	Percentage 1971[a]	Percentage 1982–83	(N)
News Magazines	88.2	93.7	63
Wire Services	80.4	95.7	47
Daily Newspapers	62.6	74.4	462
TV	58.7	80.2	121
Weekly Newspapers	43.6	69.8	182
Radio	36.6	52.5	118
Total Print Sector	59.4	76.4	754
Total Broadcast Sector	47.7	66.5	239
Total Sample	58.2	73.7	998

[a]Johnstone's number of cases are not reported here because they were weighted and not directly comparable to ours. From Johnstone, Slawski, and Bowman, *The News People*, p. 200.

in 1982-83, but the differences between news media are less dramatic than they were in 1971, when the difference between news magazines and radio were nearly 52 percentage points. In 1982-83, the difference between the medium employing the highest percentage of college graduates (the wire services) and the medium employing the lowest percentage (radio) is 43 points. And the differences between the top four media (news magazines, wire services, daily newspapers, and television) are much less pronounced in 1983 than in 1971.

The percentages in this table show that the news magazines and wire services still employ journalists who are most likely to be college graduates, as was true in 1971. The order is reversed for daily newspapers and television in 1982-83, however, with TV journalists slightly more likely to be college graduates than daily-newspaper journalists (80.2 percent as compared to 74.4 percent). As in 1971, weekly-newspaper and radio journalists are least likely to be college graduates, but even these kinds of journalists are more likely than not to have graduated from college.

Print journalists are more likely than broadcast to have graduated from college, as was true in 1971, and the increases in percentage of college graduates have been roughly equal for print and broadcast media. The largest increases have occurred among television and weekly-newspaper journalists.

Overall, then, our study shows a dramatic increase in the proportion of journalists who are college graduates in all media from 1971 to 1983. No medium employs fewer than 50 percent college graduates, whereas in 1971 both radio and weekly newspapers had fewer than one-half college-graduate journalists, and television was not far above this mark.

Johnstone and his colleagues attributed much of the difference in percentage of college graduates among the different news media to differences in sizes of media organizations and the communities in which they operate. Table 3.3 indicates some difference in the percentages of college graduates working for large versus small news organizations, but not nearly as much difference as Johnstone and his colleagues found in 1971. This table supports the conclusion that there has been a dramatic increase in the proportion of college graduates working for all kinds of news organizations, especially those with twenty-five or fewer editorial employees.

Johnstone also concluded that the very high percentages of college graduates in news magazines and wire services could be interpreted largely as a result of both organization size and size of city in which they were located, with city size a slightly stronger predictor than organiza-

Table 3.3 Number of Journalists Who Are College Graduates
by News Organization Size

Size of Editorial Staff	Percentage 1971[a]	Percentage 1982–83	(N)
1–10	44.0	68.7	415
11–25	48.1	76.7	176
26–50	58.1	75.9	133
51–100	59.4	77.8	117
More than 100 (101 +)	76.2	81.0	142
			983

[a]Johnstone's cases are not reported because they are weighted and not directly comparable to ours. From Johnstone, Slawski, and Bowman, *The News People* p. 201.

tion size.[21] We did not include city size in our study, but it appears to us that in 1983 it would not be a significant predictor of proportion of college graduates, because organization size is no longer an important factor. In addition, it comes as little surprise to us that the proportion of college graduates has increased markedly in the smaller news organizations, given the tremendous increase in the numbers of journalism school graduates from 1971 (6,802) to 1982 (18,574).

Regional Differences. In 1971, Johnstone and his associates found what they called "a surprising consistency" in the percentages of college-graduate journalists working in the nine regions of the country.[22] Table 3.4 shows less consistency across regions in 1982-83 than in 1971, with about 17 percentage points difference between regions with the fewest and most college-graduate journalists, as compared to about 10 points in 1971. That suggests that somewhat more of the college-educated journalists are being attracted to certain regions of the country than to others, especially to the Middle Atlantic, Pacific, and New England areas, where the largest and most prominent news organizations are located.

But table 3.4 also shows that the percentage of journalists who have graduated from college has increased in every region of the country from 1971 to 1983, with the largest increases occurring in New England and the West South Central regions, and the smallest in the East South Central and South Atlantic areas. As was true in 1971, the Middle Atlantic and Pacific states boast the largest percentages of college

Table 3.4 College Graduate Journalists
by Region of Employment
(Percentage Graduating from College)

Region of Country[d]	Journalists (1971)[a]	Journalists (1982-83)	U.S. Population (1970)[b]	U.S. Population (1980)[c]
New England	52.2	76.3	12.1	19.3
Middle Atlantic	61.0	81.3	10.9	17.1
East North Central	58.5	71.9	9.5	14.5
West North Central	52.4	71.9	9.8	15.1
South Atlantic	58.1	67.2	10.5	15.8
East South Central	59.1	64.7	7.7	12.0
West South Central	52.9	79.5	10.0	14.9
Mountain	58.2	68.2	14.6	18.3
Pacific	61.8	79.3	15.8	19.5
TOTAL U.S.	58.2	73.9	10.7	16.3

[a]From Johnstone, Slawski, and Bowman, *The News People*, p. 202.
[b]From U.S. Bureau of the Census, *Statistical Abstract of the U.S., 1973*, 94th edition, p. 117. Percentages are for those residing in each region.
[c]From U.S. Bureau of the Census, *Statistical Abstract of the U.S., 1982–83*, 103d edition, p. 144.
[d]*New England* includes Maine, New Hampshire, Vermont, Massachusetts, Rhode Island, and Connecticut. The *Middle Atlantic* region includes New York, New Jersey, and Pennsylvania. The *East North Central* region includes Ohio, Indiana, Michigan, Illinois, and Wisconsin. The *West North Central* area includes Minnesota, Iowa, Missouri, North and South Dakota, Nebraska, and Kansas. The *South Atlantic* region includes Delaware, Maryland, Washington D.C., Virginia, West Virginia, North and South Carolina, Georgia, and Florida. The *East South Central* area includes Kentucky, Tennessee, Alabama, and Mississippi. The *West South Central* region includes Arkansas, Louisiana, Oklahoma, and Texas. The *Mountain* region includes Montana, Idaho, Wyoming, Colorado, New Mexico, Arizona, Utah, and Nevada. The *Pacific* area includes Washington, Oregon, California, Alaska, and Hawaii. Source is U.S. Bureau of the Census, *Current Population Reports*, series P-25, no. 913.

graduates, but the West South Central area is now equal to the Pacific region in proportion of college-graduate journalists.

The proportions of journalists who majored in journalism or communication in college vary more widely by region than do the percentages of college graduates. Table 3.5 indicates that the highest proportions of the college graduates majoring in journalism come from colleges in the West North Central states (Minnesota, Iowa, Missouri, the Dakotas, Nebraska, and Kansas) and the East North Central area (Ohio, Indiana, Illinois, Michigan, and Wisconsin). That is not surprising, considering

Table 3.5 College Major of U. S. Journalists
by Region of College
(Percentage of College Graduate Journalists in 1982–83)

Region of College[a]	Journalists Majoring in Journalism/Communications[b]
New England	31.7%
Middle Atlantic	33.3%
East North Central	62.4%
West North Central	68.9%
South Atlantic	45.5%
East South Central	44.1%
West South Central	55.6%
Mountain	56.7%
Pacific	59.8%
TOTAL	53.2%

[a]See table 3.4 for a listing of states included in each region of the country.
[b]Includes journalism, radio-TV, telecommunications, and other communications.

the numerous large and well-established journalism schools in the Midwest, but it does suggest that the influence of journalism education is not felt uniformly across the country, especially not in the New England and Middle Atlantic states, where the majority of the most prominent news media are headquartered.

This conclusion about the impact of journalism education assumes that graduates of journalism schools in various regions of the country tend to work as journalists in those same regions. Table 3.6 supports this assumption, showing that a majority of journalists attending college in each region tend to work as journalists in that same region. That is especially true in the Pacific area, where nearly 80 percent of the journalists attending college find work, and in the Southern states, where more than 70 percent do. In several of the regions, the next-highest proportion of journalists is found working in an adjacent region, which suggests that even if they do take a job in a different area from that where they attended college, most journalists do not move far from their place of college education. In the Northeast, for example, 63.5 percent of those attending college there end up working there, but another 20.6 percent end up working in the nearby Middle Atlantic states of New York, New Jersey, and Pennsylvania. Likewise, although

Table 3.6 Region of College by Region of Employment
of U.S. Journalists

Region of College[a]	Percentage of Journalists Employed in 1982–83 in the Same Region in Which They Attended College
Northeast	63.5%
Middle Atlantic	54.1%
East North Central	63.6%
West North Central	55.6%
South Atlantic	61.4%
East South Central	70.6%
West South Central	72.8%
Mountain	61.3%
Pacific	79.3%

[a]See table 3.4 for a listing of states included in each region of the country.

only 54.1 percent of the journalists attending college in the Middle Atlantic region find work there, another 15 percent find work in the Northeastern states of Maine, New Hampshire, Vermont, Rhode Island, and Connecticut.

This tendency to work in another region adjacent to the one where college is attended is particularly striking in the Northeast and Middle Atlantic areas, reinforcing the stereotype of the Eastern journalist who is isolated from the rest of the country, but it is also notable between the East North Central and West North Central (the Midwest) regions and between the Mountain and West South Central areas. In short, these findings argue against the popular view that most journalists are a nomadic sort who roam throughout the country as they advance in their careers. We find, instead, surprising loyalty to the various regions of the country, which probably reflects the job placement practices of journalism schools as much as or more than the desire to live in a certain region of the country.

Fields of Study in College and Graduate School. In 1971, Johnstone and his colleagues found that journalism represented the most popular major field of study at both the undergraduate and graduate levels of university education, but that formal training in journalism was not typical among practicing journalists, because only 22.6 percent held journalism undergraduate degrees, and just 6.9 percent had completed graduate degrees in journalism.[23] In 1982-83, we find the same thing, although the proportion of working journalists holding an undergraduate degree in journalism has risen by about 7 points to 29.5 percent, and the proportion holding a graduate degree in journalism has increased from 6.9 to 7.5 percent. (See table 3.7.)

When radio and television (telecommunications) and other communication subjects, such as public relations and advertising, are included with journalism, it is apparent from table 3.7 that slightly more than 40 percent of all working journalists majored in communication in college, and more than one-half of all college-graduate journalists chose communications as their major. Thus, if only college graduates are considered, formal training in communications is more typical than not among practicing journalists in this country in 1982-83, in contrast to the situation in 1971.

Johnstone cited data compiled by the Newspaper Fund showing that just 25.2 percent of journalism graduates in 1971 found employment in the news media. He concluded from this figure and his survey results that most working journalists were not trained in journalism in school, and most of those trained in journalism in college did not enter the news media.[24] In 1982, the picture is considerably different: the annual Dow Jones Newspaper Fund/Gallup survey of journalism/communications graduates shows 53.2 percent of them going into media jobs, and our survey shows that more than half (54.7 percent) of all working journalists who graduated from college had majored in journalism or communications.[25] These figures together suggest that formal training in journalism is becoming a necessary condition for entry into the U.S. news media.

Table 3.7 also indicates that the increase in journalism/communication majors has occurred largely at the expense of English and creative writing. The largest decline in the proportion of college-graduate journalists is in the English and creative writing category — from 22.9 percent in 1971 to 14.7 percent in 1982-83. There were also decreases in the proportions of journalists majoring in history and political science, although these were smaller and possibly due to sampling error. Overall, though, the liberal arts and social sciences combined suffered a drop in college-graduate journalists from 53.4 percent in 1971 to 40.2 percent in 1982-83. In contrast, the proportion of journalists who majored in the hard sciences and other fields remained very small and stable during the 1970s.

The same patterns apply to the relatively few journalists (8.1 percent in 1971 and 11.1 percent in 1982-83) who have completed graduate degrees. There has been a notable increase in the proportion majoring in journalism, and a decrease in the percentage majoring in English, history, and political science. The proportions of graduate-degree holders majoring in the hard sciences and other subjects such as business, agriculture, and education has remained very small and stable during the 1971-83 period, with a slight increase in the percentage studying law.

When compared to the U.S. population at large who completed college, it is clear that journalists are much less likely to major in business and education, and somewhat less likely to major in math and the physical and biological sciences.[26] And, not surprisingly, journalists are much more likely to major in journalism and English than are college students in general. That is true in graduate school, as well, although the likelihood of journalists majoring in education, law, and humanities is higher than at the undergraduate level.

It is also true that journalism is the most popular undergraduate major for those earning graduate degrees in journalism or communications. Forty percent of those journalists who earned graduate degrees in journalism majored in this same subject as undergraduates, and 21 percent of them majored in English. Of those majoring in other communication subjects in graduate school, 31 percent majored in journalism as undergraduates, and 15 percent majored in communications.

Thus, the "high degree of educational diversity" of journalists found in the Johnstone study in 1971 is eroding, for better or worse.[27] In 1982-83, more journalists have graduated from college than in 1971, more have majored in journalism or communications at the undergraduate and graduate levels, and nearly half of those majoring in journalism at the graduate level also majored in it at the undergraduate level. A journalism degree is becoming the necessary condition for working in the U.S. news media as a reporter or editor. And typically this journalism degree includes a minor in English, history, political science, or other social sciences. Three-fourths of those majoring in journalism report these minor subjects, with political science the most popular (24.5 percent).

Are Journalism Majors Different? Given the increases in proportions of journalists, especially younger ones, majoring in journalism at both undergraduate and graduate levels, it is tempting to ask what difference that makes. We find no indication that majoring in journalism or

Table 3.7 Fields of Study of U.S. Journalists
in College and Graduate School
(Percentage of U.S. Journalists)

Subjects	Major Field in College (1971)[d]		Major Field in College (1982–83)	
	% of Sample	% of All Subjects Who Finished College	% of Sample	% of All Subjects Who Finished College
Journalism	22.6	34.2	29.5	39.8
Radio-TV	1.8	2.8	4.4	5.9
Other communication specialties	3.1	4.7	6.7	9.0
Total communication field	27.5	41.7	40.6	54.7
English, creative writing	15.1	22.9	10.9	14.7
History	6.4	9.7	4.7	6.3
Other humanities	2.9	4.4	4.9	6.6
Political science, government	5.0	7.5	3.6	4.9
Other social sciences	3.6	5.5	3.3	4.4
Liberal arts, unspecified	1.1	1.6	1.0	1.4
Mathematics	.4	.6	.2	.3
Physical or biological sciences	.8	1.2	1.2	1.6
Total liberal arts and sciences	35.3	53.4	29.8	40.2
Agriculture	.2	.3	.4	.5
Business	1.0	1.5	1.7	2.3
Education	.5	.8	1.3	1.8
Law	a	.1	.1	.1
All other fields	1.5	2.3	.3	.4
Total other fields	3.2	5.0	3.8	5.1
TOTAL	66.0[b]	100.1	74.2[b]	100.0

[a]Less than one-tenth of 1 percent.

Table 3.7 (continued)
(Percentage of U.S. Journalists)

Subjects	Major Field in Graduate School (1971)[d]		Major Field in Graduate School (1982–83)	
	% of Sample	% of All Subjects Who Finished Graduate School	% of Sample	% of All Subjects Who Finished Graduate School
Journalism	6.9	34.2	7.5	41.9
Radio-TV	.3	1.6	0.0	0.0
Other communication specialties	1.6	8.0	1.3	7.3
Total communication field	8.8	44.5	8.8	49.2
English, creative writing	2.0	10.3	.9	5.0
History	1.6	8.2	.8	4.5
Other humanities	.9	4.7	2.1	11.7
Political science, government	2.2	10.9	1.1	6.1
Other social sciences	1.3	6.4	.8	4.5
Liberal arts, unspecified	.1	.5	.1	.6
Mathematics	.1	.5	.2	1.1
Physical or biological sciences	.1	.5	.1	.6
Total liberal arts and sciences	8.3	42.0	6.1	34.1
Agriculture	.1	.7	0.0	0.0
Business	.1	.7	.4	2.2
Education	1.0	5.2	1.1	6.1
Law	.6	2.9	.9	5.0
All other fields	.8	4.1	.6	3.4
Total other fields	2.7	13.6	3.0	16.7
TOTAL	19.8[c]	100.1	17.9[c]	100.0

[b]Does not total to 100 percent because some journalists are not college graduates, and does not total to percentage of college graduates because some majored in more than one subject.

[c]Does not total to 100 percent because many journalists did not attend graduate school, and does not total to percentage attending graduate school because some studied more than one field.

[d]From Johnstone, Slawski, and Bowman, *The News People*, p. 203.

communications is associated with job stability (number of previous jobs in journalism) or job satisfaction, but a journalism education is a predictor of plans to stay in the news media during the next five years. (See chapter 4 for details.) We also find no relationship between the type of ownership of news organizations (group, independent, or other) and the proportions of journalism majors employed, which indicates that journalism majors are just as likely to work for group-owned as independently owned media. In addition, majoring in journalism or communications is not associated with sex or race.

The most notable differences between journalism/communications majors and journalists majoring in other subjects are found in type of media, size of media organization, region of employment, and age. Table 3.8 indicates that the college-graduate journalists working for news magazines are much less likely to have majored in journalism or communications than are college graduates working for other kinds of news organizations. Table 3.9 shows that the largest news organizations have the lowest percentage of college-graduate journalists who majored in journalism or communications, and table 3.5 reveals that college-graduate journalists employed in the New England and Middle Atlantic regions are far less likely to have majored in journalism or communications than are college graduates employed in the other areas of the country.

These findings, when coupled with earlier ones illustrated in tables 3.2, 3.3, and 3.4, suggest that the influence of journalism education is least in those news organizations and regions of the country that are most likely to employ college graduates. Although news magazines, organizations with more than 100 editorial employees, and media located in the Northeast are most likely to employ college graduates, they are also *least* likely to employ journalism majors. Because the larger news organizations (especially news magazines) are likely to be located in the Northeast, and because the majority of journalists tend to work in the same region where they attended college, the relative scarcity of journalism/communications majors in the Northeast is most likely due to the relative scarcity of major journalism schools in that area. Whatever the reasons for the relatively low percentages of journalism majors at large Northeastern news magazines, however, the fact remains that these prestigious and influential news media are the least influenced by journalism education in the United States. And that may help to explain why large Northeastern media are less favorable toward journalism education than are other news media.

Table 3.8 College Major of U. S. Journalists by Media Type
(Percentage of College Graduate Journalists in 1982–83)

Media Type	Journalists Majoring in Journalism/Communication[a]	N
News Magazines	25.9	58
Wire Services	53.3	45
Daily Newspapers	56.3	348
Television	62.9	97
Weekly Newspapers	50.4	127
Radio	53.1	64
		739

[a]Includes journalism, radio-TV, telecommunications, and other communications.

Table 3.9 College Major of U. S. Journalists
by News Organization Size
(Percentage of College Graduate Journalists in 1982-83)

Size of Editorial Staff	Journalists Majoring in Journalism/Communication[a]	N
1–10	53.3	287
11–25	62.5	136
26–50	54.5	101
51–100	58.7	92
More than 100	35.3	116
		732

[a]Includes journalism, radio-TV, telecommunications, and other communications.

In their 1971 study, Johnstone and his colleagues found that prior to 1945, the most typical college major of journalists was in English or the humanities, but from the end of World War II until about 1960, the media recruited heavily from journalism school graduates.[28] From 1960 to 1971, the emphasis on journalism majors seemed to level off, and recruiting from majors in political science and history increased. Johnstone also found that the number of journalists with undergraduate degrees in professional fields other than journalism/communications was fewer among more recent graduates, which led him to question whether that reflected a trend toward declining media recruitment of persons from other occupations.[29]

Table 3.10 College Major of U. S. Journalists by Age
(Percentage of College Graduate Journalists in 1982-83)

Age	Journalists Majoring in Journalism/Communication[a]	N
Under 25	65.9	88
25–34	59.8	373
35–44	39.6	154
45–54	40.3	62
55 +	45.8	59
		736

[a]Includes journalism, radio-TV, telecommunications, and other communications.

We also find that among more recent graduates, there are fewer majoring in fields other than journalism, and more majoring in journalism or communications. Table 3.10 shows that nearly two-thirds of U.S. college-graduate journalists under twenty-five years old majored in journalism/communications, whereas only about 40 percent of those thirty-five years old and older were graduates of journalism schools. These data suggest that the news media are indeed recruiting more heavily than in the past from journalism schools, at least with regard to those just entering journalism from the universities. The percentages of young college graduates from journalism schools in 1982-83 (65.9 and 59.8) are especially striking when compared to Johnstone's percentages of 49.3 (for those graduating between 1945 and 1959) and 42.4 (for those graduating in 1960 or later).[30] Our data clearly suggest that most news media, except the news magazines, are recruiting more heavily from journalism schools than in the past.

Continuing Education of Journalists. In 1971, Johnstone and his colleagues found that just over a third — 35.7 percent — of the journalists in their national sample said they had participated in some kind of education program since becoming journalists, and more than half — 57.7 percent — said some type of additional training would be helpful.[31] We did not repeat the question on actual participation in a program, but we did ask journalists in 1982-83 the same question asked in 1971 about whether they would like additional training in journalism or other subjects, and if so, what kind of training they would want. Table 3.11 reveals a dramatic increase from 1971 to 1982-83 in the

Table 3.11 Preferences of U.S. Journalists
for Continuing Education
(Percentage of Total Sample Mentioning)

	1971[a]	1982–83
Total who said they would like some kind of additional training	57.7	76.8
Journalism	10.1	15.4
Political science, government	8.9	4.3
English, literature, writing	7.2	8.9
History	3.9	3.1
Economics	3.6	3.6
Law	2.7	3.3
Business	2.6	9.2
Photography	2.2	2.1
News analysis, clinics, seminars	1.7	12.9
Shorthand	1.5	0.0
Modern languages	1.5	2.2
Total who said they would not like additional training	42.3	23.2
	100.0	100.0
	(n ≅ 1,000)	(n = 987)

[a]From Johnstone, Slawski, and Bowman, *The News People*, pp. 45, 207. Subjects mentioned by fewer than 1.5 percent of journalists are not included in this table; therefore, the percentages for the individual subjects do not total to the percentages wanting additional training.

percentage of U.S. journalists who say they would like additional training in journalism or other subjects — from 57.7 to 76.8 percent. And table 3.11 also indicates that there are more journalists in 1982-83 interested in additional training in journalism, business, and news-analysis clinics and seminars than in 1971, which suggests an increased desire for vocational continuing education that is consistent with nationwide trends in university enrollments. Johnstone found in 1971 that academic subjects were cited more frequently than vocational and technical ones, but in 1982-83 we find that academic and vocational subjects are cited about equally, if one considers business an academic subject, as

Johnstone and his colleagues do.[32] If business is considered a vocational subject, then the balance has shifted to vocational continuing education.

In general, the younger the journalist and the less time spent in journalism, the more likely he or she is to want additional training. More than 85 percent of those journalists thirty-four and younger say they would like additional training, whereas less than 45 percent of those fifty-five and older say so. And slightly more than 85 percent of those with ten or fewer years in journalism desire additional training, compared to 47.4 percent of those with more than thirty years' experience in the field.

It is not surprising that younger, less experienced journalists are more likely to want some form of continuing education, especially education that will help them advance in their careers. In their 1981 study of daily-newspaper journalists, the Burgoons and Atkin concluded that many young journalists aspire to management positions but lack the training to perform many of the tasks required of media managers.[33] Nor is it surprising that those journalists who are dissatisfied with their jobs are more likely to want additional training than those who are very satisfied. Likewise, those who think their news organization is doing a less than outstanding job of informing the public are more likely to want additional training than those who rate their organization as outstanding.

But at the same time that it is those journalists who are youngest, least experienced, and most dissatisfied with their jobs and their news organizations who are most likely to want additional training, it is also true that those journalists planning to stay in journalism and those with college educations are more likely to want additional training. Thus, dissatisfaction with one's job and the performance of one's organization should not be interpreted as a lack of commitment to the field of journalism or a lack of interest in education.

As journalists gain more experience, they are more likely to want something besides journalism, such as law or history. Other predictors of a preference for nonjournalistic continuing education are working for a daily newspaper, holding an advanced university degree, being a supervisor of others, working for a very large organization, and not doing very much reporting.[34] Thus, it seems that those journalists most interested in continuing education that focuses on journalistic or vocational subjects are likely to be less experienced reporters working for news media other than daily newspapers (especially weekly newspapers and radio) who do not hold graduate degrees and do not supervise other staff members. That is consistent with the earlier finding that younger, less experienced journalists are more likely to desire some form of continuing education that will help them advance in their careers. Those who are supervisors and/or editors in larger news organizations are more likely to be interested in broadening their horizons, even if the subject matter is not directly related to their jobs.

CONCLUSIONS

Although it is still true that there is no single set of educational requirements for becoming a journalist in the United States, as Johnstone pointed out in 1971, we find that U.S. news media have relied increasingly upon journalism schools for hiring since 1971. Our findings support Johnstone's prediction that differences in educational backgrounds of journalists will become less pronounced as those in the oldest age groups are replaced by younger persons. Not only are U.S. news media hiring mostly college graduates, but these media also are hiring mostly journalism and communications majors — except for news magazines, which still employ a minority of journalism and communications majors.

This emphasis on recruiting journalists from journalism and communication schools has come largely at the expense of English, creative writing, history, and political science, which suggests that the trend identified by Johnstone of hiring more college graduates in history and the social sciences since 1960 has been reversed during the 1970s.

The influence of journalism education has not been felt uniformly across the country or across all media, however. Very large news organizations located in the Northeast, especially news magazines, are far less likely to employ journalism school graduates than are other news media, despite the fact that these very large and prominent media are the most likely to employ college graduates. Thus, it appears that Johnstone's conclusion that journalism in the United States is an occupational field with diverse entry routes applies more to the very large Northeastern media, especially the news magazines, than to the other news organizations throughout the country.

Our survey findings do not provide ready explanations for these patterns of hiring, but they do suggest that the majority of journalists find work in the same regions of the country where they attended college, and the universities in the Northeast have not emphasized journalism education to nearly the extent that those in the Midwest, South, and West have. But it may be that the very large and prominent news organizations in the Northeast are seeking journalists with more diverse educational backgrounds because of the increased specialization required for reporting and editing jobs within these media. It may also be that these Northeastern news media, like the older universities in their areas, have a less favorable view of journalism and communication education in general.

Certainly not everyone within the field of journalism or journalism education would agree that it is desirable for more and more journalists to be professionally educated in schools of journalism and communication.[35] Even among journalism educators, there is not agreement on how much professional training and how much instruction in the liberal arts and sciences are needed to be a well-educated journalist. The Accrediting Council on Education in Journalism and Mass Communication (ACEJMC) has for years endorsed a ratio of 25 percent professional training and 75 percent liberal arts and sciences for undergraduate journalism students, but that recently has been criticized as being too restrictive by a number of schools of journalism and communication that want to offer more vocationally oriented instruction in such topics as advertising and public relations.[36]

Because the entry routes to journalism in the United States are not as diverse as they were in 1971 when the Johnstone study was conducted, one might expect somewhat less differentiation among journalists on other issues such as professional values and ethics, standards of journalistic excellence, and the relative importance of different aspects of journalistic work. The following chapters discuss these and other subjects related to the profession and practice of journalism in the United States, and they show that less diversity in educational backgrounds does not necessarily mean less diversity in professional orientations.

—4—

Job Conditions and Satisfactions

Modern studies of journalism organizations sometimes describe them as engaging in the "politics of newswork," with the beat system of news coverage as the focus of activity. They picture journalists as working in a labor-intensive bureaucracy, with a news staff only as large as required to fill the allotted news space. Newsroom staff size has little to do with the size of the community to be covered, or with the number of things the journalists may think are newsworthy. These analysts of the "manufacture of news" see the reporter beat system as the dominant, yet arbitrary, mode of gathering the news. The end result is a dependence on government and business bureaucracies' needs for publicity to generate sufficient copy to meet deadlines and fill news space.[1] In this view of the news business, journalists are engaged largely in "wage labor."[2]

Some others, particularly journalists, reject the assembly-line analogy and say that independence from sources is the measure of good journalism. A few see the problem in much more down-to-earth terms. Gene Miller, two-time Pulitzer Prize winner for reporting and an associate editor of the *Miami Herald*, says newspapers are run on "momentum" and "hysteria."[3]

Herbert Gans, a sociologist, says, "The analogy with the factory is not entirely accurate, for news is a more variegated product than an

65

automobile." He adds, though, that the assembly of news is remarkably similar in all news organizations, because "they are all creating a similar product under deadline conditions, and the workers are members of a single profession."[4] As a result, Gans notes, media organizations tend to "defy textbook generalizations about organizational practices."[5]

Johnstone's work a dozen years ago concluded that journalism in the United States took place in a wide variety of organizational environments. The Johnstone team concluded that "these settings differ markedly in the types of editorial personnel they recruit and in the kinds of influences they exert on those who work for them."[6] Therefore, the job context of journalists is extremely important to study.

This chapter analyzes journalists' perceptions of their jobs. We are concerned particularly about journalists' perceptions of the tasks they perform, how much autonomy they have, the extent of editing and the nature of supervision, their communication patterns within journalistic organizations, and their job satisfaction.

PROFILES OF NEWSWORK

Most journalists have worked for more than one news organization. About three-quarters of the respondents in our sample say they had worked for at least one other organization than their present one. As noted in chapter 2, one of the major changes over the last decade is the drop in median age of journalists. That change is most dramatic in supervisory personnel, who are now almost seven years younger than they were in 1971. (See table 4.1.) Journalists still begin their careers as reporters, but with increasing seniority, management is an option. It appears that the opportunity for supervisory duties comes much earlier now than during the previous decade. By the time the typical journalist has reached a professional age of twenty-one years, it is more likely that he or she is in management than in full-time reporting. That is about five years earlier than in the period Johnstone studied. (See figure 4.1.) So the "typical" manager now has only four more years' journalistic experience than the reporters who work for him or her.

Reporting is done regularly by about 68 percent of the journalists we studied. But more than half of all journalists (54 percent) say they regularly report *and* edit, just as Johnstone found a dozen years ago. (See table 4.2.)

Table 4.1 Comparison of 1970 and 1981 Median Ages of Print
and Broadcast Journalists Who Perform
Various Journalists' Functions

Type of Function	Median Age	
	1970	*1982–83*
A. Print journalists		
Covers a specific news beat	35.2	31.8
Does reporting regularly	35.6	31.8
Writes features	37.0	48.0
Writes a column	40.6	46.8
Manages a news desk	41.5	35.0
Does a great deal of editing	41.7	33.5
Has an influence on hiring and firing	45.2	37.0
Manages a daily newspaper	48.5	38.7
All print journalists	38.1	33.5
B. Broadcast journalists		
Does a great deal of editing	29.7	28.3
Covers a specific news beat	30.6	27.8
Does reporting regularly	31.0	28.6
Has an influence on hiring and firing	32.8	30.8
Manages a news department	36.2	31.0[a]
All broadcast journalists	30.8	28.3

[a]In data collected during 1982, Vernon Stone found the median age of TV news directors to be 35.5, and the age of radio news directors to be 30.1. See Vernon A. Stone, "Then and Now: News Directors' Profiles and Problems, Noteworthy Changes in a Decade of RTNDA Surveys," *RTNDA Communication* 37 (October 1983), pp. 27–29.

Writing and editing, or the management of those functions, are the tasks most central to journalism. In a world that sometimes seems dominated by visual images, that may make journalism sound provincial. But most journalists spend the majority of their time on the reporting and writing arts. In fact, successful broadcast journalists, such as Walter Cronkite and Dan Rather, often refer to the importance of the traditional skills.

While touring new broadcast educational facilities at the dedication of a new communications building at a major state university, Dan Rather, a newsman for CBS Television, was asked what he thought of them. He replied that he would change only one thing: "I would put a little plaque every six feet along these beautiful corridors, and on each plaque would

Types of Journalistic Functions Performed by Years of Experience in News Media

^aPercent who do reporting "regularly"

^bPercent who have managerial/supervisory responsibility

^cPercent who do "a great deal" of editing

Figure 4.1

be the same message . . . 'Learn to Write.' "'[7] As we see later in this chapter, it is difficulties with writing that supervising editors complain about most when evaluating their staffs' performance.

The dominant job titles among reporters are general-assignment reporting and specific-beat reporting. A little more than half of those in our sample who said they did reporting *regularly* were general-assign-

Table 4.2 Types of Job Functions Journalists Perform,
by Media Sector
(Percentage Engaged in Each Type of Activity)

Functions	Print Sector (N=756)	Broadcast Sector (N = 240)	Total Sample (N = 1,001)
A. Reporting, news-gathering,. and news-writing functions			
Total who do reporting	78.7%	83.3%	79.8%
Covered a specialized newsbeat	41.8%	27.5%	38.4%
B. Editing and news-processing functions			
Total who edit or process other people's work	70.2%	75.0%	71.4%
C. Managerial and supervisory functions			
Total with managerial or supervisory duties	46.7%	48.3%	47.1%
Influence hiring and firing	34.4%	33.7%	34.2%
Supervise one or more reporters	41.7%	46.1%	42.9%

ment reporters who cover a variety of areas. Specific beats, such as police or government, are covered by 48 percent of those who report regularly. Beat reporters are still in a minority, then, as they were in 1971, even though there has been a slight increase in their numbers over the decade. Print reporters are more likely to cover a specific beat than are their broadcast colleagues (42 percent compared to 28 percent).

Reporting is just one of the several things most journalists do on the job. A little more than half of the journalists who do reporting regularly have jobs that include other duties, mainly editing. That is especially true for journalists who work for the smaller media. Staff size, of course, varies widely among the various media, with print organizations typically employing larger staffs than broadcast news operations. (See table 4.3.)

Profile of the General-Assignment Reporter. The typical general-assignment reporter has been in journalism about eight years, is thirty-one years old, and has worked three years for a present employer. Most

THE AMERICAN JOURNALIST

Table 4.3 Median News Staff Size by the Various Media

Medium	Median Staff Size
News Magazines	100.9
Daily Newspapers	41.5
Television	21.8[a]
Wire Service Bureau	6.2
Weekly Newspapers	4.6
Radio	3.0[a]

[a]In 1979, Vernon Stone found that the median news staff size for television was 15, and 2 for radio (full and part-time). See Vernon A. Stone, "Survey Shows TV News Staffs Expanding But Radio Newsrooms Are Little Changed," *RTNDA Comnunicator* 34 (January 1980), pp. 8–9.

have held jobs in other organizations, with thirty-five different job titles mentioned. The variety of journalistic work experience is great, but more than half of the reporters had been employed as reporters before coming to their present organization, mostly in general assignment. Editing posts were mentioned by one-fifth of the reporters as previous jobs in either a former or present organization. (See figure 4.2.)

Profile of the Beat Reporter. Beat reporters, similar to their general-assignment colleagues, are about thirty-one years old, with eight years' journalism experience. Typically they have worked four years for their present employer, a year longer than the general-assignment reporters we studied. Their profile of employment in previous organizations is very similar to that of general-assignment reporters. A majority had been reporters prior to joining their present organization, typically doing general-assignment work. They are a little more likely to have moved through several posts in their present organization and to have had an editing responsibility than are their general-assignment colleagues. (See figure 4.3.)

In general, then, reporters in the United States have had fairly extensive experience, concentrated mainly in editorial journalism.

Profile of Desk Editors and Producers. Supervising editors, typically "desk" editors or news "producers," are about thirty-five years old, with twelve years' experience. They have worked five years for their present organization, about a year longer than the reporters who work for them. Thus, the typical manager is considerably younger and is less experienced than a decade ago, when the median age was about forty-two. Supervisors are still likely to be male, but 28 percent of them are women, compared to about 12 percent in 1971.

A majority of the editors had jobs in other journalism organizations prior to joining their present one, and typically they were reporters. Most of them moved around in their present organization, but they usually had come directly into other editing posts. About one-third of them entered their present organization through a wide variety of posts, ranging from production to advertising sales. (See figure 4.4.)

Profile of Managing Editors and News Directors. It is in top management that youth has taken over even more dramatically than in desk management and reporting. The median age of managing editors on daily newspapers has dropped by about ten years. The typical managing editor was forty-nine in 1971. The median age in 1982 was thirty-nine. Almost two out of ten managing editors are now women. Typically, the managing editor came to the present job in early 1976, meaning that the editor had held the post about seven years and had been in journalism for a total of fifteen years.

News directors in broadcasting are even younger than their print colleagues, with a median age of thirty-five for television and thirty for radio. The news director typically came to the present job late in 1979, and had about thirteen years' professional experience if in television and about six years' if in radio. About 8 percent of the TV news directors and 18 percent of the radio news directors were women in 1982.[8]

PERCEIVED AUTONOMY OF JOURNALISTS

Increased bureaucratization and specialization were occurring in journalism, just as in other fields, when Johnstone looked at the profession in 1971. He speculated that these developments would make it increasingly hard for the journalist to enjoy professional autonomy over his or her work.

In spite of the organizational growth in journalism that Johnstone saw in 1971, he found that journalists tended to claim substantial autonomy. About three-quarters of them said they had almost complete freedom to decide which aspects of a news story should be emphasized. More than

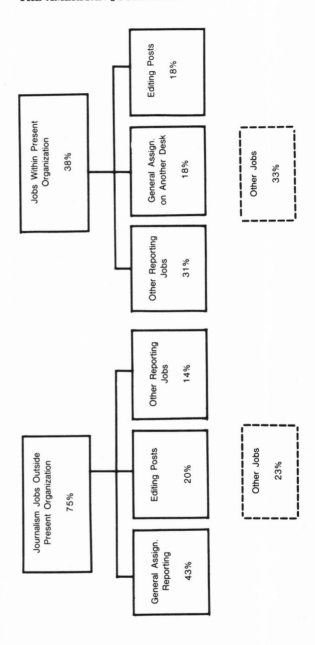

Figure 4.2

Career Patterns:

Previous Jobs Held by
General Assignment Reporters
(N = 188)

Jobs Within Present Organization — 38%

Other Reporting Jobs — 31%

General Assign. on Another Desk — 18%

Editing Posts — 18%

Other Jobs — 33%

Journalism Jobs Outside Present Organization — 75%

General Assign. Reporting — 43%

Editing Posts — 20%

Other Reporting Jobs — 14%

Other Jobs — 23%

Figure 4.3

Career Patterns:

Previous Jobs Held by Beat Reporters

(N = -114)

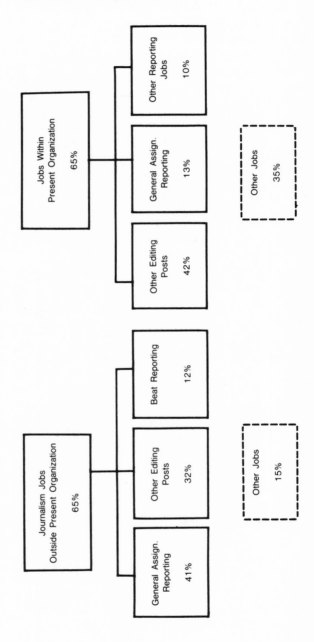

Figure 4.4

Career Patterns:

Previous Jobs Held by Desk
Editors and Managing Editors
(N = 86)

60 percent of the journalists went even further, saying they had almost complete freedom to select stories on which they worked.[9]

Since Johnstone wrote, new technologies have swept the media industry. (See chapter 6.) Concentration of ownership has continued, with the larger group-owning companies acquiring additional media properties. Another significant development has been scandal.

Janet Cooke's fabrication of principal elements of a Pulitzer Prize-winning story for the *Washington Post* in 1983 was the harbinger of an ethical storm that will plague newsrooms for a long time.[10] Had reporters been given a blank check? Was there merely a hairline fracture, or was there a cancer on the editorial fabric of the profession? In a convocation speech to journalism students at Indiana University, Eugene Patterson, publisher of the *St. Petersburg Times*, said, "We've had a time in the last decade or so when on some newspapers, the sailors were running the ship." That has changed, he said: "Editors are beginning to edit again."[11]

The implication of these developments, of course, is that the authority of the editor has limited reporter autonomy somewhat. Using a similar approach to Johnstone's, we attempted to find out what journalists thought about this subject.

Journalists in our sample were asked how much freedom they had in selecting the news stories they work on and in deciding which aspects of a story should be emphasized. They also were asked about the extent of editing their copy receives.

The responses suggest little change in the freedom to select stories, with about 60 percent of our sample saying they have almost complete freedom on story selection. Significant decline *is* registered in the reporters' perceptions of their freedom to decide news story emphasis, however. Sixty-six percent say they determine news story emphasis, 10 percentage points fewer than twelve years ago. Among journalists who work in organizations with 100 or more newsworkers, the decline in those deciding story emphasis is even greater — 18 percentage points less than in 1971 — with only a little more than half saying they have complete control over story emphasis.

Another question asked whether copy produced by the reporters in our study was edited by other persons in the organization. The results show a significant decline across all sizes of media organizations in the number of journalists who say their copy is *not* edited. In a classic linear pattern, the larger the organization, the less likely the journalists are to

Table 4.4 Indicators of Professional Autonomy among Those Who Do Reporting, by Type of Medium

Indicators of Autonomy	Medium Type						
Percentage Who Say	Dailies	Wires	News Magazines	Weeklies	TV News	Radio News	All Reporters
A. They are almost always able to get a story covered that they think should be covered.	64%	63%	45%	50%	61%	60%	59%
B. They have almost complete freedom in selecting the stories they work on.	56%	46%	39%	67%	47%	73%	60%
C. They have almost complete freedom in deciding which aspects of a news story should be emphasized.	67%	63%	32%	64%	67%	73%	66%
D. Their stories are not edited by other people.	14%	8%	23%	29%	39%	59%	29%
	N=253	N=24	N=30	N=117	N=72	N=90	N=794

say their copy gets no editing, with only 8 percent of those from the largest organizations making such a claim.

Considerable media differences emerge with regard to these factors. Not surprisingly, radio, which tends to have very small news staffs, is the medium in which reporters are least likely to have their copy edited by someone else. News magazine reporters, on the other hand, who work with very large news staffs, appear the least likely to have professional autonomy. This finding is corroborated by another item, which asked how often the journalists could get a story idea followed up by their organization. Only about 45 percent of the magazine journalists said they could almost always do so, compared to about 60 percent of journalists from other media. (See table 4.4.)

Most striking, though, is the finding that it is in the daily print organizations — daily newspapers and wire services — that the great majority of reporters have their copy edited by someone else. The broadcast journalist, particularly in radio, is much less likely to have copy edited by others in the organization. The underlying explanation for the differences, however, may be news staff *size* rather than medium. The broadcast media typically have smaller news staffs, making editorial supervision less likely.

So, it appears that with regard to two of three items that are associated with professional autonomy, fewer reporters perceive absolute independence from editors than did so a decade ago. If reporters who also have some management responsibilities are excluded, the proportion claiming complete autonomy decreases even further, by about 6 percentage points on all three items.

On the other hand, an overwhelming majority of the nation's reporters say that they can get a story covered if they think it should be. About two-thirds of the reporters said they almost always got subjects covered when they desired. Another 30 percent said they could do so more often than not. Similar majorities of reporters say they have "a great deal" of or "near total" freedom to select the stories on which they work and to decide news-story emphasis. So, while it seems clear that fewer journalists in 1982-83 than a decade ago perceive absolute autonomy from editors, reporters still think they have considerable autonomy in delivering news.

EXTENT OF COMMUNICATION WITH OTHERS

Earlier research has suggested that the newsroom context dominates the reactions by which reporters gauge their work and how well they are doing. A common assumption is that "feedback" from audience and sources is a weak link of American journalism. We attempted to assess reporters' views of the extent of external and internal communication about their work.

Surprisingly, significantly more reporters say they regularly get reactions or comments from their audience members than say they get them from either news sources or persons in their news organizations. About half of the reporters say they get audience response regularly. Forty percent hear comments regularly from peers in their organization. The same number say they get regular response to their work from news sources. About one-third of all reporters say they regularly hear about their work from persons higher up in the organization. Only a very small minority of reporters (17 percent), typically those in larger organizations, say they get regular comments on their work from peers in other media organizations. (See tables 4.5 and 4.6.)

Media differences concerning "feedback" are slight. Reporters for daily and weekly newspapers are less likely to receive comments from superiors than are their broadcast colleagues. Daily-newspaper reporters are more likely to get comment from news sources than reporters for other media. Audience comment about their work is acknowledged about equally by those in all media, except wire reporters.

Supervising journalists — desk editors and news producers, primarily — follow a similar pattern of communication about their work. They are slightly more likely to get responses from audience members than from peers or their supervisors, just as are the reporters they manage. And, there are only slight differences among the various media. One significant difference between reporters and supervisors, however, is that a greater percentage of them say they regularly get comment about their work from their supervisors than do reporters. The difference is especially great on daily newspapers, where 29 percent of the reporters, compared to 46 percent of the supervisors, say they get regular comment from supervisors about their work. (See table 4.7.)

A little less than half of the journalists who have management responsibilities say they meet daily with individual reporters to talk about ideas for future stories. Another 18 percent of them say they meet at least several times a week with reporters.

Perceived Faults in Performance. Supervising journalists were asked to estimate the most common faults in the work of their subordinates.

Table 4.5 Reporters Who Regularly Receive Comment about Their Work, by Source of Comment and Type of News Organization

Source of Comment	Medium						
	Dailies	Weeklies	News Magazines	Wires	Radio	TV	All Combined
Superiors	29%	28%	41%	42%	49%	42%	35%
Peers	38%	41%	20%	42%	46%	45%	40%
Journalists Outside Own Organization	15%	16%	17%	33%	17%	16%	17%
News Sources	48%	32%	33%	21%	33%	36%	39%
Audience	48%	56%	40%	13%	50%	55%	49%
	N = 254	N = 118	N = 30	N = 24	N = 90	N = 288	N = 589

Table 4.6 Sources of Reactions to
Journalists' Stories, by Medium

Reaction Type	Daily Newspapers (N = 460)	Television (N = 121)[a]	Total Print (N = 748)[a]	Total Broadcast (N = 240)[a]	Total Sample (N = 993)[b]
Readers or Viewers	3.33	3.49	3.30	3.45	3.33
People of Same Level	3.22	3.25	3.18	3.29	3.21
People Above	3.10[c]	3.21	3.09	3.23	3.12
News Sources	3.14	3.08	3.09	3.05	3.08
People in Other Organizations	2.52	2.69	2.52	2.72	2.57

[a]The total number for each category—daily newspapers, television, total print, and total broadcast—varies somewhat from variable to variable. The ranges are: daily papers, 451 to 460; television, 120 to 121; total print, 732 to 748; total broadcast, 233 to 240.

[b]The total number for the sample also varies. The range is from 964 to 993.

[c]A value of 4 indicates regularly; 3 indicates occasionally; 2 indicates seldom; 1 indicates never.

More than 100 different flaws were cited, ranging from sloppiness to poor taste. The most frequent weaknesses were said to be writing problems. About a fifth of the problems cited were described as writing difficulties with organization, clarity, repetition, or awkwardness. Another 16 percent of the flaws were labeled as grammar and syntax errors. Spelling mistakes made up about 11 percent of the complaints. Reporting problems rarely were mentioned. Less than 2 percent of the complaints mentioned factual errors, and a similar number of mentions suggested that stories sometimes contained unanswered questions. Significantly, there were no differences between the complaints of broadcast and print supervisory personnel.

JOB PERCEPTIONS:
REWARDS AND SATISFACTIONS

Newswork rarely has been lucrative. The median income for journalists in 1970 was $11,133, according to the Johnstone study. Johnstone also found considerable variation in salaries among regions of the country and by job type, and serious disparities between the incomes of men and women. He concluded, however, that general income levels in the field

Table 4.7 Supervisors[a] who Regularly Receive Comment about Their Work, by Source of Comment and Type of News Organization

Source of Comment	Medium						
	Dailies	Weeklies	News Magazines	Wires	Radio	TV	All Combined
Superiors	46	31	44	50	49	58	45
Peers	45	43	46	29	55	46	45
Journalists Outside Own Organization	14	16	35	21	24	25	18
News Sources	43	36	37	26	47	39	40
Audience	57	65	67	4	54	61	57
	N = 202	99	27	24	59	57	468

[a]Supervisors include all journalists who answered yes to this question: "Do you have any managerial responsibilities, or do you supervise any editorial employees?"

in 1970 were roughly comparable to those in other fields characterized by similar amounts of education and training. In spite of the optimistic interpretation of salaries, Johnstone also concluded that there was a "manpower dilemma" in the field — that the "organizational realities" of newswork were incompatible with the professional aspirations of the best-educated young journalists.[12] On the other hand, those journalists who said they wanted to leave the news media in 1971 tended to be the lowest paid, least educated persons, with less perceived autonomy than their peers.[13]

Annual Income of Journalists. Salaries and intangible rewards do not appear to have improved over the decade since the Johnstone study. The median personal income of journalists during 1981 was $19,000. That figure, while much more than the median of $11,133 reported a decade earlier, represents an actual loss of purchasing power for the median journalist. Using the Consumer Price Index as a base of constant dollars, the median journalist in our study had about $7,000 *less* in purchasing power than if salaries had kept up fully with inflation.[14] (See table 4.8.)

But it is obvious that not all journalists suffered equally. Those with graduate degrees and those forty-five to fifty-five years old experienced the largest increases in salary from 1970 to 1981. Likewise, news magazine and wire service personnel — those working for the largest organizations — appear to have suffered least from inflation over the decade, because their median salary figure rose dramatically compared to that of personnel in the other media. Daily-newspaper salaries rose slightly, while weekly-paper personnel reported slight declines in income relative to the median figures for all journalists. Television journalists show the greatest losses, with a median annual income now lower than the overall median salary for journalists.[15] Radio journalists also make comparatively less money than others, but their relative losses are not as great as those of their TV colleagues. (See table 4.9.)

The most significant finding concerning salaries, though, is that the serious disparity between male and female journalists' income appears to have lessened considerably, and it has almost disappeared at the entry level. (See table 4.10.)

Johnstone found in 1971 that the median annual income of men younger than age twenty-five was 36 percent higher than that of women. Our data show essentially *no* disparity at that age level. Furthermore,

Table 4.8 Median Income in 1970 and 1981
by Sex, Age, and Years of Schooling

Factors		Median Income	
		1970	*1981*[a]
A.	Sex		
	Male	$11,955	$21,000
	Female	7,702	14,984
B.	Age		
	Under 25	6,492	10,991
	25–34	10,031	17,012
	35–44	13,322	22,999
	45–54	12,847	27,000
	55 and older	12,000	22,000
C.	Years of School		
	High school graduate or less	10,992	16,000
	Some college	10,164	18,022
	Graduated from college	11,617	17,999
	Some graduate training	11,424	21,000
	Graduate degree	12,823	25,012
			N = 939

[a]Sixty-two people were excluded because they had worked less than one year, making their estimates of 1981 income invalid.

among those twenty-five to thirty-four, the disparity between men's and women's salaries has dropped from 17 percent to 13 percent over the decade. Overall, the median male-female salary disparity has dropped from 55 percent to 40 percent since 1971.

Salary discrepancies by gender are still present in specific job areas. Full-time male reporters had a median income of $20,000 in 1981, compared to $14,500 for women. Part of the disparity is explained in differential experience, with the men having worked in journalism an average of three years longer than women colleagues. At supervisory levels, the disparity is slightly less, with males earning a median income of $22,000, and their women colleagues $17,010. The men, however, have worked in the field a median of four years longer than the women supervisors. And, as in the overall sample of journalists, beginning supervisors appear to have more equitable incomes in 1981. Supervisors

Table 4.9 Median Income in 1970 and 1981 by Media Sector, Region, and Size of News Organization

Factors	Median Income	
	1970	1981
A. Media Sector		
News Magazines	$15,571	$34,750
Television	11,875	17,031
Wire Services	11,833	24,100
Daily Newspapers	11,420	21,000
Radio	9,583	15,000
Weekly Newspapers	8,786	14,000
B. Region		
New England	11,274	30,000
Middle Atlantic	11,622	24,000
Total Northeast	11,532	27,000
East North Central	11,702	18,000
West North Central	9,600	15,993
Total North Central	11,187	16,999
South Atlantic	11,484	19,100
East South Central	7,846	16,033
West South Central	8,920	14,000
Total South	10,005	17,550
Mountain	9,118	15,933
Pacific	13,573	22,050
Total West	11,661	18,975
C. Size of News Organization		
1–10 editorial employees	8,632	15,000
11–25 editorial employees	9,866	15,985
26–50 editorial employees	11,657	21,000
51–100 editorial employees	10,892	23,960
Over 100 editorial employees	13,550	30,025

N = 939

with one to three years of journalism experience were earning salaries similar to those of their women colleagues with comparable journalism experience in 1981.

Regional variation in journalism salaries in 1981 appears to be much different from that a decade ago. The Northeast has moved significantly ahead of the other regions of the nation, with a median income of

Table 4.10 Median Income of Journalists
in 1981, by Sex and Age

Median Income[a]

Age	Men	Women	Difference
Under 25	$11,017	$10,967	$ 50
25–34	$18,013	$15,995	$ 2,018
35–44	$26,000	$16,900	$ 9,100
45–54	$29,960	$17,050	$12,910
55 and older	$25,125	$12,150	$12,975
TOTAL	$21,000	$14,984	$ 6,016

[a]Sixty-two people were excluded because they had worked less than one year.

$27,000. Median salaries for the South and North Central regions are closer to parity than in 1970, but the South is now ahead, with a median income of $17,550, compared to $16,999 in the North Central states. (See table 4.9.)

Even more dramatic salary disparities have emerged between small and large news organizations. Media with more than 100 editorial employees now have a median 1981 income of $30,021, more than double the median salary of the smallest organizations. (See table 4.9.) Editorial staff size, in fact, is one of the strongest predictors of annual income. When considered with a dozen other factors, ranging from region to professional age, organizational staff size is second only to years of journalism experience as a salary predictor. More important, staff size and years of experience are much more powerful predictors of salary than they were a decade ago. In addition, working on a unionized editorial staff emerged as a significant predictor of larger salaries in 1981. Regional salary differences, then, appear to be accounted for largely by professional age and staff size differences, with other factors (such as gender, education, and scope of managerial responsibilities) also causing regional differences in salary. (See table 4.11.)

Although Johnstone saw journalists' income as roughly equivalent to incomes of other comparable occupations in 1971, that certainly is not true today. The median journalist's salary has been eroded by the inflation of the 1970s, and his income hardly compares with other professionals'. In 1981, the *average* salary for corporate public-relations practitioners was $24,876, compared to $21,520 for journalists. The

Table 4.11 Predictors of Income Level of Journalists

Predictors	Standardized Regression Coefficients	Simple r
1. Professional age (number of years in news media)	.41	.49
2. Size of organization	.27	.43
3. Editorial staff unionized	.14	.35
4. Managerial responsibilities	.14	.18
5. Years of schooling	.13	.17
6. Sex (being female)	−.10	−.25
7. Media Sector		
a) Daily newspapers	−.002	.03
b) Radio	.07	−.11
c) Weekly newspapers	−.01	−.19
d) News magazines	.27	.35
e) Television	.15	.02
8. Region		
a) Northeast	−.06	.26
b) North Central	.41	−.14
c) South	−.025	−.08
9. Prominence of news organization	.05	.40
10. Reporter	−.03	−.16
11. Graduate degree	−.03	−.11
12. Chronological age	−.02	.37
13. Journalism major	−.02	−.10
14. Journalism minor	−.01	−.009
15. Group-owned medium	−.009	−.003
16. Editor	.002	−.12

$R^2 = .54$

average education and experience levels of the two fields are comparable, yet the salary disparity is significant.[16]

Furthermore, journalists' salaries do not compare favorably to those of other jobs of similar stature. For example, accountants and auditors for the U.S. government had *average* salaries of $27,700 in 1980.[17] With a bachelor's degree and two years' experience, an accountant could command $18,600 with the federal government in 1980, considerably more than the median journalist with four to seven years' experience ($15,035).[18] Even more telling is the fact that other professionals have fared better over the inflationary decade than have journalists. Engineers, accountants, directors of personnel, and job analysts appear to have ridden the crest of inflation to maintain their real purchasing power over the decade.[19] Journalists, in general, have not.

JOURNALISTS' IMAGES OF AUDIENCES

Critics of the news media sometimes claim that journalists underestimate the intelligence of their audiences. The Burgoon-Atkin study suggested that "far too many" newspaper journalists "express beliefs that the public is unsophisticated and plebian in its tastes."[20] David Altheide, a sociologist who has studied television news organizations, says that a major element of the television news "perspective" is seeing the audience as "essentially stupid."[21] And an old anecdote tells of the proverbial journalist who has on his desk a miniature statue of a baboon on which is carved "My typical reader."

How true are these claims? Journalists in our sample were asked three questions about their audiences. A majority (74 percent) agreed, either somewhat or strongly, that their audiences preferred breaking news to analysis of trends. On the other hand, a little less than a third of our sample thought their audience had little interest in reading about social problems such as racial discrimination and poverty.

More important, only a very small minority (16 percent) agreed, either somewhat or strongly, that their audience members were gullible or easily fooled. These results are roughly similar to findings by Burgoon, Burgoon, and Atkin in their 1981 case studies of eight U.S. newspaper staffs.[22]

Media differences on audience image were slight. Broadcast journalists were somewhat more likely than their print colleagues to see the audience as preferring breaking news. There was virtual unanimity on the question of audience interest in social problems, with a small minority in all media agreeing that there was little interest in such news. There was a slight tendency for broadcast journalists to be more likely to say their audiences were gullible than were their print colleagues, with radio journalists being the most likely to have such an image of the audience.

JOURNALISTS' RATING OF THEIR ORGANIZATION

News-media performance in informing the public is rated more highly by journalists in the 1982-83 study than in Johnstone's research of a dozen years ago. (See table 4.12.) When asked how well their organization

Table 4.12 Journalists' Rating of How Well Their Organization
Informs the Public, 1971 and 1982–83

Rating	Respondent's Own Organization	
	1971 (%)	1982–83 (%)
Outstanding	14.9	17.9
Very Good	38.1	49.1
Good	31.2	24.9
Fair	13.1	7.0
Poor	2.0	1.1
No Opinion	.7	.1
TOTAL	100.0	100.0

informed the public, almost 70 percent say either outstanding or very good, compared to little more than half the sample responding that way in 1971.

There were no significant differences among journalists of the various media in their rating of media performance. Broadcast journalists and their print colleagues were equally likely to say that their organization was doing a very good or outstanding job of informing the public.

JOB SATISFACTION AND JOB PERCEPTIONS

Journalists appeared satisfied with their jobs in 1971, expressing considerably higher levels of job satisfaction than the labor force at large. A similar picture emerged a decade later, although significantly fewer journalists see themselves as "very satisfied" than did so in 1971. (See table 4.13.) The slight decline would not appear to be serious were it not such an essential factor in journalists' commitment to the field.

In case studies of several journalism organizations, the Burgoons and Atkin found that journalists complain about their jobs, but that they love their work "even though it causes stress."[23] They also found that journalists who said they received clear and consistent "directives" from supervisors and who had autonomy in their jobs expressed greater job satisfaction. Older journalists, with the exception of those thirty-five to forty-four, were more likely to be satisfied with their jobs than were their younger colleagues. Those journalists in their late thirties and early forties were least likely to be satisfied. Finally, journalists who held their organization in high esteem also tended to express higher rates of job satisfaction.

Table 4.13 Job Satisfaction

	1971	*1982–83*
Very Satisfied	49%	40%
Fairly Satisfied	39	44
Somewhat Dissatisfied	12	15
Very Dissatisfied	1	2
		N = 1,001

Our research, done about one year later than the Burgoon-Atkin study of eight daily newspapers, suggests both differences and parallels. As in Johnstone's work a decade ago, we find the context of job satisfaction to be a great deal more complex for older journalists. For journalists who are forty or younger, six significant predictors emerged, as compared to fourteen for those older than forty.

For journalists who are forty or younger, the major predictor of job satisfaction is how well they thought their news organization was doing in informing the public. The higher their esteem for the organization, the more likely the journalists were to be happy in their job. (See table 4.14.) That appears to be a very stable factor, because it was also the strongest correlate of job satisfaction a dozen years ago.

The second-most important predictor of job satisfaction by younger journalists is the frequency of comments made by superiors about journalists' work. This finding appears to be consistent with that of the Burgoon-Atkin study. Their research found clear directives from supervisors and job autonomy together to be their strongest predictor of job satisfaction.[24] We found two elements of job autonomy — choosing stories to work on and determining the emphases of those stories — to be related to job satisfaction for younger journalists.

In general, the correlates for job satisfaction for younger journalists have remained stable over the decade, with one significant exception. Salary level no longer predicts job satisfaction. Instead, the relative *importance* journalists place on salary in evaluating journalism jobs is associated with job satisfaction. In general, the more important salary is as a criterion for evaluating the job, the less job satisfaction the journalist expresses. That relationship is even stronger for older journalists, even though salary level is a predictor of satisfaction among those forty and older, just as it was a dozen years ago. Older journalists with higher salaries are a little more likely to express greater job satisfaction than their less-well-paid colleagues.

Table 4.14 Relative Strength of Several Predictors of Job
Satisfaction among Journalists in Two Age Groups

Predictors	Standardized Progression Coefficients (Beta)	Simple Correlation Coefficient (r)
A. Journalists 40 or younger ($R^2 = .37$)		
1. Rating of performance of the employing news organization.	.32	.39
2. Frequency comments received from supervisors about work.	.27	.35
3. Extent of freedom to choose news stories on which to work.	.15	.17
4. Importance of salary in evaluating a job.	−.14	−.11
5. Working for a news magazine.	.14	.10
6. Extent of freedom to decide which aspects of news stories to emphasize.	.12	.14
B. Journalists older than 40 ($R^2 = .61$)		
1. Editorial staff members of a labor union.	−.36	−.17
2. Importance of editorial policies in evaluating a job.	−.33	−.19
3. Being unmarried.	−.29	−.18
4. Majoring in journalism in college.	.27	.09
5. Perceived importance of autonomy in evaluating a job.	−.23	−.16
6. Salary level.	.24	.09
7. Importance of salary in evaluating a job.	−.23	−.19
8. Ability to get an important subject covered in news.	.20	.19

Table 4.14 (continued)

Predictors (Beta)	Standardized Progression Coefficients (r)	Simple Correlation Coefficient
9. Subscribing to the information transmitter/disseminator role.	.19	.20
10. Rating of performance of employing organization.	.17	.31
11. Frequency of comments from supervisors.	.14	.21
12. Number of social friends who are journalists.	−.14	−.12
13. Subscribing to an adversarial role for the journalist.	−.12	−.17
14. Stress on journalism's importance to helping people.	.12	.12
15. Being a reporter.	.10	.10

Several other factors are common to the job satisfaction of both older and younger journalists. Esteem for the organization and frequent communication from superiors were job satisfaction predictors for both groups. Key differences, though, are apparent.

The more important the organization's editorial policies and job autonomy to the older journalists' evaluation of their jobs, the *lower* the level of reported job satisfaction. And those older journalists who think they almost always can get a news subject covered that they think is important express higher job satisfaction.

Some surprising factors emerged in our work that did not appear in the earlier Johnstone study or in the Burgoon-Atkin research. Older journalists who were on unionized editorial staffs, who were unmarried, or who tended to have a preponderance of other journalists as social friends expressed less job satisfaction than their colleagues. In line with that, those who strongly endorsed the adversarial role of journalism reported less job happiness. In contrast, those older journalists who felt strongly about the importance of the information-disseminator role of mass media, who had been journalism majors in college, or who stressed the importance of helping people in a journalism job claimed higher job satisfaction.

Some factors which appear to be *unrelated* to job satisfaction in the 1980s are as interesting as some of those that predict satisfaction. For example, job satisfaction levels appear to be similar among all media, with the exception of news magazines. Younger journalists working on the magazine staffs — who tend to have higher incomes than their other print colleagues — express higher job satisfaction than journalists in general. A decade ago, broadcast journalists tended to be less happy with their jobs, but that appears to have changed. Another significant change is that organization size is no longer a factor, with journalists in the larger organizations just as satisfied as personnel in smaller media, unlike the situation a decade ago.

Other factors that make *no* difference in job satisfaction are whether one works for a group-owned organization, the professed importance of advancement opportunity or job security, and the journalist's political leanings. And, in contrast to the situation in 1971, gender makes no difference in job satisfaction. A decade ago, women tended to express higher job satisfaction than men. Now that one journalist in three is a woman, the men no longer are expressing lower levels of job satisfaction than are women journalists. In addition, being a manager no longer predicts greater job satisfaction as it did in 1976.[25] And, surprisingly, older reporters tended to show higher levels of job satisfaction than did their younger colleagues.

In summary, the most important predictors of job satisfaction — esteem for the organization's performance, frequent communication with supervisors, and perceived job autonomy — appear to have remained stable over the last dozen years. The major changes appear to be among older journalists, where the pattern of factors has changed significantly. The older journalists' attitudes about the role of journalism in the society, and whether they majored in journalism now appear to be factors in job satisfaction. Personal circumstances, such as being single or having a majority of social friendships with other journalists, appear now to have a negative effect on job attitudes of older journalists. So the major changes, for older journalists particularly, appear to be the strengthening of *professional* and *personal* factors as elements of job satisfaction.

Importance of Aspects of the Job. American journalists have an image of altruism that is traceable at least as far back as the early-1900s "muckraking" period of Ida Tarbell, Ray Stannard Baker, and Lincoln Steffens. Johnstone found in 1971 that the image had a ring of authenticity, at least in the minds of journalists. Public service — the chance to help people — was the top-rated factor from a list of items pertinent to "judging" jobs in journalism. Job autonomy was second, with job security middle-ranked. Pay and fringe benefits, while viewed as important, were at the bottom of the list. (See table 4.15.) The agreement among journalists from the various media was striking. There were no significant differences among journalists from print or broadcast media in the ranking of the items. (See table 4.16.)

The most dramatic change over the years is in the increased importance of job security, which is now almost as salient as public-service job values. Pay and fringe benefits remain the least important of the items. This upward shift in the importance of job security, which was most dramatic among daily-newspaper journalists, was, no doubt, influenced by the timing of the interviewing at the height of the early 1980s recession, when unemployment was dominating the headlines, and by the fact that there were more applicants for each journalism job in the early 1980s than in the early 1970s.

In our survey, we asked journalists to consider the importance of several job attributes that were not included in Johnstone's earlier work. Editorial policy, the chance to advance in the organization, and the opportunity to develop a specialty were not considered as important as autonomy and altruism, but they were ranked above pay and fringe benefits.

Table 4.15 Factors of Job Satisfaction

	Percentage Saying Very Important
Helping people	61%
Job Security	57
Editorial Policy	57
Autonomy	50
Chance to Advance	47
Developing a Specialty	45
Fringe Benefits	26
Pay	23

$$N = 1,001$$

Table 4.16 Importance Journalists Assign to Different Job Aspects, by Media Sector, with a Comparison of the 1982–83 and 1971 Total Sample Results

Job Aspects	Daily Newspapers (N = 463)	Television (N = 121)	Total Print (N = 756)	Total Broadcast (N = 240)	1982–83 Total Sample (N = 996)	1971 Total Sample (N = 1,313)
Importance of						
helping people	1.48[a]	1.62	1.50	1.61	1.53	1.59
Job security	1.49	1.36	1.46	1.48	1.47	1.34
Autonomy	1.48	1.46	1.45	1.40	1.44	1.48
Editorial policy	1.36	1.31	1.44	1.24	1.40	—[b]
Chance to get						
ahead	1.23	1.43	1.27	1.48	1.32	—[b]
Developing a						
specialty	1.24	1.46	1.24	1.41	1.28	—[b]
Freedom of						
supervision	1.24	1.07	1.23	1.12	1.21	1.39
Pay	1.06	1.16	1.06	1.12	1.07	1.06
Fringe benefits	1.06	1.02	1.04	1.05	1.05	.97

[a]Where 2 = very important; 1 = fairly important; and 0 = not too important, with the mean scores for all respondents reported in the table.
[b]Not reported in John Johnstone, Edward Slawski, and William Bowman, *The News People*. Urbana: University of Illinois Press, 1976, p. 229.

On-the-job values, when analyzed extensively, reveal three basic orientations. Some journalists tend to emphasize economic issues — pay and fringe benefits — more than their colleagues. Others are more apt to cite personal-development items, advancement, and developing a specialty. A third group values job autonomy to a slightly greater extent.

If on-the-job values are grouped into three clusters of economic welfare, autonomy, and personal development, the most striking finding that emerges is that the orientations tend to be subscribed to by quite similar types of journalists. However, three very faint profiles of job-value correlates do emerge.

Economic Values: Those news personnel most likely to place high value on pay and fringe benefits tend to emphasize the information-disseminator role of the journalist, to work for unionized editorial staffs, and to be older.

Autonomy Values: Journalists who place a high value on autonomy as an on-the-job requirement tend to put greater stress on the interpreter role of the journalist.

Personal Development: The personal-development items of organizational advancement and developing a specialty tended to be valued slightly more by younger journalists who emphasized the information-disseminator role and were more conservative politically, or who were in television news.[26] (The journalistic roles mentioned above will be discussed thoroughly in chapter 5.)

In conclusion, perceptions of important attributes of journalism jobs tend to be quite similar among various types of journalists. Media sector makes very little difference, except that daily-newspaper journalists rate job security a bit higher, and TV news personnel see personal development as more important. Older journalists tend to focus more on economic factors, while younger journalists emphasize personal development. Job autonomy is more likely to be favored by those journalists more strongly endorsing the interpretive role of journalism. Again, though, the most significant finding is that the pattern of job perceptions is roughly similar for all journalists. The type of ownership of news organizations, the region of the country where employed, educational background, and a host of other variables make virtually no difference in how journalists rate various job attributes.

Job Disenchantment. A dozen years ago, Johnstone painted a generally positive picture of job satisfaction and aspirations among journalists. Yet, the portrait contained some worrisome blemishes. Johnstone feared that while only a small minority of all journalists were dissatisfied with their jobs in 1971, among the dissatisfied were often the best-educated personnel.[27] On the other hand, those whose dissatisfaction was great enough to say they planned to leave the news field (only 6 percent) tended to be in their late twenties and the least educated, lowest-paid persons.[28]

Lee B. Becker and several colleagues analyzed the responses of the reporters in Johnstone's sample, and found a somewhat different portrait of those who intended to leave the field. Neither salary nor education levels appeared related to the reporters' plans. Job satisfaction was the key predictor of intention to remain a career journalist. Reporters who said they were very satisfied with their jobs were much more likely to say they planned to stay in the field. Married reporters with families, and those who placed higher importance on salary, job security, fringe benefits, and the chance to get ahead, also were more likely to say they wanted to remain in journalism. So job- and family-related matters in 1970 appeared to be more predictive of reporters' career plans than the philosophical-professional sentiments.[29]

Commitment to Journalism. Since the early 1970s, the quality of students entering the major accredited schools of journalism has risen dramatically. Journalism graduates now boast Rhodes and Marshall scholars among their ranks, and the education level of the average professional is considerably higher than it was a decade ago. Some worry, however, that the cream of the young journalists quickly becomes disillusioned with the field.

In 1971, Johnstone found that most persons in the field intended to remain there. Seven percent said they planned nonmedia jobs, and another 8 percent were undecided.[30] Twelve years later, the proportion of journalists who plan to remain in the field is about the same as in 1971. Eighty-three percent say they want to be in the field in five years. But, although not statistically significant, a slightly greater percentage of journalists than in 1971 planned to change careers. Eleven percent of our sample said they had decided to leave the news media. (See table 4.17.) In contrast to the earlier picture, professional values and educational background emerge as significant predictors of career plans.

Table 4.17 Employment Aspirations of U.S. Journalists
in Five Years, by Age
(Percentage in Each Grouping)

Employment Aspirations

Age	Work in News Media[a]	Work outside News Media	Retire	Undecided	Total
Under 25	80	10.4	—	9.6	100.0
25–29	84.8	11.2	—	4.0	100.0
30–34	81.4	10.2	—	8.4	100.0
35–39	87.9	7.6	—	4.5	100.0
40–44	84.2	13.2	—	2.6	100.0
45–49	91.9	6.5	—	1.6	100.0
50–54	85.1	10.6	—	4.3	100.0
55–59	71.2	11.5	7.7	9.6	100.0
60–64	75.0	—	25.0	—	100.0
65 and Older	88.5	—	11.5	—	100.0
Total	82.6	10.6	1.7	5.1	100.0

[a]The Johnstone survey asked respondents if they would work for the same organization or elsewhere in the media. Respondents in this study were asked only if, in five years, they would be working in the media or elsewhere outside the media.

An intensive analysis of career plans focused on the 419 persons in the sample who said they did reporting as a substantial part of their jobs.[31] The respondents were divided into those who said they planned to remain in the news media and those who desired to change fields.[32] (See table 4.18.).

The most striking difference between the two groups is in their professional values. Reporters who say they want to leave the profession are much likelier to rate these factors as important in judging jobs: the chance to help people, the editorial policies of the organization, freedom from supervision, and the amount of autonomy they have. Ironically, though, reporters who say they *have* considerable autonomy on their jobs are *also* likelier to say they plan to leave journalism than are those with *less* autonomy.

Similarly, the longer the reporter has been in the field, the more likely he or she is to plan to change professions. Journalists who intend to leave the profession also see the information-disseminator role as less important than do those who want to remain in the field.

Table 4.18 Comparison of the Importance of Various Factors
That Discriminate between Reporters Who
Plan to Change Careers and Those Who
Wish to Stay in Journalism[a]

	1971[b]	*1982–83*
Education and Background		
Education Level	—	− .24
Journalisn Major	—	.24
Journalism Minor	—	.31
Age	—	− .15
Married	.33	− .14
Have Children	.16	− .12
Organizational Characteristics		
Print Journalist	—	− .25
Group-owned	—	.30
Size of Organization	− .16	.25
Guild Organization	− .15	− .03
Peer Feedback	—	.18
News Source Feedback	—	.22
Years in Journalism	—	− .24
Income	—	.14
Job Sentiments		
Evaluation of Organization	—	.04
Perceived Autonomy	—	− .33
Job Satisfaction	.36	.38
Professional Factors		
Stress on Professional Values	—	− .40
Stress on Nonprofessional Values	.18	—
Stress on Information-Disseminator Role	.11	.32
Membership in Journalism Organizations	.18	.21

[a]Discriminant analysis was used to determine the "power" of the various factors to discriminate between reporters who were "defectors" and "stayers." The coefficients are analogous to beta weights in regression analysis. A positive number means the factor is a characteristic of "stayers." A negative number means the factor is associated with "defectors."

[b]Data for 1971 are from Lee B. Becker, Idowa A. Sobowale, and Robin E. Cobbey, "Reporters and Their Professional and Organizational Commitment," reprinted in G. Cleveland Wilhoit and Harold de Bock, eds., *Mass Communication Review Yearbook*, vol. 2. Beverly Hills, Calif.: Sage Publications, 1981, pp. 339–50.

Reporters who chose journalism as a minor or major subject in college are more apt to want to stay in the field than those who studied another field. There is also a tendency for those with the highest degrees to say they plan to leave the field.

Job satisfaction remains a substantial factor in predicting commitment to the profession. Journalists who say they are very satisfied with their jobs are considerably more likely to say they plan to remain in the field than are those who are less satisfied. Reporters working for larger organizations and those that are group-owned are likelier to be among the committed. And broadcast reporters are a bit more likely than those in print to say they want to remain in journalism.

Over the last decade, then, the characteristics of reporters desirous of leaving journalism have changed somewhat. The bulk of the disenchanted now are in the prime age group of thirty to forty-four. Unlike those a dozen years ago, the "defectors" are no longer "journalists who are not particularly well-placed within the industry and those whose earnings are low."[33] Being married and a parent no longer is associated with professional commitment. The tendency is just the opposite. Single reporters with no children are a little less likely now to say they want to leave the field than are their married colleagues. Older journalists with lengthier reporting experience are more apt to plan to leave the field than their younger counterparts, unlike those ten years ago. Numbered among those likely to leave are the most highly educated journalists who say they have been entrusted with more job autonomy. The "defectors" also include a larger number of reporters who feel strongly about professional values in the field.

That is a disturbing shift. While the problem should not be exaggerated — the proportion of journalists intending to leave the field is only slightly greater than it was a decade ago — it is vexing that highly educated, experienced journalists with strong feelings about the role and purpose of the field are overrepresented among those who intend to leave the profession. Why they may wish to leave is, of course, a complex question. But salary and fringe benefits top a long list of reasons they cite for wanting to get out of the field. More than half of the reporters (58 percent) mentioned money matters as their leading problems. Other reasons cited ranged from stress to boredom. That pattern of responses, however, is similar to what we were told by journalists who said they have no plans to leave the field. When asked what factors, if any, they could imagine leading them to leave journalism for a job in another field, the "confirmed" reporters listed money matters more frequently. About half of them mentioned salary or fringe benefits first, and another 15 percent mentioned money as second. Twenty other reasons, ranging from stress to burnout, were cited by very small percentages of these journalists.

In an attempt to probe more deeply into the reasons for disenchantment with journalism as a career, this open-ended question was asked of *all* respondents, not just reporters: "What factors, if any, could you imagine leading you to leave journalism for a job in another field?"

Given the decline in journalists' purchasing power over the decade, the responses to our query should have been no surprise. A little more than half of our sample mentioned pay and fringe benefits first. Of more than eighty other replies, only stress and the need for other challenges were mentioned by as many as 5 percent of the respondents. Of the remainder of the reasons cited, these were mentioned by at least 2 percent of all journalists: lack of freedom, lack of advancement opportunities, difficulties with management, dislike of editorial policy, job security, and lack of recognition.

Among those who had told us they *intended* to leave the field in the next five years, the pattern of responses was similar. Fifty-four percent of them noted money-related matters as their first reason. Another 10 percent said they had decided they "liked" another field better than journalism. Stress, lack of freedom, lack of challenge, time demands, and boring assignments were each mentioned by 4 percent of the respondents.

The irony of the obvious crisis of financial rewards in journalism is that those who intend to leave the field, ostensibly because of pay, tend to be those who claim the strongest commitment to professional values of altruism, editorial policy, and autonomy. Furthermore, those leaving, who tend to be experienced journalists, are among those who see themselves as having reached a high degree of autonomy on the job. They appear to be the kinds of personnel the field can least afford to lose.

CONCLUSIONS

The administrative path to advancement in journalism appears to be attracting journalists at a much younger age now than it did a decade ago. Journalists in management positions are much younger now. That is likely a result of three forces. First, the editorial workforce has grown markedly, creating additional management opportunities. Technological changes in the newsroom have placed a premium on young persons in management to cope with the rapid innovation. But most important, it seems logical to conclude that the rate of turnover in personnel leaving the field is greater now than in 1971. Journalism is now truly a young people's business.

Perceived autonomy is still high among journalists, even though their assessment of the amount of autonomy suggests that they have less than in 1971. The significant decline in perceived autonomy may be a result of a younger workforce's not having "proven" itself yet. But it is likely that public criticism of isolated cases of story fabrication and of adversarial journalism has encouraged editors to increase control.

Having job autonomy and a sense of altruism are still said to be highly important factors in journalism as a job, but job security has risen markedly as a value. Ironically, even though journalism earnings in general have not kept up with inflation, salary remains on the bottom of most journalists' lists of important job factors.

Professionalism factors on the job — such as the importance of autonomy and the estimate of how well the employing organization is doing in informing the public — appear to have become stronger predictors of work satisfaction, particularly for journalists aged forty and older. Overall job satisfaction has declined slightly, although the rate of satisfaction remains high in comparison to that of the adult workforce in general.

The most disturbing development is, of course, the evidence that the one journalist in ten who has decided to leave the field in the next five years is more likely now to be among the most highly educated, committed journalists who are at mid-career. Their reasons for the decision to leave, however, appear to boil down to issues of salaries and benefits.

In summary, our analysis of job conditions and satisfactions of U.S. journalists in 1982-83 reveals these major findings:

1. The typical reporter is thirty-one years old, with eight years of journalism experience, reflective of the younger work force described in chapter 2.

2. Most journalists do some reporting and editing, just as they did a dozen years ago.

3. As the workforce has grown younger, so has management; the

typical journalist with management responsibility is now thirty-five years old, with about four years' more professional experience than the staff.

4. Of those with supervisory responsibility, 28 percent are now women, a significant increase over the decade.

5. Journalism training, supervisors, and news sources are seen as the top influences on the definition of news; but the better the job the journalist perceives the organization as doing, the more important supervisors and staff peers are judged to be.

6. Journalists still perceive substantial autonomy in their work, with an overwhelming majority feeling they have the ability to get important subjects reported. On the other hand, there is significant decline in the number of journalists who think they have the freedom to determine story emphasis, or whose copy is not edited by someone else.

7. While the newsroom context is extremely important in all aspects, feedback from the audience and news sources is greater than might be expected. Audience response is obtained regularly by about half of the journalists and is the top-rated source of feedback. News sources, peers, and supervisors also provide frequent feedback.

8. Journalistic salaries have been eroded seriously by inflation over the decade; the median salary is $19,000, with about $7,000 less in purchasing power than the median salary in 1971.

9. The disparity between income received by male and female journalists has narrowed considerably, with salaries of beginning men and women journalists (including management) now the same.

10. Editorial staff size, years of experience, and Guild membership are strongest predictors of income level.

11. Journalistic salaries are considerably lower than those in occupations requiring comparable education and experience, such as public relations and accounting.

12. Job satisfaction, while higher than general job satisfaction of the U.S. labor force, is down significantly from that a decade ago.

13. Salaries are generally so low that income is no longer a predictor of job satisfaction for journalists younger than forty. Instead, the relative *importance* placed on salary is related to job satisfaction.

14. The two most important predictors of job satisfaction for younger journalists are their esteem for the job their organization is doing and the frequency of feedback received from their supervisors. These factors are related to job satisfaction of older journalists, too, but job satisfaction for older journalists is more complex to predict.

15. Job satisfaction is similar among journalists of all media, except that news magazine journalists, the most highly paid sector of the media, express generally higher satisfaction.

16. Job security is a much more important element of journalists' job perceptions than it was in 1971, but altruism and autonomy remain important elements of how journalists evaluate their jobs.

17. The proportion of journalists who say they plan to leave the field has increased slightly over the decade, from 7 to 11 percent. That increase is not statistically significant, but the profile of the would-be "defectors" has changed. Those who plan to leave the field tend to be the most highly educated and experienced journalists from the prime age group of thirty to forty-four. They tend to be the journalists who emphasize the professional aspects — altruism and autonomy — of the field.

18. Pay and fringe benefits are cited most often when journalists are asked what might make them want to leave the field, both by those who say they *are* leaving and by those who plan to be in journalism after five years.

—5—

Professionalism: Roles, Values, Ethics

No intellectual occupation defies sociological categories of professionalism as robustly as journalism. Yet, there is an irresistible attraction to couching the values and roles of journalists in the context of professionalization.[1]

Arthur Lawrence, who reported from the Lobby of the House of Commons for the *London Daily Mail*, appears to have been among the first to write a book describing journalism as a profession. His 1903 work *Journalism as a Profession* portrayed newspapering as a "model of scientific sub-editing," and described the journalist's role as diverse. In his view, journalism accommodated the desire to "ameliorate the lot of the people," and the possibility to "reform the public service" in a "most interesting and engrossing occupation."[2] Lawrence, who wrote the book at the young age of thirty-two, even advised "a year at a university" for aspiring journalists, which surely made him a visionary among British writers of his time.[3]

The modern journalist often is called a professional. But so is almost everybody, as Harold Wilensky observed in his article "The Professionalization of Everyone?" Wilensky, a sociologist, argued that the hasty use of the term *professional* obscures an understanding of newer occupational forms that are emerging.[4]

Journalists have become increasingly eager to call themselves professionals. James Boylan, historian and journalism educator, says acceptance of the term reached its peak during the 1960s upheaval in covering
the civil rights movement and the Vietnam War. By calling themselves
professionals, Boylan wrote, "journalists could, like doctors or lawyers,
claim special rights, notably a degree of individual autonomy in writing
and reporting."[5] The implications of the rhetoric of professionalism,
Boylan said, were that individual journalists, and the larger media
institutions they served, were "free-floating" bodies, answerable to no-
one.[6]

Johnstone and his colleagues concluded from their analysis a decade
ago that journalism *was* a profession, in an "abstract formal sense."[7]
The major question was whether working journalists *behaved* as professionals. The answer, in short, was yes and no. Journalists valued public
service, autonomy, and freedom from supervision. They leaned toward
altruism, at least in ranking economic rewards as less important than
public service. But in their nurturance of the field, journalists were
unlike other professionals. Their rate of membership in professional
groups was remarkably low. And this reticence to join professional
associations appeared to be reflected in considerable divergence of purpose and lack of unity.[8]

The following analysis of a wide range of survey questions about
organizational memberships, roles, ethics, and values will suggest that
journalists are more pluralistic in their professional attitudes than they
were a decade ago, despite their less diverse educational backgrounds,
documented in chapter 3. The tendency to see the journalist's role as
either "participant" or "neutral" seems to have given way to a blending
of the two approaches, and perhaps a more realistic view of journalistic
purpose.

THE PROFESSIONAL COMMUNITY
OF THE JOURNALIST

The professional "community" of news journalism is extremely diverse.
Memberships in thirty-five different groups — ranging from the American Society of Newspaper Editors and the Radio-Television News Directors Association to the Baseball Writers Association of America — were
claimed by the journalists in our sample. As the journalistic workforce
grew substantially over the last decade, the proportion of journalists

claiming membership in professional organizations declined slightly. In 1972, about 45 percent of American journalists said they were members of national or local groups that were primarily for journalists.[9] Only 40 percent of the 1982 respondents said they belong to such groups.

The proportion of journalists who claim membership in *national* professional groups has increased substantially. About 22 percent of U.S. journalists now belong to one or more national groups, compared to 13 percent a decade ago.[10] That suggests an emerging professional identity, even though no *single* organization commands a very high proportion of U.S. journalists on its membership roles.

The Society of Professional Journalists, Sigma Delta Chi (SPJ/SDX) is the largest professional association in the field, with 17 percent of all U.S. journalists claiming membership. Having shed its status as an honorary Greek-letter society many years ago, SPJ/SDX has been a leader over the last decade in the discussion of ethics and standards for the field. It has national committees on professionalism and ethics and publishes widely circulated commentaries on professional issues.[11] It is the dominant national voice for professionalism among rank-and-file journalists, because no other voluntary organization commands more than 2 percent of U.S. journalists as members.

The weak institutionalization of journalism is shown quite dramatically when the field is compared to law, medicine, and public accounting. All three professions are much larger than journalism, but each has a single national organization that claims a large proportion of practitioners. The American Bar Association consists of about half of the 620,000 attorneys in America.[12] The American Medical Association, although it has declined in proportional membership during the last decade, still has about 44 percent of the roughly 500,000 physicians in America on its roster.[13] Of about 250,000 public accountants in the United States, 70 percent are members of the American Institute of Certified Public Accountants (AICPA).[14] Journalism, then, has much weaker organizational identity than other major professional occupations.

Television news personnel are somewhat more likely to have professional memberships than their radio or newspaper colleagues. A little less than half of the television news people say they are members of some journalistic association or society, compared to 38 percent of the daily-newspaper journalists. Overall, print associational allegiances exceed broadcast memberships in one or more journalistic associations. (See table 5.1.) Still, the main point is that only a minority of journalists

Table 5.1 Number of Professional Associations
Belonged to, by Media Sector
(Percentage)

	Media Sector				
Number of Associations or Societies	*Daily Newspaper*	*Television*	*Total Print*[a]	*Total Broadcast*	*Total Sample*
More than one	16.2	13.2	15.5	12.3	15.1
One	22.2	33.9	24.3	20.2	25.3
None	61.6	52.9	60.2	67.5	59.6
TOTAL					100
N	463	121	756	163	1001

[a]Includes wire services

claim memberships in nonunion associational groups, which suggests a very weak institutional structure for a claim to traditional professionalism.

About 17 percent of our sample are members of trade unions, primarily The Newspaper Guild (TNG) and the American Federation of Television and Radio Artists (AFTRA). That statistic is down from 29 percent a decade ago. In 1982-83, the Guild claimed about 13 percent, with the remaining 4 percent belonging to broadcast unions, primarily AFTRA.[15]

FACTORS INFLUENCING IDENTIFICATION WITH JOURNALISM ASSOCIATIONS

Membership in journalism associations and societies, a choice made by only a minority of U.S. journalists, is an affirmation of commitment to the field that goes beyond the confines of the job. What are the characteristics of those journalists who make that commitment?

Extensive analysis of the backgrounds of those journalists who are members of one or more professional associations suggests that leadership in the field may be changing. Those who join organizations still tend to come from management and from among those with more extensive journalism experience. But the most striking change over the decade is the tendency for journalists from smaller media to be more likely to join associations than their colleagues in larger organizations. Secondly, journalism education, while only a weak predictor, is a more important factor than general education level in influencing the tendency to make a commitment to professional associations. (See table 5.2.)

Another indicator of professional identity may be the amount of socializing journalists do with other news people. Johnstone and his colleagues, at least, suggest such a possibility in their earlier work.[16] In

Table 5.2 Factors Influencing Formal and Informal
Identification with Journalism

A. *Formal Identification* (Number of Professional Organizations
Belonged to)

Predictors	Standardized Regression Coefficients	Simple r
1) Professional Age	.21	.10
2) Scope of Managerial Responsibilities	.17	.19
3) Organization Size	−.10	−.10
4) Years of Schooling	.03	.07
5) Chronological Age	−.14	.04
6) Media Sector (being in broadcast)	−.04	−.02
7) Organizational Prominence	−.03	−.08
8) Journalism Education—major	.08	.08
9) Journalism Education—minor	.05	.05
10) Journalism Education—graduate	.08	.09

$R^2 = .08$

B. *Informal Identification* (Percentage of People Seen Socially Who Are
Connected with Journalism)

Predictors	Standardized Regression Coefficients	Simple r
1) Professional Age	−.14	−.17
2) Scope of Managerial Responsibilities	−.06	−.13
3) Organization Size	.19	.15
4) Years of Schooling	.01	.10
5) Chronological Age	−.37	−.27
6) Media Sector (being in broadcast)	.07	.09
7) Organizational Prominence	.0005	.08
8) Journalism Education—major	.05	.11
9) Journalism Education—minor	.06	.07
10) Journalism Education—graduate	.06	.06

$R^2 = .13$

Table 5.3 Extent of Informal Social Contacts
Among Journalists, by Media Sector

Percentage of Social Contacts Which Are with Journalists	Daily Newspapers	Television	Total Print[a]	Total Broadcast	Total Sample
50 or more	44.3	61.2	39.8	34.4	41.7
11–49	21.6	16.5	20.2	27.0	21.0
1–10	25.9	19.8	29.8	27.6	28.1
zero	8.2	2.5	10.2	11.0	9.3
TOTAL	100	100	100	100	100
BASE	463	121	756	163	1,001
MEAN	37.4	47.9	33.8	30.9	35.3

[a]Includes wire services

our study, as in the earlier work by Johnstone, the journalists were asked to estimate the percentage of persons they saw socially who were in newswork. Analysis of those findings reveals a picture very similar to the pattern of a dozen years ago. About one-third of the typical journalist's social friends were said to be other journalists. (See table 5.3.)

Younger journalists, particularly personnel from larger media without extensive professional experience, were more likely to have more extensive social ties to other journalists. Broadcast journalists were a little more likely than their print colleagues to socialize with journalistic friends, as were those who took journalism courses in their college years. (See table 5.2.)

As a dozen years ago, then, professional groups appeal more significantly to experienced journalists with management responsibilities. The informal ties to colleagues as friends, on the other hand, are stronger for younger journalists in large organizations. The most provocative difference in the 1980s is that journalists from smaller nonelite media are most attracted to formal identification with the field.

READERSHIP OF PROFESSIONAL JOURNALS

Journal and trade-publication reading among news people may be considered an important indicator of professional identity. The journalists in our sample were asked about their use of fifteen magazines and journals that are published on subjects having to do with news.

The oldest magazine in the field, *Editor & Publisher*, which began publication in the early 1900s, has the largest readership. About 60 percent of all journalists — and almost 80 percent of daily-newspaper journalists — read the weekly trade magazine at least "sometimes." (See table 5.4.)

Columbia Journalism Review, a bimonthly journal of criticism that is published by the Graduate School of Journalism at Columbia University, and the *Quill*, the magazine of the Society of Professional Journalists, Sigma Delta Chi (SPJ/SDX), are the next-most widely read journals.

Table 5.4 Readership among All Journalists of Professional
Journals and Trade Publications
(N = 1,001)

	Frequency of Readership		
	Regularly[c]	*Sometimes*	*Never*
Editor and Publisher[a]	29%	34%	37%
Columbia Journalism Review	20	36	44
Quill	18	32	50
Washington Journalism Review	13	30	57
Journalism Quarterly	6	28	66
APME News	7	12	82
ASNE Bulletin	6	13	81
Journal of Broadcasting	6	11	84
Nieman Reports	3	17	81
Editor's Exchange	4	8	89
Wirewatch	4	7	89
ANPA News Research Reports	3	10	87
presstime[b]	3	8	90
Journal of Communication	2	7	92
Newspaper Research Journal	2	8	91

[a]Of daily newspaper journalists, 39 percent regularly read and 40 percent sometimes read *Editor & Publisher*.

[b]A publication of the American Newspaper Publishers Association, *presstime* was a new journal at the time of interviewing. It is likely the journal is read by a larger audience now.

[c]Regular readership is defined as reading "almost every issue."

Table 5.5 Regular Readership of Major Professional Journals
and Magazines, by Organizational Membership
(Percentage of Regular Readership)[a]

| | *Organizational Status* | |
	Member (N = 404)	*Nonmember* (N = 589)
Editor & Publisher	37%	23%
Columbia Journalism Review	23	18
Quill	34	7

[a]Regular readership is defined as reading "almost every issue" of each publication.

Journals that are much more specialized, not surprisingly, are read by only a very small minority of journalists. *Journalism Quarterly*, a scholarly publication of academic research, is read regularly by only 6 percent, but is read sometimes by another 28 percent.

As would be expected, those journalists who are members of journalism associations, such as SPJ/SDX, are more likely to say they read the journals than are nonmembers. *Quill* and several others are publications of prominent associations, so membership is obviously a factor in those cases. The relationship holds, though, for the large publications that are not products of associations. (See table 5.5.)

Other factors are associated with journal reading, but none is as consistent as organizational membership. Educational level, particularly having a graduate degree, is associated with journal readership. And the more editing responsibility the journalist has, the more likely it is that the major journals are read.

Media differences generally are along the lines one would expect. Weekly-newspaper and radio journalists are much less likely to read either *Quill* or *Columbia Journalism Review* than are journalists from daily newspapers, the major news services, and television. Those journals tend to focus on problems that are more relevant to large news operations. News magazine journalists are much less likely to read *Quill* and *Editor & Publisher* than are their other print colleagues.

Few broadcast journalists, of course, read *Editor & Publisher* regularly, because the content is written primarily for newspaper people. However, television journalists are just as likely to read *Quill* and *Columbia Journalism Review* as are their print colleagues. That suggests that television news personnel identify as strongly with professional discussion of the field as do print journalists, despite some critics' suggestions to the contrary.

It may be disturbing to some that the top professional journals, with material that is critical of practices in the field, reach only about half of U.S. journalists. An essential question, though, is how that finding compares to the situation in other fields. Some evidence suggests that the general professional information flow from journals to journalists may be roughly comparable to that of some of the established professions. Figures supplied by the American Medical Association show that about half of the physicians in the United States read, to some degree, the *American Medical News*, a magazine similar in content to *Quill*. Research publication readership, of course, is much higher for physicians than among journalists.[17]

JOURNALISTIC ROLE CONCEPTIONS

Debate among journalists about the role of the press has reached high levels during the last decade. Ethics and responsibility issues have become popular topics for industry seminars and working papers. Courses dealing with these subjects, which have been offered at major schools of journalism for at least thirty years, suddenly have become popular. They are no longer viewed as required drudgery.

Articles such as "Are Journalists a New Class?" in *Business Forum*, and *Time* magazine's cover story on "Journalism under Fire" show the breadth of public concern.[18] The rhetorical image of journalists that emerges in the popular discussion of the 1980s portrays journalists as an arrogant, meddlesome elite, bent on being adversaries. *Time* aptly summarized: "They are rude and accusatory, cynical and almost unpatriotic."[19]

Distinguished journalists are among the most severe critics. Eugene Patterson, publisher of the *St. Petersburg Times*, said, for example, "Our system of assault journalism has diminished the majesty of the democratic process."[20]

Louis Boccardi, executive vice-president of the Associated Press, told the 1984 annual meeting of the AP membership that the cause of the firestorm of criticism rested on public perception of the journalistic role. "To much of our audience," Boccardi said, "we have not simply been the messengers of Vietnam, Watergate, the flower children and all the rest." Instead, journalists "are perceived by many not as messengers but as *agents*" of change.[21]

To what extent have journalists viewed themselves as messengers, or as agents, in our time? Johnstone's work addressed the question extensively. His research found evidence of two "pure" ideological types among working journalists in the early 1970s. The value cleavage reflected old arguments about objectivity, detachment, involvement, and advocacy. Johnstone and his colleagues characterized the competing belief systems as a *neutral*, "nothing-but-the-truth" orientation versus a *participant*, "whole-truth" mentality. The researchers found that most journalists adhered to some parts of both views, but that there were occupational subgroups organized around the two "ideologies."[22] The participant values were more prevalent among journalists in large cities and those who socialized extensively with other journalists. Neutral views of the journalistic role tended to be reflected by journalists from small towns and those with fewer social acquaintances among news people.[23]

Our research attempted to replicate Johnstone's inquiry into journalistic roles so that we could look for change and continuity in professional values. In addition to the questions asked by the previous research, we added important items to try to assess the depth of the participant role. Specifically, we attempted to see whether the participant orientation included the "adversarial mindset" that Michael J. O'Neill, editor of the *New York Daily News*, deplored in his 1982 address to the convention of the American Society of Newspaper Editors.[24]

The 1,001 journalists in our sample were questioned about nine "things that the media do or try to do today." Specifically, each journalist responded to questions such as this: "How important is it for the news media to get information to the public quickly? Extremely important, Quite important, Somewhat important, or Not really important?"

Investigating government claims and statements and getting information to the public quickly were said to be either quite or extremely important by a large majority of journalists. But only a minority thought being a skeptical adversary of public officials (or businesses) was important for the press. (See table 5.6.)

Journalists' views on press roles appear to be generally similar to those a decade ago, but some slight shifts are apparent. While the percentage differences are small, the items calling for analytical ap-

Table 5.6 Importance Journalists Assign to Various
Mass Media Roles

Media Roles	Percentage Saying Extremely Important	
	1971[a]	1983
Investigate Government Claims	76%	66%
Get Information to Public Quickly	56	60
Avoid Stories with Unverified Content	51	50
Provide Analysis of Complex Problems	61	49
Discuss National Policy	55	38
Concentrate on Widest Audience	39	36
Develop Intellectual/Cultural Interests	30	24
Provide Entertainment	17	20
Serve as Adversary of Government[b]	—	20
Serve as Adversary of Business[b]	—	15
	N = 1,313	N = 1,001

[a]Data are from John Johnstone, Edward Slawski, and William Bowman, *The News People*
Urbana: University of Illinois Press, 1976, p. 230.
[b]These items were not included in the 1971 survey.

proaches — investigating claims, analyzing complex problems, discussing national policy, and developing intellectual interests — are less likely to be ranked as important now than they were ten years ago. In contrast, entertaining and providing quick information are considered important by more journalists than in the earlier years. (The questions about the adversary role were not included in the 1971 survey.)

The Johnstone team noted that the overall results of the questions about roles in their study suggested that more journalists appeared to endorse the "participant" role than the "neutral" orientation, but that a majority appeared to accept functions common to *both* roles. Only after complex statistical analysis could they show distinguishable patterns of separate, competing belief systems among journalists.[25]

Our overall results suggest a similar picture. Investigating government claims (a "participant" item) and getting information to the public quickly (a "neutral" item) are endorsed about evenly in the sample. More important, though, is the unpopularity of the items that ask about an adversarial relationship.

The adversary items were included in the battery of role questions to test the limits of the so-called participant role. In spite of the easy acceptance the labels have received among scholars, we argue that *participant* and *neutral* are misnomers. Investigating government claims is, of course, an active, rather than passive, role, just as is discussing national policy. But neither necessarily means sharing of policy making. Getting information to the public quickly may be, in fact, just as participatory, and it certainly is not always neutral. If, then, the participant and neutral factors are still present in the most recent study, the factors must be labeled more appropriately.[26] Secondly, the adversary questions may enable us to show whether journalists claim a truly participatory role.

The ten questions about journalistic role were subjected to factor analysis, a complex statistical procedure, to determine whether news personnel's beliefs were patterned.[27] Three clusters of items emerged.

The most distinct factor to emerge had very high positive relationships with the two items about adversarial stances on government and business. In fact, this factor explained 57 percent of the common variance among *all* the items.

A second factor consisted of the same items that made up the participant attitude found by Johnstone. Analyzing and interpreting complex problems, investigating claims made by government, and discussing national policy while it is being developed were related strongly to this factor. The adversary items were related only weakly to this factor, so it seems reasonable to conclude that the items represent a separate cluster of values.

A final factor showed linkages with two of the four items that Johnstone labeled as neutral values. Getting information to the public quickly and concentrating on the widest possible audience were related strongly to this element. Two other items — staying away from unverifiable stories and entertaining the audience — were related weakly to this factor. They also were related slightly to other factors, so they are not considered a part of this cluster.

This analysis, then, suggests that *three*, rather than two, relatively distinct belief systems dominate journalists' attitudes about press functions: *adversarial*, *interpretive*, and *disseminator*.[28] The next section attempts to assess the relative importance of the three factors for American journalists.

After it had been established which of the various role questions relate to each other, the factor groupings were made into three scales, with each item in each factor weighted equally. The result enables us to look at upper and lower quartiles of each scale to estimate the proportions of journalists who predominantly favor one or more of the three roles.

The most striking finding is that the dominant professional role of contemporary journalists is interpretive. A majority of our sample scored in the top quartile on the interpretive scale. (See figure 5.1.)

The disseminator orientation is also important, with about half of the journalists ranking high on getting information quickly to the widest possible audience.

Only a very small minority of the sample felt that the adversary role was important.

The most important finding here is that contemporary journalists are extremely pluralistic in their conceptions of media roles, with about a third of them embracing fully both the interpretive *and* disseminator roles. Only about 2 percent of the respondents are exclusively one-role-oriented, tending to reject the other two roles, compared to 18 percent in 1971 who identified strongly with only one role. That greatly strengthens Johnstone's conclusion that journalists typically hold patterns of beliefs from several perspectives.[29] More important, these data illustrate that what the Johnstone group called the participant role — what we have labeled the interpretive role — does not extend to the full acceptance of an adversarial stance. In spite of the public clamor about the aggressiveness of the post-Watergate press, only a small minority of journalists strongly endorse a skeptical, adversarial mentality as a central role of journalism.

FIGURE 5.1

**JOURNALISTS' ROLE
PERCEPTION**

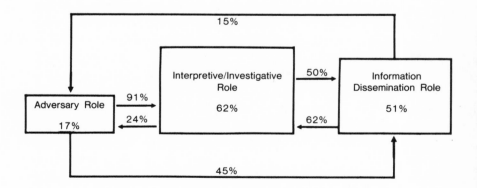

Does this general pattern of pluralism extend to all sectors of the press, or are there certain types of journalists who are more likely to be adversarial, interpretive, or disseminator in orientation? The next section addresses these questions.

CORRELATES OF PROFESSIONAL VALUES

In an attempt to trace the antecedents of professional values, the Johnstone research group looked at a host of factors. The results were disappointing, because nothing predicted journalistic roles very strongly. Considered together, however, a number of general points could be made. Educational experiences, aging, gender, types of career paths, demographic and organizational environments, and patterns of social relationships all seemed to contribute, if only weakly, to professional values.[30]

Using the three professionalism factors described earlier, a similar analysis was performed on the recent survey data. Again, the surprising thing is that so little of the variance in professional attitudes could be explained, although we were able to account for twice the amount Johnstone found.[31] The significant finding, though, was that factors in the *organizational* environment — as opposed to education and background variables — were most predictive of journalistic role orientation.

Organizational Status. Of about twelve factors that "predicted" journalistic role, five of them are associated with the job situation of respondents. Journalists with higher salaries favor the interpretive role and tend to avoid the disseminator stance, a pattern similar to that of a decade ago. Because the analysis controls for the effect of higher income resulting from being in management, a plausible interpretation is that it is the "star" reporters with higher salaries who have the strongest leanings toward the interpretive role.[32] In contrast to the findings of the earlier study — where medium appeared to be unrelated to perceived role — journalists working in print journalism today are more likely to subscribe to the interpretive orientation than are their colleagues in other media.

Persons with supervisory, editorial authority tend to lean toward the disseminator role and to avoid either the adversarial or interpreter positions. Reporters, on the other hand, are slightly more likely to be interpretive and adversarial than their editors. (See table 5.7.)

Table 5.7 Predictors of Professional Values among Journalists

VARIABLES	Interpretive Values ($R^2 = .25$)		Disseminator Values ($R^2 = .17$)		Adversarial Values ($R^2 = .19$)	
	Standardized Regression Coefficients	Correlation Coefficients	Standardized Regression Coefficients	Correlation Coefficients	Standardized Regression Coefficients	Correlation Coefficients
A. Region						
North Central	−.12	−.11	—	—	−.11	−.09
South	−.14	−.10	—	—	—	—
B. Education (years of schooling)	—	—	−.11	−.18	—	—

C. Organizational Status						
Income	.19	.20	-.12	-.11	—	—
Medium Print	.14	.21	—	—	—	—
Reporter	.14	.10	—	—	.14	.07
Supervisor	-.12	-.11	—	—	—	—
Editorial authority	-.18	-.11	.13	.12	-.18	-.12
D. Job Circumstances						
Importance of autonomy	.15	.20	—	—	—	—
Importance of job security	—	—	.13	.21	—	—
Amount of comment from news sources	.10	.07	—	—	—	—
E. Political Leanings						
Being conservative	—	—	.10	.18	-.14	-.19

Job Attitudes. Journalists who value autonomy highly or who receive a lot of comment from news sources tend to favor the interpreter role. Journalists who place greater importance on job security tend to be disseminator in orientation.

Region. Geographic location is the second-best predictor of professional roles. Journalists working in the South slightly favor the disseminator role, while avoiding both the adversary and interpretive stances. Those from the North Central region tended to follow a similar pattern.

Education. The higher the journalist's educational level, the less likely he or she is to subscribe to the disseminator role. The predictive power of educational level is less, however, than it was a decade ago. That is probably a result of less variation in years of schooling, with most journalists now having baccalaureate degrees. As then, majoring in journalism does not seem to predict any professional role orientation.[33]

Political Leanings. Journalists who claim to be conservative in political views tended to hold disseminator values, while avoiding the adversarial mentality.

It appears, then, that job context has become more important over the decade in affecting expressions of professional values among journalists. From the 1971 portrait, the Johnstone group concluded that professional orientations were reinforced more by external environment of journalistic work than by media characteristics.[34] That suggests that we should take a closer look at those statistical relationships, to see whether they appear to make a substantive difference. For example, what real differences are there between print and broadcast journalists in expression of roles? How serious is the philosophical difference between reporters and their supervisors on professional values?

COMPARISON OF DIFFERENT
KINDS OF JOURNALISTS

The *interpretive* function, while a dominant factor in all media, is most clearly salient for *print* journalists, particularly wire service and news magazine staffs. Broadcast journalists tend to see this function as less important than do their print colleagues. For example, large majorities from all media except radio said that investigating claims of public

Table 5.8 Percentages of Journalists of Various Media
Who See Elements of the Interpretive Function
as Extremely Important

	Investigating Official Claims	Analyzing Complex Problems	Discussing National Policy	N
Wire Service	81	57	64	47
News Magazines	73	75	43	63
Dailies	69	52	43	463
Weeklies	66	46	31	183
TV	64	48	29	121
Radio	44	27	23	119
ALL	66	49	38	996

officials was extremely important. Somewhat similar patterns were found regarding the importance of providing analysis of complex problems and discussing national policy. (See table 5.8.)

Editors and reporters do not differ strongly on the salience of the interpretive function, but reporters are a bit likelier to place higher value on it. For example, about half the reporters and 38 percent of the editors say discussing national policy is extremely important. The other factors of investigating official claims and analyzing complex problems are viewed with virtual consensus by reporters and editors. The greater the editor's authority — to hire and fire, and to determine news content — the less likely the interpretive function is to be viewed as extremely important.

Information *dissemination*, the second-most salient press function in the eyes of journalists, has two dimensions, each showing a different profile among the various media. (See table 5.9.) Print and broadcast emerge with quite similar patterns on the salience of getting news quickly to the public. Roughly 60 percent of journalists in all media say that that is extremely important. The importance of concentrating on news for the widest possible public shows some differences. Radio journalists are likeliest to view that as extremely important, with news magazine staffs, predictably, least likely to see news for the widest audience as a highly important goal. No significant differences in attitudes about the disseminator role appeared between editors and reporters in general. However, the *more authority* editors have, the likelier they are to place high value on the dissemination role.

Table 5.9 Percentages of Journalists of Various Media Who See Elements of the Dissemination Function as Extremely Important

	Getting Information to Public Quickly	Concentrating on Widest Audience	N
Radio	66	48	119
Wire Service	64	34	47
Dailies	62	38	463
News Magazines	56	11	63
Weeklies	54	41	183
TV	53	26	121
ALL	60	36	996

The *adversary* role, a distinctly minority view among American journalists, is likelier to be found among print journalists than among their broadcast colleagues. (See table 5.10.) Again, it is the radio journalists who are least likely to say the adversary role has usefulness.

Wire service and daily-newspaper journalists are likelier than broadcast and weekly newspaper journalists to see being constantly skeptical of the actions of public officials as extremely important. An even smaller minority sees the business adversarial role as highly important, but the pattern of responses is roughly similar.

Reporters and editors are fairly similar in their response to the adversary role, although editors with supervisory responsibilities are slightly more likely to avoid adversarial views. More important, the greater the authority of an editor, the less likely the adversary role is to be viewed as highly important. (See table 5.7.)

The entertainment and relaxation function of the news media, which Johnstone found clustered with the neutral conception of journalism, did not appear to be correlated with what we have called the disseminator role among contemporary journalists. It is somewhat surprising, then, that we found significantly more journalists in 1982-83 who accepted the importance of entertaining the audience. Perhaps it was news coverage of the Watergate scandal, which tended to unfold in episodes similar to soap opera, that rekindled an awareness that news does provide entertainment. More important, with the emergence of television news as a highly profitable commodity and the concern that newspaper circulation is not keeping up with population growth, some critics have charged that entertainment has become too great a factor in news

Table 5.10 Percentage of Journalists of Various Media
Who See Elements of the Adversarial Role
as Extremely Important

	Adversary of Officials	Adversary of Business	N
Wire Service	25	19	47
Dailies	25	18	463
News Magazines	19	19	63
Television	17	15	121
Weeklies	15	10	183
Radio	9	10	119
ALL	20	15	996

Table 5.11 Percentages of Journalists from Various Media
Who Say Providing Entertainment and Relaxation
Is Extremely Important

	Entertainment	N
Dailies	26	463
Weeklies	18	183
Radio	18	119
News Magazines	13	63
Television	10	121
Wire Service	9	47
ALL	20	996

formats. Ironically, though, television journalists — perhaps responding defensively — are among the least likely to acknowledge entertainment as important. Flanked by their wire service colleagues, only one in ten television journalists says providing entertainment and relaxation is extremely important for the journalist.

It is, then, on daily newspapers that entertainment is likeliest to be acknowledged as an important function. (See table 5.11.) Furthermore, it is the editor rather than the reporter who is most likely to say entertainment is important. Sixty-four percent of newspaper editors, as compared to 49 percent of reporters, say entertainment is either quite or extremely important.

In general, then, the pluralism of roles that seems to have increased over the decade of the 1970s extends to all media. The small cadres of journalists with extreme views about their professional roles that Johnstone found in 1971 have become even smaller in the 1980s.[35]

Still, it is possible to see some significant, if slight, differences in the professional portraits of various types of journalists. Print personnel tend to lean more toward the interpretive role and to show a slightly greater tolerance of the adversarial stance than do their broadcast colleagues. Broadcast journalists, particularly radio, lean more toward the disseminator philosophy. Reporters are slightly more sympathetic to interpretive and adversary stances than are their editors, especially those editors who have greater managerial authority. The differences, though, are slight.

NEWS VALUES

A basic commodity of journalistic professionalism is the determination of newsworthiness. Nothing is more controversial and sensitive in the field than the decisions about what is and what is not worthy of publication or broadcast.

Notions about what makes something newsworthy are many: conflict, drama, official sources; the list is long. A certain element of newsworthiness, however, often rests with journalists themselves and the news-gathering context. To get an idea about the dynamics of that setting, we asked journalists how influential a number of factors were in determining what was newsworthy in their day-to-day work.

Journalistic training — both on the job and in college courses — was the factor most often mentioned as very influential. Friends and acquaintances were the least often cited. (See table 5.12.)

To assess whether there were patterns of influence on newsworthiness, we subjected the items to factor analysis. Three factors emerged that explained a little more than half the variance in response to the questions. The first cluster of items — labeled *media staff* — was staff peers and supervisors, which suggests that journalists tended to rate both of these high in influence, if they mentioned any one of them. The second factor linked network news, wire services, and competing media — which we called *external media* influence. A third cluster showed audience research and news sources — a factor we called *audience/sources* — as being correlated for many journalists.[36]

Table 5.12 Factors Influencing Concept of Newsworthiness, by Medium

Factors	Percentage Saying Very Influential						
	Daily	Radio	Weekly	News Magazines	Wire	TV	Total
Journalistic Training	77.5	77.3	70.9	76.2	89.3	81.8	77.3
Supervisors	62.5	55.5	47.5	67.8	55.3	60.4	58.3
Sources	44.0	69.0	62.9	61.9	27.7	62.5	53.1
Staff Peers	43.0	42.2	39.9	55.5	46.8	39.7	42.8
Readership/ Audience Research	40.9	47.5	51.4	25.4	21.3	41.4	41.8
Local Competing News Media	33.2	44.6	41.7	22.5	54.7	36.4	36.4
Network News and Prestige Papers	25.5	37.8	21.3	31.7	40.4	30.6	27.9
Wire Service Budgets	23.0	30.3	9.5	14.3	29.8	25.6	21.5
Friends	16.4	15.1	21.3	42.8	10.6	17.4	18.7
	(N = 461)	(N = 118)	(N = 179)	(N = 62)	(N = 47)	(N = 120)	(N = 991)

PREDICTORS OF NEWSWORTHINESS

Regression analysis was performed in an attempt to assess the correlates
of the three factors that were perceived to be major influences on
newsworthiness. This section discusses the highlights of that analysis.[37]

The first factor, *media staff*, was a significant influence on newsworthiness for those journalists who said their organization was doing
an outstanding job of informing the public, and for those who were high
on the disseminator role of the press. *External media* also tended to be a
salient influence on newsworthiness for those who valued the disseminator role. The third cluster, *audience/sources*, was a comparatively strong
factor for the disseminator journalists, especially those at smaller media,
where they might reasonably be expected to be in closer touch with
individual sources and audience members.

Few differences with regard to newsworthiness influences are attribut-
able to specific media, but some significant patterns should be noted.

Wire service journalists were especially likely to see their professional
training as influential on their notions about newsworthiness. Wire
service personnel, flanked by their radio colleagues, were also likelier
than other journalists to say that competing media were an influential
factor in determining newsworthiness. News magazine journalists were
least likely to view competing media as influencing news definitions.
News service staffs were much less likely to see news sources as influencing their ideas about what is news. Daily-newspaper people were also a
little less likely to stress the importance of news sources as an influence
on newsworthiness than were journalists as a whole.

News magazine staff were the likeliest to see peers and supervisors as
influential on newsworthiness. As expected, magazine journalists, along
with those on weekly newspapers, were least likely to cite wire service
budgets as influencing newsworthiness. Radio journalists were the most
likely to see the wires as influencing newsworthiness.

Friends and acquaintances seem to be important only for news magazine journalists, but even for them, less than half said friends were
influential in determining what is news.

In summary, then, the organizational context — including media staff
and journalistic training — tends to be perceived by most journalists as
the most influential factor with regard to newsworthiness. Although
there are some predictable media differences, the most significant predictors of influences on newsworthiness appear to be a strong leaning

toward the disseminator role and how well the journalists see their organization doing in informing its audience. Those who felt most positive toward the disseminator orientation and those who had high esteem for their news organization's performance seemed to be more sensitive to all the possible influences on newsworthiness than were their peers. Age, income, demographics, and a host of other factors were unrelated to perceptions of what defines news.

ETHICAL PERCEPTIONS ABOUT
VARIOUS REPORTING PRACTICES

Flagellation of the press over matters of ethics reached a historic high in 1982 during the controversy about the ill-fated Pulitzer award to Janet Cooke, then of the *Washington Post*, for what turned out to be a fabricated story about the drug-infested world of an imaginary six-year-old child. The same year, *Absence of Malice*, a successful motion picture written by former journalist Kurt Luedke, dramatized other ethical dilemmas of the press and suggested the extent of public concern.

The domain of press ethics covers a broad landscape, but one of the most crucial problems is the handling of news sources. Our inquiry into journalistic attitudes about ethics focused on reporting practices directly involving sources.

Journalists were asked to assume that they were dealing with an important story in the context of eight reporting situations, ranging from the possibility of paying for confidential information to undercover reporting. The questions were identical to those used in major studies of German and British journalists, in which the respondents were asked whether the reporting practices "may be justified on occasion" or would not be approved "under any circumstances." (See table 5.13.)

Disclosing Confidential Sources. American journalists agree overwhelmingly on one principle: divulging a confidential source is *not* approved under any circumstances by 95 percent of the interviewees. So, rulings by federal and state courts that have undermined journalists' claim of a constitutional right of source privilege have not shaken their belief that a promise of confidentiality must be honored.

Other studies suggest, however, that the absolutist position suggested from our data might not hold for some journalists in actual situations. For example, Philip Meyer's 1982 survey for the American Society of

Table 5.13 Journalists' Acceptance of Various Reporting Practices

	Percentage Saying May Be Justified
(1) Getting employed in a firm or organization to gain inside information	67
(2) Using confidential business or government documents without authorization	55
(3) Badgering unwilling informants to get a story	47
(4) Making use of personal documents such as letters and photographs without permission	28
(5) Paying people for confidential information	27
(6) Claiming to be somebody else	20
(7) Agreeing to protect confidentiality and not doing so	5

N = 1,001

Newspaper Editors found that a considerable number of his sample thought confidentiality could be broken in "unusual circumstances," such as when the source has, in reality, lied to the reporter.[38]

Using False Identification. Lou Cannon, reporter for the *Washington Post*, in his book on reporting tells about the late Chicago journalist Harry Romonoff, the "Heifetz of the telephone," who impersonated public officials to get news stories. Cannon says few reporters today would use such tactics, but that many journalists "have benefited" because their sources "did not know they were reporters and were not told."[39] For example, Carl Bernstein and Bob Woodward, in their book about the *Washington Post*'s Watergate investigation say they "dodged, evaded, misrepresented, suggested and intimated" in gathering evidence on the Watergate story.[40]

Our interviews suggest that Cannon is right in that only a small minority of contemporary journalists say that using false identification

Table 5.14 Opinion on Using False Identification, by Medium

Medium	Percentage Saying May Be Justified	N
Television	31	121
News Magazines	30	62
Radio	25	119
Daily	19	463
Wire	15	47
Weekly	12	183
TOTAL SAMPLE	20	995

p<.001

may be justified. Weekly- and daily-newspaper journalists were significantly less likely to accept such practices than their broadcast and news magazine colleagues. (See table 5.14.)

Payment for Confidential Information. A former aide to President Richard Nixon, John Ehrlichman, recently claimed, "There are various types of raconteurs who are paid money by publishers, news syndicates and the networks." These persons "peddle" their "secrets never before revealed" to the "highest bidder."[41] A celebrated example was Mr. Nixon, who sold "news" interviews to CBS Television's *Sixty Minutes* in 1984.

A little less than a third of American journalists say that payment for confidential information is justifiable. Differences among the media on this question are relatively slight. Some journalists do not think that the practice occurs very often for most journalists. Steve Knickmeyer, a former managing editor of the Ada (Oklahoma) *Evening News*, says, "A small town editor's budget barely includes reporters' salaries, much less payoffs for sources."[42] David Hawpe, managing editor of the Louisville *Courier-Journal*, agrees that the practice is unusual for most newspapers.[43] (See table 5.15.)

Using Personal Documents without Consent. A respected book on journalism ethics tells of a classic case of a West Coast newspaper that wanted a photograph of a murdered man. The family refused to supply one. A reporter for the newspaper stole a photograph from the man's home, published the picture, then returned it to the distraught family.[44]

Table 5.15 Opinion on Payment for Confidential
Information, by Medium

Medium	Percentage Saying May Be Justified	N
News Magazines	35	62
Television	32	121
Wire	30	47
Daily	26	463
Radio	26	119
Weekly	23	183
TOTAL SAMPLE	27	995

p>.05

Table 5.16 Opinion on Unauthorized Use of
Personal Documents, by Medium

Medium	Percentage Saying May Be Justified	N
Wire	49	47
Daily	33	463
News Magazines	32	62
Television	26	121
Weekly	21	183
Radio	12	119
TOTAL SAMPLE	28	995

p<.000

That is likely not a frequent occurrence in journalism, and only a minority of the journalists in our sample say such a thing may be justified. There were, however, considerable media differences. Daily-print journalists were likelier to accept the practice than journalists in broadcast or weekly newspapers. (See table 5.16.)

Badgering Sources. Scarcely anyone who saw CBS Television's Mike Wallace goading the defenseless Terre Haute, Indiana soldier who was a witness-participant in the My Lai tragedy during the Vietnam War will

Table 5.17 Opinion on Badgering Sources, by Medium

Medium	Percentage Saying May Be Justified	N
Wire	68	47
News Magazines	67	62
TV	52	121
Dailies	47	463
Radio	43	119
Weekly	38	183
TOTAL SAMPLE	48	995

p<.0000

ever forget it. Michael O'Neill, former editor of the *New York Daily News*, says that the "militant techniques" of programs such as *Sixty Minutes* and "the bullying tactics" of ABC Television's Sam Donaldson are symptoms of the "temptations of excess" that occur in an adversary press.[45] Obviously, television news has dramatized the problem of source badgering, but the problem has existed for years in all media.

American journalists are deeply divided on badgering unwilling informants to get a story. About half say that badgering may be justified on occasion. Ironically, broadcast journalists, particularly radio, are less likely to accept the practice than are their print colleagues. (See table 5.17.)

Unauthorized Use of Confidential Documents. Publication of the secret Pentagon Papers, and the Supreme Court case that invalidated the prior restraint suffered by the *New York Times* and other newspapers, marks one of the most controversial episodes in American journalism history.[46] While the Pentagon Papers case is extraordinary, the ethical questions underlying it are not. Lou Cannon says, "Reporters on investigative stories frequently are given glimpses of closed records or see copies of testimony that has been sworn to secrecy."[47]

A majority of journalists say that unauthorized use of confidential business or government documents may be justified. Daily print journalists seem more willing to permit the practice than are broadcast personnel. (See table 5.18.)

Table 5.18 Unauthorized Use of Confidential
Documents, by Medium

Medium	Percentage Saying May Be Justified	N
Wire	68	47
News Magazines	67	62
Dailies	62	463
Television	55	121
Weekly	46	183
Radio	33	119
TOTAL SAMPLE	56	995

p<.000

Undercover Employment. The frequent investigations of abuses of the elderly in nursing homes often have used clandestine employment by the journalists doing the stories. CBS Television hired journalism students to get jobs in the offices of a national credit rating company. Chicago reporters got jobs as ambulance drivers in order to disclose abuses in emergency services. The *Indianapolis Star* permitted one of its reporters to get a job with an operation that claimed to raise money for volunteer fire department charities for handicapped children. The reporter was able to document that none of the money ever reached the children.[48]

Lawrence "Bo" Connor, managing editor of the *Indianapolis Star*, summarized the issue well in commenting on the charitable-fund-raising investigation his newspaper conducted. He said that at one level under- cover investigations may violate an "unwritten" code, but that "when you are dealing with a rat" there may be "no other way to get that story. . . ."[49]

A majority of journalists say that a reporter may be justified in obtaining a job to gain inside information. Television and wire service journalists are more likely than some of their radio and weekly col- leagues to accept such practices. (See table 5.19.)

PATTERNS OF REACTION
TO JOURNALISTIC PRACTICES

Intensive analysis of the questions about reporting practices suggests that the responses to the various situations are fairly similar among all

Table 5.19 Opinion on Using Undercover
Employment, by Medium

Medium	Percentage Saying May Be Justified	N
Television	78	121
Wire	77	47
News Magazines	71	62
Dailies	68	463
Radio	64	119
Weekly	58	183
TOTAL SAMPLE	67	995

p<.02

Table 5.20 Predictors of Justification of
Various Reporting Practices

Variables	Standardized Regression Coefficients (Beta)	Correlation Coefficients
Age	−.19	−.23
Professional Age	−.10	−.18
Radio Journalists	−.15	−.17
Craft Union in Organization	.13	.24
Size of Organization	.12	.20
Income	.19	.17

$R^2 = .35$

types of American journalists.[50] The differences between broadcast and print, between large and small media, between old and young journalists, are modest. But taken as a whole, the set of items suggests some differences. (See table 5.20.)

Older journalists and those who have been in the field longer are a little less likely to say that the various reporting practices may be justified. Of all the media, radio journalists are more conservative than others in approving the use of the various reporting tactics. Journalists who work for larger organizations, particularly those in which a craft union is present, or who make higher salaries are likelier to say that the various reporting tactics may be justified than are journalists who work for smaller media.

The most striking thing is that the cleavage one might expect between reporters and editors on the reporting practices does not emerge. And, a host of other factors — such as education and college major, geographic location, or whether the journalist works for a group-owned or independent organization, for example — appear unrelated to whether the various reporting tactics may be justified.

CORRELATES OF ETHICAL ORIENTATIONS
IN JOURNALISM

Moral and ethical development among professionals in medicine, law, and business has been a subject of considerable concern in the 1980s. Colleges and universities have rediscovered applied ethics, and the professions have responded by attending ethics workshops and short courses.

Journalists, too, have shown great interest in ethical questions recently. Ironically, ethical issues have been dealt with in schools of journalism for decades, with a major book on the subject having been published in 1924 by the late Nelson A. Crawford, head of the Department of Industrial Journalism of Kansas State Agricultural College. Crawford's aim was to contribute to a "professional consciousness" and an ethical philosophy that was "realistic, discerning, intellectually honest, and applicable to the press as a social institution."[51] He realized that the goal was ambitious and that it might never be accomplished, but he certainly would take pride in the concern today about professional ethics among journalists.

Salient Shapers of Journalists' Ethics. Few journalists have the time or the inclination to ponder the influences of their past or present circumstances on their professional work. But that is what they were asked to do in a question probing the influence of a set of factors — ranging from family upbringing to their publisher or general manager — on their ideas in matters of journalism ethics. The respondents were asked whether each subject was extremely, quite, somewhat, or not very

Table 5.21 Sources of Influence on Ethics

	Percentage Saying Influential
Newsroom Learning	88
Family Upbringing	72
Senior Editor	61
Coworkers	57
Journalism School Teachers	53
Senior Reporter	52
College/University Teachers	50
Religious Upbringing	35
Publisher	25
High School Teachers	24

N = 1,000

influential in developing their ideas about what is right and wrong in journalism. (See table 5.21.)

Day-to-day newsroom learning is the factor cited most frequently as influential in matters of journalism ethics. In spite of that, family upbringing exceeded the perceived importance of senior editors, coworkers, or senior reporters in the eyes of the respondents.

Journalism school teachers and other college and university instructors were cited as influential shapers of ideas on ethics by about half of the journalists. Although more than 90 percent of the journalists say they went to church while growing up, only about a third cited religious upbringing as important to them in matters of journalism ethics.

Patterns of Influence. Intensive analysis of the sources of ethical influence suggested that the items could be grouped into three clusters: the newsroom context, college teachers, and family-religious influences.[52] These clusters were used to search for different patterns of ethics influences among journalists.

The most striking, but certainly not surprising, finding is the perceived importance of the newsroom context in shaping the ethics of journalists in all media, regardless of size or location. Of a host of factors — ranging from age and educational background to number of years of experience — only two made appreciable differences in journalists' perceptions of the importance of the newsroom context on ideas about journalism ethics. The presence of an ombudsman in the organization and working in a newsroom where supervisors commented regularly about the staff's performance appeared to be associated with placing a higher value on the newsroom context.[53]

Family and religious upbringing appeared to vary somewhat as an ethical influence. Journalists working for group-owned media were a little less likely to cite family-religion as important in matters of ethics. Older journalists were somewhat likelier than younger persons to say that family and religious upbringing were important to them as shapers of their ideas on ethical matters.[54]

Most journalists now have bachelor's degrees from colleges and universities; those who majored in journalism or took courses in journalism are more likely to cite instructors as an influence on their thought about ethics. Younger journalists working for smaller media — both print and broadcast — and with smaller salaries are somewhat likelier to perceive an influence from their professors. Most of them are recent college graduates, so it is not surprising that they would be more likely to cite the influence of their teachers.[55] On the other hand, the pattern was reversed in the case of religious-family influences, as the older journalists found them more salient than did their younger colleagues.

In conclusion, this analysis of ethical influences finds that journalists see newsroom environment as the most powerful force in shaping their ideas about ethical matters. That, of course, is not unexpected. What is surprising is that family upbringing is ranked so high, and that college teachers are seen as important by half of the journalists we interviewed. How these elements of past learning compete with, complement, or counterbalance the impact of social control in the newsroom cannot be determined from this work.

But an analysis of thirty-one cases written by editors about their toughest ethical dilemmas led Frank McCulloch, executive editor of McClatchy Newspapers, to conclude "that in journalism, the practice of ethics is inescapably situational."[56] He noted the power of the editor in such matters, though, in suggesting that "a newspaper takes on the personality of its top editor." That personality is transmitted by day-to-day management, but the informal vestiges of power may be even greater.

"Because journalists are storytellers and gossip mongers," McCulloch says, "anecdotes about senior editorial behavior are saved and passed on from reporter to reporter, sometimes for generations." Those anecdotes, McCulloch believes, "for better or worse . . . become the parables which shape the behavior of journalists."[57]

Arthur L. Caplan, an ethicist at the Hastings Center, read the same cases and agreed with McCulloch that each one was "both difficult and unique," but said they made clear that "journalists engage in ethical thinking throughout their professional lives." He was impressed that valid "moral rules" formed a "constant background" for the journalistic decisions he studied.[58]

Our work suggests, then, that the "parables" of the newsroom are, indeed, important in matters of journalism ethics, but so are those from family and teachers.

Philip Meyer, a journalism researcher and educator, conducted survey research in 1982 that supports the notion that the newsroom context is extremely important in ethical decision making. Our finding that the extent of communication with superiors was related to the importance of the newsroom context to ideas about ethics seems particularly consistent with Meyer's ideas about the "ethically efficient" news operation. However, our finding that journalists are unlikely to see the publisher as important to their ideas about ethics suggests that the "active role" for the publisher in ethical consideration, called for by Meyer, may not be a reality in most newsrooms.[59]

CROSS-CULTURAL RESEARCH ON ACCEPTANCE OF JOURNALISTIC PRACTICES

Comparative research on the organization and behavior of professional journalists has begun to build some evidence of similarity of professional attitudes of journalists across various cultures. Jack McLeod and Ramona Rush, in work published in 1969, compared Latin American and U.S. journalists on a number of professional values. They found the journalists roughly in agreement on job performance and newspaper organization factors, but in much less agreement on their ideas about professional training and the role of professional organizations.[60] McLeod and Rush found the Latin American journalists receptive to much stronger professional enforcement of journalistic standards than U.S. journalists were willing to accept. They concluded, however, that the journalists showed far greater similarity than dissimilarity.[61]

Wolfgang Donsbach, a German researcher, compared data on German and Canadian journalists with the results obtained by McLeod and

Rush on U.S. and Latin American news people. He found that the major difference hinged on the Latin American journalists' regarding political power as much less important than did journalists from the other countries, particularly the Federal Republic of Germany. The Latin Americans also seemed less concerned with career and prestige than the journalists from the other Western societies studied.[62]

In 1982, Donsbach presented major new research on British and German journalists' conceptions of their professional roles. He argued that journalists from the Federal Republic of Germany tend to emphasize their political power within a democracy, whereas the British concentrate on the information function as their foremost professional task. Based on his earlier analysis of American and Canadian data, Donsbach concluded that journalists from Germany, then, are quite different from those of other democratic cultures.[63]

New Comparative Work. This section builds on data collected in a cooperative survey by the Institut für Demoskopie Allensbach, the Institut für Publizistik at the University of Mainz, and the Centre for Mass Communication Research at the University of Leicester in Britain.[64] The objective is to compare U.S., British, and German journalists with regard to the various reporting practices dealt with earlier and their attitudes about the impact of media on public opinion in the three societies.

Legitimacy of Reporting Practices: Protecting Confidential Sources. A common thread among journalists in three of the world's great democracies is almost complete agreement on honoring source confidentiality. Overwhelming majorities of journalists in the United States, Germany, and England say that a promise of confidentiality always must be kept. The importance of confidentiality is shared by all media and all types of journalists in the three countries, with no more than 5 percent in any country saying breaking confidentiality may be justified. Frank McCulloch succinctly explained this finding: "The need to protect sources, especially vulnerable ones, exists for journalists in all cultures and environments. Too often, whistle-blowers are punished for their actions."[65] (See table 5.22.)

Undercover Employment. Most journalists in the United States and Britain think getting employed in a firm or organization to gain inside

Table 5.22 Stance on Reporting Methods[a]

	Percentage Saying May Be Justified		
	U.S.	German[b]	British[c]
Employment under False Pretenses	67	36	73
Using Confidential Documents	55	57	86
Badgering Sources	47	8	72
Using Personal Documents without Permission	28	5	53
Paying for Confidential Information	27	25	69
Using False Identification	20	22	33
Divulging Confidential Sources	5	1	4
	N = 1,001	N = 450	N = 405

[a]"Journalists have to use various methods to get information. Given an important story, which of the following methods do you think may be justified on occasion and which would you not approve under any circumstances?''

[b]Data are from Institut für Demoskopie Allensbach, Prof. Dr. Elisabeth Noelle-Neumann, director; Konstanz, Federal Republic of Germany.

[c]Data are from the Centre for Mass Communication Research, Professor James Halloran, director; University of Leicester, England.

information may be justified. Journalists from both print and broadcast sectors of the British media appear in harmony on the matter of clandestine employment by journalists. Journalists for prestige dailies such as the *Times* of London were more apt to be uncertain about the technique than other British journalists, but 63 percent said such reporting may be justified. British editors and reporters, like their American counterparts, have similar views on the practice.

German journalists, particularly those in print media, are deeply divided on the ethics of undercover reporting. A little less than half of the print journalists and 59 percent of the broadcast news people sampled say they never would approve clandestine employment to gain inside information.

Several years before the interviewing was conducted for the German study by the Allensbach Institute, a controversial book by Gunter Wallraff revealed an unfavorable portrait of the editorial management of Axel Springer's *Bild-Zeitung*, the largest newspaper in Europe.[66] Wallraff, who had been criticized editorially in *Bild-Zeitung* for his undercover investigation of Melitta Industries, disguised himself so cleverly that he was able to get a reporting job with the newspaper. Later he published a book exposing the inner workings of the controversial *Bild-Zeitung*. Wallraff's work, too, is very controversial, which perhaps reflects the greater reticence of German journalists to accept undercover reporting through clandestine employment.

Using Confidential Documents. The American and German journalists are deeply divided on use of confidential documents, but not so the British. In England, fewer journalists on the small provincial dailies (78 percent) justify use of unauthorized official documents, compared to the overwhelming majority of the prestige national daily-newspaper journalists (97 percent) and BBC press people (88 percent). As in the United States, there are no differences between British reporters and editors on the issue. Although a slight majority (57 percent) of German journalists say illicit use of official documents may be justified, about 20 percent were unsure, with broadcast journalists likelier to be unsure than print journalists.

Badgering Sources. The question of source badgering produces considerable differences in attitudes among journalists. The Germans appear to reject overwhelmingly the practice of badgering sources. The majority of British journalists think badgering unwilling informants to get a story may be justified. American journalists are evenly split on the problem.

British acceptance of source intimidation appeared consistent across all media, with no differences between editors and reporters. German print and broadcast journalists largely opposed badgering sources.

Using Personal Documents without Permission. When asked about the use of personal documents such as letters and photographs without consent, German and American journalists differ from the British. Most German journalists and a majority of Americans say they do not approve. More than half the British think illicit use of personal documents may be justified.

Journalists for the BBC and the British provincial newspapers are likelier to oppose use of personal documents without consent than other

British journalists, but the differences are small. Journalists from both print and broadcast in Germany overwhelmingly appear to be against illicit use of personal documents.

Paying for Confidential Information. Significant majorities of U.S. and German journalists say they would not approve under any circumstances paying sources for confidential information. British journalists, on the other hand, say the practice may be justified (69 percent). National tabloid journalists lead the way in justifying payment for information (87 percent), but a majority of British broadcast journalists (65 percent) and prestige print people (67 percent) also approve.

Opposition to payment for confidential information is consistent throughout all U.S. media. A similar pattern holds for West German journalists in both print and broadcast.

Using False Identification. Substantial majorities of American and German journalists, and a smaller majority of British journalists, oppose using false identification in reporting.

British tabloid journalists working for national publications are a little more likely to approve of claiming to be someone else than are journalists from the prestige dailies and the broadcast media. Reporters in England are a bit more likely than their editors to approve false identification in reporting.

In general, then, the British journalists appear more willing to accept the reporting practices outlined here than are the German or American journalists. The Germans were least likely to say the various practices may be justified.

The reasons for the differences are, no doubt, complex. Harold Evans, former editor of the *Times* and the *Sunday Times* of London, argues that it is much harder to get information in Britain than in the United States. For example, if a British journalist wants to find out whether it is safe to eat on the *Queen Elizabeth* or a similar cruise ship, the information cannot be obtained in England. Instead, the journalist comes to the United States and obtains the inspector's report through the Freedom of Information Act.

According to Evans, "That goes through a whole range of political, economic and social questions, from medicine to old age, to treatment in mental hospitals." These restrictions on information occurred, Evans argues, "by an accretion of common law decisions, by statute, by inertia, by habit and lousy press behavior . . ."[67] So, perhaps that explains, in part, the greater willingness of British journalists to justify reporting practices such as paying for confidential information.

In contrast, the German press is accorded a special right of access to government information, under the Land Press laws. Some argue that that results in a freer flow of official information in Germany, which perhaps leads to greater conservatism about the reporting practices considered here.[68]

Of course, there are likely to be many other explanations for the differences found here, such as educational background. It appears that German and American journalists are much more likely to have university degrees than are British journalists. For certain, journalism education as a university-related field of study is much less prevalent in Britain.[69]

For whatever reasons, though, American journalists seem to be more in agreement with journalists in the Federal Republic of Germany than with those in England.[70]

Media Influence on Public Opinion. The final section of this chapter presents comparative data on journalists' estimates of their impact on public opinion in their countries. The three samples of journalists were asked to estimate, on a scale of zero to ten, how strong they thought the influence of the media was on the formation of public opinion. The question was followed by a similar item asking how strong they thought the press *ought to be* on public opinion. Both questions attempted to get at how much political clout the journalists thought they had, and should have. (See table 5.23.)

Table 5.23 Comparative Estimates by Journalists of Actual and Ideal Influence of the Mass Media on Public Opinion[a]

	U.S. Journalists (N = 991)	*German Journalists*[b] (N = 450)	*English Journalists*[b] (N = 405)
Actual	7.39	5.93	7.30
Ideal	5.96	6.01	5.90

[a]Mean (average) results of a scale where zero was no influence and ten was a very great influence.
[b]Data for these are from Wolfgang Donsbach "Journalists' Conceptions of Their Audience," *Gazette* 32 (1983): 19–36.

The American and British journalists were very close in their estimates that they have considerable impact on public opinion. The German journalists were more conservative in their guess of their actual impact on public opinion.

Again, the American and British were very similar in their estimates of how much power they ought to have, agreeing that it should be somewhat *less* than they thought it actually was. The Germans, who were very close to the British and American journalists' estimate of ideal clout, felt their power was about what it ought to be.

In the United States, broadcast journalists see the mass media as being slightly more influential on public opinion than do their print colleagues (7.74 compared to 7.27 on a scale from zero to ten, where ten indicates most influence). And, while both print and broadcast journalists agree that the impact of the press should be less than it is, the broadcast journalists say the mass media should be a little less powerful than do the print journalists (5.57 compared to 6.09).

The American journalists were asked a more general question about the role of public opinion in democratic government. Specifically, the respondents were asked to say how strong they thought the influence of public opinion *should be* on governments. The results suggest that U.S. journalists think public opinion ought to have great influence in the American governmental system. (The mean response was 8.02 on a scale of 0 to 10.) There were no significant differences among the media, or among various types of journalists.

CONCLUSIONS AND SUMMARY OF FINDINGS

The professional culture of journalism remains quite weak compared to the more established professions of law and medicine. The one sign of strengthening professional identity is the striking rise in membership in national associations over the decade of the 1970s. More than 20 percent of all journalists now belong to a national professional group, compared to 13 percent a decade ago.

Membership trends in those national organizations suggest that leadership in the field may be shifting to the smaller media. That is because journalists from smaller organizations, often with higher educational backgrounds in journalism, are somewhat more likely to join national organizations than their colleagues from larger, elite media.

The overwhelming conclusion from the intensive analysis of role conceptions among American journalists is that a large majority see their professional role as highly pluralistic. They cannot be described simply as interpreters or disseminators; they are *both*. Nor can it be said that they see *no* utility in the adversary role. While few journalists find an adversarial stance to be extremely important, only a little less than a third of them completely reject the adversary role. Martin Linsky, a political scientist at Harvard, suggests that anecdotal evidence supports the pluralistic view of the journalist's role. "It is not adversarial, it is not symbiotic, it is not independent, it is not under the tent." Instead, he said, "It's clearly a marble cake. It's a combination of all those things."[71]

In this sense, the modern journalist attempts to blend the classical *critical* role of the journalist — as interpreter or contemporary historian — with the technical requirements of disseminating great volumes of *descriptive* information.[72] This duality of roles apparently is not viewed by journalists as the "bifurcated professional existence" described twenty years ago by Bernard Cohen.[73] Rather, the two major roles, interpretive and disseminator, appear to be complementary. Or, as Linsky so aptly put it: "At 9 o'clock it's adversary, at 10 o'clock it's symbiotic. At 11 o'clock it's independent and at 12 o'clock the politicians are manipulating the press. It goes back and forth, it's all over the place."[74]

And, while there are *slight* tendencies for the role conceptions to be stronger among certain types of journalists, the more significant fact is that these basic roles are almost universal perceptions among journalists. They are, in a sense, the primary colors of the profession: their pigment and hue may be grayer or darker in some, but they are present in virtually all journalists of all media, large and small, Eastern and Western, young and old.

Another noteworthy finding is that American journalists are more conservative than their British colleagues in acceptance of various reporting practices that contemporary critics have associated with the excesses of an "adversarial mindset." In addition, U.S. journalists seem to be quite idealistic in their conception of the role of public opinion as deserving to have great impact on American government.

Of various factors that may play a part in shaping the professional values of journalists, the newsroom environment appeared to be the most important. The day-to-day interactions with editors and colleagues is perceived by the journalists themselves to be the most powerful force over their conceptions of values, ethics, and professional practice.

Just as Johnstone noted a decade ago, journalists seem to meet the abstract criteria of what it is to be professional. Or, as Stephen Hess concluded in his study of Washington reporters, "The press has created for itself most of the trappings of professionalism."[75] They are educated, altruistic, and principled. Yet, they are deeply divided on many questions of journalistic practice. And they refuse to join professional organizations in large numbers.

The modern journalist, then, is *of* a profession but not *in* one. The field has come to represent the prototype of the occupational form that Wilensky foresaw some twenty years ago. The journalist is in a "hybrid organization" that combines both professional attributes and bureaucratic controls. The career journalist values "professional standards of work" and is "an important link between professional culture and civil culture, the man of knowledge and the man of power."[76] The institutional forms of professionalism, however, likely will always elude the journalist.

—6—

New Technology and the Job

Technology always has fascinated Americans. Throughout our history, we have tended to stress the economic and technical aspects of our society. Indeed, it is a measure of the success of American democracy that we have accomplished so much in both areas, and it is largely because of technological developments that we have become one of the most economically successful civilizations in the history of mankind. But at the same time that we have been amazingly successful in developing new technologies, we have been much less successful at predicting how these inventions would affect our society, and we have not kept pace socially, ethically, and philosophically with technological advancement.[1]

Past developments in technology have had significant, often unexpected effects on various occupations in our society, including journalism. Nineteenth-century technological developments such as railroads and high-speed presses helped to turn the press into a mass audience medium and contributed to the broadening of the concept of "news" from the mercantile and the political to the experiences of more "common" people, especially those recorded in reports from the police and the courts.[2] The telegraph, which newspapers began using in the 1840s to bring in timely outside news, had a significant impact on news values. A study of the Wisconsin English daily press from 1852 to 1916 suggests that political news "bias" (defined in terms of the number of value-laden words present in the news story) dropped dramatically in the 1880-1884 period, during which there was a large increase in the proportion of wire service news used. The analysis of the news coming in by telegraph showed that it contained significantly fewer value-laden words than the news provided by the newspapers' own reporters or clipped from other papers or other sources.[3]

Telegraph news also appeared to influence journalistic writing techniques and the scope of news coverage. Reporters learned to imitate the more "objective" news style of the wire services and to write news stories in the "inverted pyramid" style, with the "who, what, where, when, why, and how" crammed into the first few paragraphs for quicker and less costly telegraph transmission. Telegraph news also appeared to alter newspaper readers' mental pictures of the political world, because the news stories after 1884 much more often pertained to a political candidate himself, regardless of where he was located, than to the supporters of the candidate located in nearby areas. In other words, the readers were taken more directly to the political event, regardless of whether or not it occurred in their part of the country. Thus, the telegraph enlarged the daily newspaper's area of coverage to the nation and the world, and seemed to heighten the public's desire for more timely national and international news.[4]

Other technologies have had major effects on journalism and journalists, as well as on the larger society. In 1877, the telephone was used to send newspaper dispatches. It soon became not only a way of transmitting news, along with the telegraph, but also a way of collecting news from faceless news sources both near and far who could more easily avoid (and perhaps mislead) reporters than in face-to-face encounters. With the increase in news gathering and transmitting capabilities came the invention of a device in the mid-1880s to simplify and speed up the mechanical processing of news — the Linotype machine. Twenty years later, the development of the vacuum tube opened the way for voice broadcasting, and the first American radio stations began to seek regular public listenership in the 1920s, with the result that the journalist's voice became as important as his ability to gather information accurately and quickly.

In 1927, Bell Telephone Laboratories publicly demonstrated black-and-white television. After World War II, television quickly took its place in most American homes, and it created a new kind of journalism where not only the voice but also the looks of journalists are important, and where the visual aspects of an event play a large part in the determination of its newsworthiness.

The advent of radio and television also made it possible for politicians sometimes to bypass the press and speak directly to listeners and viewers. Although allowing leaders to speak directly to their followers may be a contribution to the survival of democracy, the electronic media also have given rise to some negative effects on the overall society, and on journalism in particular. For example, a top official of CBS News has argued that television is not best at covering issues, but instead is more suited to covering personalities. He claimed that TV news is more interested in strategies of campaigns than in substance.[5] In addition, there are numerous studies that suggest that dependence upon television for news is associated with less political knowledge and less participation in politics, whereas dependence upon newspapers is associated with more knowledge of politics and more participation in elections.[6]

In short, it is clear that the technological developments of the nineteenth and twentieth centuries have contributed greatly to the creation of printed and electronic media capable of very quick dissemination of news to enormous audiences. But in providing the means to distribute more messages to more people faster, these technological developments also have changed the nature of these messages and the role of journalists in society. Not only have these technologies changed the role of the journalist, they also have changed working conditions in dramatic ways — from hot type to cold, from noisy, clacking typewriters to quiet, clicking video display computer terminals, from blue-collar production workers to white-collar professionals, from the use of musty records to the use of computer terminals, and from calling in stories to rewrite persons to electronically transmitting them to the newsroom.

For nearly one hundred years, the use of hot (melted-lead) type for producing newspapers remained relatively unchanged, but in the mid-1960s several changes were begun — from hot type to cold (letters and characters printed on film which is pasted to page sheets to be photographed), from letterpress printing to offset, and, more recently, from typewriters to video display terminals (VDTs). As recently as 1970, most newspaper publishers in the United States were trying to decide whether to buy a computer system for writing, editing, and production. The annual survey of the American Newspaper Publishers Association's

(ANPA) Research Institute showed no use of video display terminals in 1969, but by 1981 the 666 newspapers replying to the survey reported 46,217 VDTs in use.[7]

In addition to VDTs and computer systems for writing and editing, other new technologies, mostly computer-driven, are being developed to speed up production of printed media and to deliver information electronically. Such technologies include pagination (the use of a computer system for designing pages, eliminating the need for manual paste-up), electronic libraries and data bases, computer graphics, robotics (to transfer papers from conveyor belts to inserting machines), and videotex systems (where printed information is delivered via broadcast signals, cable, telephone, or satellite to home television screens).

But many of these new technologies are still in the planning and testing stages, and thus have not had much impact on the work of journalists to this point. On the other hand, video display terminals, attached to so-called "front-end" computer systems for writing, editing, and typesetting, are now nearly ubiquitous at American newspapers and magazines (and are becoming more common in television stations),[8] so their real and perceived effects on the work of journalists can be assessed. In addition, videotape technology is widely used throughout the television industry, so its effects can be studied.

STUDIES OF THE IMPACT OF TECHNOLOGY

Although the available studies of the impact of computers and video display terminals (VDTs) on journalists and the news are fairly few in number, they may be divided into two major categories: those that try to assess the actual effects of new technology on the newsroom and news content, and those that try to gauge journalists' *perceptions* of the impact of new technologies on their jobs. Some studies do both, but most research can be placed into one or the other of these categories.

Research on Actual Effects. Many of the studies on the effects of technology focus on the number of errors and the speed in editing news copy with pencil and paper as compared with VDTs. Most of these studies agree that editing with VDTs reduces the number of typographical and spelling errors, but most of them also show that editing speed is reduced, because of the need for more proofreading, more keystrokes to make changes, and greater manual dexterity.[9]

These studies generally find little or no impact of the technology on journalists' decisions regarding what is newsworthy, although Hess found in his 1978 study of Washington, D.C. reporters that foreign correspondents in Washington were more likely to compete directly with the U.S. wire services for fast-breaking news, because of faster electronic delivery of their copy via computers and satellites, than was the case before the use of such technology.[10] Because of the faster transmitting technology, the foreign correspondents were filing shorter stories (nearly eight per week) and fewer longer, analytical articles. Hess argues that emphasizing quantity over quality in foreign news reporting is a mistake, because "foreign audiences are better served when experienced overseas reporters try to explain the complicated, rather than to report the obvious."[11]

In a recent telephone interview, Hess observed that because of videotape technology and satellites, more television stations than ever before have Washington bureaus which can put their local congressmen on local television the same day. That contributes to the Congress's actually becoming "more provincial" than before, Hess argues, because these congressmen must be more concerned about local problems (and speak on such problems) on a day-to-day basis.[12] In a 1980 study, Lambeth also found steady growth in the number of regional correspondents reporting from Washington for local TV stations — from 20 in 1959, to 45 in 1969, to 79 in 1979.[13] He attributed this growth largely to satellite transmission and videotape technology. Lambeth concluded that the pressure on these regional correspondents to produce many stories works against reporting in depth and makes investigative reporting rare.

In a larger study of thirty-four television stations in fourteen U.S. cities during the fall of 1979 and the spring of 1980, Yoakam found that ENG (electronic news gathering) technology, consisting of videotape cameras and editors, portable microwave equipment, and satellite transmitting and receiving dishes, had changed television reporters' jobs by allowing for later deadlines and thus more visual material from later in the day, even including live broadcasts.[14] In addition, this new technology also has increased the length of TV newscasts to two and three hours in some major cities, according to Yoakam, and has created a need for more assistant news directors to coordinate the technology and camera crews.

Thus, while there apparently has been some impact of the new technologies for news gathering and processing on certain kinds of news content, this impact should not be overstated. Hess's observation that a transmission revolution does not equal a communications revolution is worth keeping in mind, and seems to be generally supported by the studies cited above.

Research on Perceived Effects. A few of the studies of journalists' perceptions of the impact of new technology on their work focus on number of errors and speed, but more of these studies simply assess whether journalists feel positive, negative, or ambivalent about such technology. These studies are divided about evenly on whether computers and VDTs speed up or slow down journalistic work, and on whether there are fewer or more errors as a result of using these devices.[15]

In a 1979 case study of the *Milwaukee Journal*, for example, Garrison found that almost all the editors he interviewed agreed that the use of VDTs results in fewer errors in a published copy, but slightly more felt that the VDT slowed editing rather than speeded it, and many said they thought it made no difference.[16] About half of the copy editors perceived no effect of VDTs on their news judgment, but others said VDTs helped them experiment with changing headlines and content of stories. Most editors thought they had to do more proofreading with VDTs than without them, because of the lack of proofreading by those who used to work in the backshop setting type. Some editors thought that attention to operating VDTs took priority over the content of stories, and most perceived headline writing to be simpler, more flexible, faster, and more accurate because of VDTs.

Killenberg concluded after more than four years of visits to newspapers with new systems that there is a conflict of opinion on whether VDTs speed up or slow down editing, but the overwhelming consensus of journalists is that few would want to return to pencil and paper.[17] An attitude survey of eighty-two newspapers in 1978 found editors divided on whether VDTs improve or reduce editing speed, but most agreed that the quality of the news copy was improved.[18] In another 1978 study of daily-newspaper editors in nine states, Fisher found that many editors perceived increased editing speed and improved editorial quality with VDTs, even though his research showed pencil-and-paper editing was slightly faster, especially on simpler articles.[19] And Kurtz found editors of small newspapers resenting the extra proofreading required by VDTs and perceiving more errors because of VDTs, although his research showed that VDTs actually improve typographical accuracy.[20] Francke and Anderson, in a before-and-after study of conversion to VDTs at the Orlando (Florida) *Sentinel Star*, also found that journalists there perceived a decline in typographical accuracy after the VDTs were installed.[21]

Thus, there are no clear conclusions to be drawn from these studies regarding the influence of VDTs on editing speed and accuracy. Such influence seems to depend upon the particular news organization, journalists' attitudes toward the technology, the ratio of machines to journalists, and the amount of training and practice on VDTs. The studies that attempt to assess journalists' feelings about VDTs and computers are more conclusive, however. Most of them indicate generally positive, or at least mixed, rather than negative feelings.

Shipley, Gentry, and Clarke, in their 1978 study of daily-newspaper editors in nine states, found that the vast majority of editors, when given a chance, prefer VDT editing to pencil and paper, and an overwhelming majority like working on VDTs.[22] A 1982 survey of top-level daily-newspaper managers by Christine Ogan also found that most respondents had positive attitudes about the use of computers in their work and were especially pleased with the increased sense of accomplishment they felt in their work since the introduction of the computer.[23]

In his 1978 study of nearly 40 percent of all reporters working in Washington, Stephen Hess found that many said they preferred VDTs to typewriters, but many also feared power failures and mechanical breakdowns as deadlines approached.[24] Some reporters were worried about editors' being more likely to rewrite their stories and do more editing on VDTs than with pencil and paper, and one foreign-news editor said that VDTs were producing an "information overload" that has added to the problems of his staff. This overload complaint was echoed recently by the National Wire Watch, a professional organization of wire editors, which claimed at a recent meeting in Chicago that the typical wire editor looks at 600 to 800 stories each day, and that wire editors in general are struggling to cope with the increasing volume of stories flowing into their VDTs. Lloyd Carver, wire editor of the *Nashville Tennessean*, said that AP and UPI are sending too much material and that wire editors are "spending 97 percent of our time just pushing buttons to leave things out."

One of the most thorough studies of the impact of new technologies on journalists was conducted in the fall of 1981 by three researchers from Michigan State University — Michael Burgoon, Judee Burgoon, and Charles Atkin. In this survey of 489 newsroom people in eight daily newspapers scattered around the country, the Burgoons and Atkin concluded that "good computer systems make the news business more fun for all except copy editors."[25] A large majority of the surveyed journalists (71 percent) agreed that they were comfortable with their ability to operate the new technology, and more than half (55 percent) agreed that the introduction of VDTs and computer systems has made their jobs more pleasant. But more than one-third were dissatisfied with the way the new technology was used in the newsrooms. This dissatisfaction was mainly with availability of and access to terminals and, secondarily, with the computer systems' reliability. Older journalists were generally less satisfied with VDTs than were the younger.

The Burgoons and Atkin also found that the most commonly cited *advantages* of VDTs and computers were speed, ease, and convenience, whereas the most common *disadvantages* were eye strain, tension, headaches, and fear of breakdowns. Because copy editors must spend long hours each day in front of VDTs, whereas many reporters may spend only a few hours, the copy editors feel least benefited and most taxed by VDTs, according to the study. The journalists perceived the effects of VDTs on news gathering to be mostly positive (more timely news, ability to cover more stories, and ease of changing stories at the last minute), whereas the effects on decision making were perceived to be mostly negative (more changing by editors, earlier deadlines, less staff contact, and difficulty getting "hard" [paper] copy when needed).

Although most of these studies reveal generally positive, or mixed, feelings about VDTs and computers on the part of newspaper journalists, a 1982 survey of 174 network affiliate television news directors in the thirty largest U.S. markets and in ninety-five smaller ones found that 52 percent of the news directors from the largest markets and 62 percent of the others perceived the influence of electronic videotape technology on news content to be negative. Only 30 percent from the largest markets and 14 percent from the smaller cities thought the influence of this technology was positive.[26]

Many of the news directors in Smith's study who perceived a negative influence of technology mentioned pressure to use the technology for "live" coverage because of its expense, even if the story content was not especially important. Some mentioned an increase in "ad-libbing" stories rather than writing and polishing them beforehand. Some mentioned the use of helicopters and live coverage primarily for promoting the TV station rather than covering the news. One news director said, "I see too many stories done simply for the reason that they can be done live, instead of being judged on the basis of importance or interest to the viewer." And another said, "Too much emphasis is placed on the 'newness' of stories, not so much on actual content and news value."

Of those news directors who thought the influence of new technology was positive, several cited an increased capability to cover stories, especially late-breaking events. Several cited later, or even nonexistent, deadlines. And several said that coverage of stories in distant locations was possible with microwave relays via helicopters. As one news director put it, the new electronic news-gathering technology "allows coverage of stories of all kinds from almost anywhere."

In addition, this new technology seems to have increased the pressure for more stories each day, as Hess and Lambeth found in their studies, at the expense of fewer in-depth reports.[27] And perhaps this technology, by creating the need for more assistant news directors, as noted in Yoakam's study, contributes to a feeling of loss of control (or autonomy) by the news director.[28]

Whatever the explanation, it seems fairly clear that new technology is not regarded in the same way by print and broadcast journalists, or even by those with different jobs (reporters versus copy editors) working in the same medium. Whereas print journalists seem to be generally more favorable toward VDTs and computers than broadcast journalists are toward electronic videotape technology, the Burgoon study suggests that newspaper copy editors are considerably less enthusiastic about computer technology than are reporters.[29] But nearly all the studies cited above are local or regional in scope, and even those that are national are not based on representative national samples of journalists working for different news media. Thus, our national survey provides a way of checking whether the patterns found in previous studies are truly national, and whether there are systematic differences in the perceptions of new technology by journalists working for different media.

JOURNALISTS' PERCEPTIONS
OF NEW TECHNOLOGIES

Journalists responding to our survey were asked, "What are your thoughts, if any, on how new technologies such as VDTs and electronic news gathering have affected your job?" Up to three answers in the

Table 6.1 U.S. Journalists' Perceptions of How
New Technology Has Affected Their Work

Perceptions	*Percentage of Journalists Mentioning*
	$(n = 846)^{a}$
No Effect	11.5
Unspecified Effect	5.0
Improves Quality of Work	100.0
Saves Time	50.2
Hurts Quality of Work	9.5
Takes More Time	17.3
Other Responses	1.7

[a]Percentages total to more than 100.0 percent because up to three answers were recorded for each journalist responding.

journalists' own words were recorded by the interviewers, who were instructed to probe for details and record the answers verbatim. The answers from the journalists later were grouped into the seven categories listed in table 6.1.

Table 6.1 indicates that virtually all of the 846 journalists responding to the question about new technology said in one of their answers that it improves the quality of their work. This category included such answers as "New technology makes for better copy," "It makes my job easier," "It gives me more control over my work," "It makes for a quieter office," "It makes the work less tedious," "It allows us to cover events live," "It leads to improved visuals," and "It leads to better impact." Obviously, the journalists in our survey as a whole perceived new technology as having at least some positive effect on the quality of their working conditions or on the quality of their written or broadcast news.

Half of the journalists responding to this question also mentioned that new technology saves time. Among those in this category, some said it saves money, is more efficient, permits more work to be done, is less cumbersome, and makes the news organization more competitive. A few said it creates new jobs. But slightly more than one-sixth of our journalists said that new technology takes more time, makes more work, is less efficient, is harder to manage, is hard to learn, or results in fewer jobs.

Table 6.1 also indicates that slightly more than one-tenth of the journalists perceived new technology as having little or no effect on their jobs. Just under one-tenth of responding journalists also mentioned that they perceived new technologies as damaging the quality of their work environment or their news reporting. Answers falling into this category included mentions of more errors in writing, a "dehumanizing" effect, regret at the loss of the "old atmosphere," less time for thinking about stories, more tedious work, eye strain, an increase in competition in the newsroom, and more emphasis on technology than on the news. But clearly the percentage of journalists voicing these concerns was a minority compared to the proportion perceiving improvements in the quality of the work.

The percentages in table 6.1 also suggest ambivalence on the part of some journalists in their perceptions of the effects of new technology. All journalists responding at some point mentioned positive effects on the quality of the work, but more than one-fourth also mentioned negative effects, such as increased time and decreased quality of work environment or news. That suggests that perceived effects of new technologies are not clearly positive or clearly negative for a substantial proportion of journalists, but are mixtures of both good and bad. Nevertheless, table 6.1 shows that for most journalists, the perceived benefits of new technology greatly outweigh the perceived liabilities.

Differences in Perceptions. The studies of the effects of new technologies reviewed earlier suggested that perceptions of these effects are not uniform across print and broadcast media, or even across different jobs within the same medium. Our study confirms this conclusion.

Table 6.2 indicates that those journalists most likely to perceive little or no effect from new technology work in broadcast media (especially radio) and for small organizations (less than 18 full-time persons), and are high school graduates. Those journalists most likely to perceive that new technology improves the quality of their work are younger college graduates working for larger news organizations (18 and more full-time employees), whereas those most likely to perceive decreases in quality are wire service journalists and daily-newspaper editors. Daily-newspaper and wire service reporters are especially likely to think that the new technology saves time, but older editors are more likely to think it takes more time and creates more work. Thus, our findings are fairly consistent with those of the Burgoons and Atkin, who found 71 percent of the daily-newspaper journalists in their study comfortable with the new technology, and copy editors most negative in their perceptions of VDTs.[30] We also find daily-newspaper editors, especially the older ones, most likely to complain about decreased quality and increased time needed to do their work.

Table 6.2 Perceptions of New Technology
by Type of Journalist

	Perceived Effects				
Journalists	Little or No Effect	Improves Quality	Saves Time	Hurts Quality	Takes More Time
1. Print			X[b]	X[c]	
2. Broadcast	X[a]				
3. Reporters			X		
4. Editors				X[d]	X
5. Small organizations	X				
6. Large organizations		X			
7. Younger		X			
8. Older					X
9. College graduates		X			
10. High school graduates	X				

[a]Especially true for radio journalists.
[b]Especially true for daily-newspaper and wire service journalists.
[c]Especially true for wire service journalists.
[d]Especially true for daily-newspaper editors.

In addition, we find an interactive effect of size and type of organization. Journalists who work for large organizations are generally more likely to perceive new technology as improving their work than are those working for smaller organizations, but daily-newspaper journalists in larger operations are *more* likely to say that new technology results in more work, whereas TV journalists in larger operations are *less* likely to think so than those in smaller ones. That may be because daily-newspaper editors in larger organizations must cope with more stories (especially from the wire services) and often find it slower to edit them on VDTs, whereas TV journalists in larger organizations can use the new videotape technology to extend deadlines and justify the hiring of more news people, as noted by Yoakam.[31] Whatever the explanation, this finding is consistent with Smith's discovery that nearly twice as many TV news directors from the largest markets (30 percent) perceived the influence of new technology as positive than did those from smaller cities (14 percent).[32] It should be remembered, however, that the majority of both print and broadcast journalists perceive the effects of new technology positively, with print journalists a bit more likely to do so than broad-cast, as was true in the other studies reviewed earlier.

Similarities in Perceptions. Although there are obviously differences in perceptions of the effects of new technology by type of news medium and type of job, there are no significant differences by level of job satisfaction, different regions of the country, management versus staff responsibilities, type of ownership of news organization, and sex of journalist. Instead, differences occur between reporters and editors, and between print and broadcast journalists, primarily because of the direct impact of the technology on the everyday work of these journalists.

CONCLUSIONS

In keeping with historical developments in technology that have had far-reaching effects on journalists and what they report as news, most journalists in our survey and in other recent studies perceive some impact of the most recent forms of technology on their work. Most perceive computers, VDTs, and electronic news-gathering technologies as improving the quality of their work and saving time, but about one-fourth also say that the new technology takes more time and hurts the quality of their work. We find, as do other studies, that print journalists are generally more likely to cite the benefits of new technology than are broadcast journalists, and reporters perceive more advantages than do editors. But reporters, especially those working for the print media, are less tied to VDTs and videotape recorders than are editors, which suggests that prolonged daily contact with the new technological devices does not lead to more favorable perceptions of them, but instead just the opposite. Even though editors are more critical of new technology than are reporters, it must be remembered that the clear majority of editors, both print and broadcast, perceive this technology as improving their work.

Studies on the effects of new technology on editing generally conclude that editing with VDTs tends to reduce the number of spelling and typographical errors, but also tends to be slower than pencil-and-paper editing. Such studies usually find little or no impact on news selection if they attempt to measure it, supporting Hess's conclusion that the new technology may be responsible for a "transmission revolution" rather than a "communication revolution."

But there are some signs that computers, VDTs, and electronic news-gathering devices such as videotape cameras and satellite transmission have affected definitions of news, as well as the speed of its transmission. Several scholars have commented on the increasing number of Washington bureaus of local TV stations, due largely to satellite transmission of words and pictures. The ability to put local congressmen on television in a matter of hours has contributed to the Congress's becoming "more provincial" than before, Hess argues. And the ability of foreign correspondents to send their copy home via satellites has led them to write more numerous, shorter stories on timely events rather than longer, analytical pieces that are less time-bound — a development that Hess does not think benefits readers in other countries who seek to understand what is happening in our nation's capital.

Thus, even though the bulk of U.S. journalists perceive new technological devices as improving the quality of their work and saving time, it may be that in the long run such devices will change the nature of the messages created by these journalists in ways that do not benefit the society at large.

—7—

Women Journalists

In the late 1940s, French feminist Simone de Beauvoir observed that employment was a key to women achieving equality with men. "It is through gainful employment that woman has traversed most of the distance that separated her from the male," she wrote, "and nothing else can guarantee her liberty in practice."[1]

This chapter addresses part of that journey for women's equality in the field of journalism, drawing on data from the 1982–83 national survey of journalists as well as the 1971 survey by Johnstone, Slawski, and Bowman.[2] It also draws upon the work of other scholars in its discussion of women in the journalistic work force and in its comparison of male and female journalists on demographic backgrounds, education, income, job duties, and attitudes about their work.[3]

AFFIRMATIVE ACTION

Massive entry of women into paid work is one of the major changes in the work force during the past few decades.[4] In 1960 there were about 23 million working women who made up more than 30 percent of the nation's work force. By the mid-1980s, there were nearly 50 million women — about 45 percent of all workers — holding jobs in the United States. Meanwhile, more than 13.5 million women entered the labor force between 1972 and 1981, compared with fewer than 8 million men joining the labor force during that same period.[5]

About one-third of the journalistic work force was made up of women in 1982–83, compared to about one-fifth found by Johnstone and his colleagues in 1971. This growth in the number of women in the field coincided with other significant occurrences, including an increase in the number of women enrolled in college and university journalism programs.[6] Women for the first time outnumbered men in journalism programs at U.S. colleges and universities in 1977. A 60:40 ratio had favored men for four decades.[7] Between 1980 and 1988, enrollment in U.S. journalism programs remained stable at about 60 percent female and 40 percent male.[8]

In addition, the decade between the study by Johnstone and his colleagues and the 1982–83 study also was one in which activists took advantage of Federal Communications Commission regulations and federal equal opportunity legislation to challenge news organizations that often fell far short of having gender-balanced newsrooms.[9]

The greatest increases in participation for women in journalism were at radio and television stations. Broadcast organizations not only expanded their work forces more than print organizations, but also were under the most pressure to comply with affirmative action programs. In 1971, the FCC added women to its equal opportunity rule that originally applied only to racial and ethnic minorities. This order prohibited discrimination against women and required television stations to file with the FCC affirmative action programs outlining their efforts at implementation of equal opportunity.[10] The FCC regulations requiring broadcast stations to apply the equal opportunity rule to women made the broadcast industry more accountable for its hiring practices than some other areas of communications, and the figures gathered for this study offer some support for the argument that affirmative action has been somewhat successful in achieving its goals.

THE GENDER GAP IN EXPERIENCE

Overall, women tended to be younger and have less professional journalism experience than men in 1982–83, a change from the previous decade when women tended to be older and less experienced than men in the field. Female journalists in 1982–83, for example, were less likely than males to have held newsroom jobs other than their current jobs (66.7 percent

Table 7.1 Years of Experience in Journalism
(Percentage in Each Category)

Experience	1971		1982–83	
	Men	Women	Men	Women
1 to 5 years	30.7	40.0	25.9	43.5
6 to 10 years	19.1	18.7	26.0	26.3
11 to 15 years	14.1	12.1	15.3	12.4
16 to 20 years	9.0	8.0	9.8	7.7
21 to 25 years	12.3	9.9	7.1	3.6
26 to 30 years	3.8	5.1	5.4	3.8
31 to 35 years	4.2	2.2	5.6	0.9
36 to 40 years	3.3	1.8	2.3	2.5
More than 40	3.4	1.3	2.6	0.3

SOURCE: Percentages for 1971 are from William Bowman's Ph.D. dissertation, "Distaff Journalists: Women as a Minority Group in the News Media," University of Illinois at Chicago, 1974, Table 3.10, p. 129.

compared with 75.5 percent). (Part of this is explained by the relative youth of women journalists.)

In 1982–83, the median number of years in journalism for men was 10 years, compared with 6.6 years for women — a pattern that was consistent with the pattern for women in the work force as a whole. A 1984 U.S. Census Bureau study found that women tended to have spent less time working at their current job than men (45.3 percent of the women and 55.2 percent of the men had spent five or more years at their current job).[11]

The percentage of men in journalism with less than 11 years of experience remained relatively unchanged between the early 1970s and early 1980s (49.8 percent in 1971 and 51.9 percent in 1983). It increased by more than 10 percentage points for women, however, going from 58.7 percent in 1971 to 69.8 percent in 1983. (See table 7.1.)

THE IMPACT OF "BABY BOOM" WOMEN

The increase in the percentage of women in journalism between 1971 and 1983 came primarily from the entrance of younger journalists into the field. The gap between women under 25 in journalism and those under 25 in the labor force as a whole closed rather dramatically in the time between the study by Johnstone and his colleagues and the 1982–83 survey, going from a 15.4 percentage point difference in 1971 to a 4.5 point difference in 1983. Likewise, the percentage of women journalists under age 54 in 1983 was closer to the percentage of women under 54 in the work force as a whole than it was in 1971.

The median age for women journalists was 39.4 in 1971, compared with 30.3 in 1982–83. Meanwhile, the median age for men journalists was 36 in 1971, compared with 33.1 in 1982–83. So while the average age of journalists decreased between the two decades, this was more the case for women than it was for men, and reflected not only the increase in the number of women, particularly younger women, entering the journalism field, but the impact of the "baby boom" generation as a whole entering the work force between 1971 and 1983.

MARRIAGE AND CHILDREN

One of the continuing challenges for women in journalism — like their counterparts in other fields — is the difficulty of combining career and family. A number of studies of women in journalism have found that they are less likely than men in the field to be married or have children.[12] "You can have it all — if you don't need too much sleep," the title of an article in a publication of the American Society of Newspaper Editors noted in 1986.[13] The "all" referred to career as well as husband and children, which amounts to at least two full-time jobs for many women. As noted earlier, both women and men were less likely to "have it all" in the 1980s than they were a decade earlier. This change seems to reflect shifts in U.S. society as a whole between the two decades, which saw an increase in the divorce rate and a delay in the age of first marriage for men and women.[14]

During both decades, women journalists were less likely than men journalists to combine career and family, although the percentage point decline in married journalists between the two decades was similar for men and women. While 76.7 percent of the men were married in the 1971 study, that figure had dropped to 62.1 percent in 1982–83 — a 14.6 percentage point decline. For women, the percentage of those married went from 58.5 percent in 1971 to 42.6 percent in 1982–83 — a 15.9 percentage point decline.

Not only were women journalists in 1982–83 less likely than men journalists to be married (42 percent versus 62 percent), but they were also less likely than men to be parents. In 1982–83, while 75.5 percent of the men who had ever been married had children, the same was true for only

64.6 percent of the women. Among journalists as a whole, 57 percent of the women had children, compared with 70 percent of the men.

A more in-depth analysis showed that the differences between never-married women and men with children were significant only for journalists who were under 30. This age group, however, is the most likely to have younger children, and the presence of children is a strong influence on women's participation in the labor force.[15]

RACE AND GENDER IN THE
JOURNALISTIC WORK FORCE

As noted earlier in this book, one of the most disappointing findings in the 1982–83 survey was the lack of progress journalists of color had made into the field since the 1970s. Further analysis showed that women of color were more likely than men of color to be represented in journalism in the early 1980s. Although Asian, Latino, Native, and African Americans are included in the category of journalists of color, this finding is largely attributed to the greater participation of black women rather than black men in journalism.[16]

The reasons for this finding are complex.[17] Women of color in the United States historically have been more likely than white women to be in the paid work force.[18] Paula Giddings, in *When and Where I Enter*, noted that the double bind of sexism and racism forced black women into the paid work force at the same time it limited the kinds of work they could perform. For many years the only occupational choices black women had were lower-status professions such as teaching, nursing, and social work (where until recently there was less competition from white women), or domestic labor. And because education is a key to moving into more lucrative fields,

Table 7.2 Race of Men and Women
Journalists, 1982–83
(Percentage in Each Category)

Race	*Men* *(n = 656)*	*Women* *(n = 334)*
White	97.1	92.8
Black	1.8	5.1
Latino	0.3	1.2
Asian	0.2	0.9
Other	0.6	0.0

African-American women historically have been encouraged to pursue education.[19]

Black women are more likely than black men to finish college, and as noted earlier in this book, the majority of journalists — particularly younger journalists — are college graduates.[20] (In fact, every woman of color interviewed in 1982–83 was a college graduate, compared with 80 percent of the men of color, 71.2 percent of the white women, and 73.9 percent of the white men.) The reason for this educational gender gap among African Americans is also complex and results from historical events, discrimination, and segregation stemming from the time of slavery. However, Giddings noted that the encouragement African-American parents have offered their daughters to pursue education has been a function of class as well as race.

"In an economy where blue-collar men earned as much as or more than white-collar women, sons dropped out of school to support themselves and their families, while daughters went to school to do so," she wrote.[21] In addition, she noted, black men have faced fiercer competition in the occupations that white men have wanted for themselves.[22]

Some have argued that white males have viewed powerful black men as potentially more threatening to their power than black women, and thus have been more willing to hire black women. Ernie Schultz, during his tenure as president of the Radio-Television News Directors Association, told *Time* that black men have fared even worse than black women in journalism, because "white males feel threatened by them."[23] Black men may also be disadvantaged by what has been called a "two for one" attitude toward hiring — a cynical attitude that holds that affirmative action guidelines can best be fulfilled by hiring a black woman rather than a black man so that two underrepresented groups can be represented by one new employee.

THE CLOSING OF THE EDUCATIONAL GENDER GAP

Another major change between the two decades was the fact that journalists were not only more likely to have earned college degrees than in the previous decade, but the 1970s gender gap in educational preparation no longer exists. As of 1982–83, women in journalism were just as likely as men in the field to have completed a college education and majored in journalism. Johnstone and his colleagues found that 60 percent of the men held at least a bachelor's degree in 1971–72, compared with 50.8 percent

Table 7.3 Amount of Formal Schooling
(Percentage in Each Category)

Highest Educational Attainment	Men		Women	
	1971	*1983–83*	*1971*	*1982–83*
Some high school	2.0	0.6	1.3	—
High school graduate	10.6	6.2	18.4	10.1
Some college	27.4	19.1	29.5	16.3
College graduate	41.4	53.6	32.6	57.3
Some graduate training	10.2	8.3	11.6	9.2
Graduate degree	8.4	12.1	6.6	7.1

NOTE: The 1971 data are from William Bowman's Ph.D. dissertation, "Distaff Journalists: Women as a Minority Group in the News Media," University of Illinois at Chicago, 1974, p. 132.

of the women. By 1982–83, 74 percent of the men and 73.6 percent of the women held at least a bachelor's degree.

Other studies suggest that women journalists may even be on their way to being more educated than men in the field. Christine L. Ogan, in her 1982 study of men and women newspaper managers, found that female managers were more likely than male managers to have a college education.[24] Meanwhile, a 1988 survey of daily newspaper journalists by the American Society of Newspaper Editors found that women had more education than men, and superior academic records.[25]

The higher educational level of women has been associated with an increase in the participation of women in the work force. Mary Frank Fox found that in 1988, among women who had completed high school, 59 percent were employed; among those with four years of college, 72 percent were employed; and among those with five or more years of college, 79 percent were employed.[26]

THE INCOME GAP

Not only did the decade see a complete closing of the educational gap between male and female journalists, but it also saw the gap in income become smaller. Women in 1982–83 earned 71 cents for each dollar earned by the average man in the field, compared with 64 cents for each dollar earned by a man in 1971. Even after statistically controlling for differences in education, years of experience, and other factors, women journalists still earned less than men.[27]

Male earnings for all full-time, year-round workers in the United States have always exceeded women's earnings. In the 1970s, the 59 cents on the dollar figure became a symbol of the failure of the marketplace to ensure equal treatment. U.S. Bureau of the Census data show that the difference in the earnings ratio of women to men in the full-time labor force remained fairly stable between 1955 and 1983, with the annual earnings of women averaging between 57 and 64 percent of those of men during the two decades.[28] By 1987, among full-time, year-round employees, women were making 65 percent of what men were earning.[29]

Researchers disagree as to why the wage gap appears to be narrowing. Gordon Greene, assistant division chief of the income branch of the U.S. Census Bureau, has argued that it is because ''women are making progress in entering higher-paying occupations.''[30] For example, from 1979 to 1986, women's representation rose from 34 to 45 percent of accountants and auditors, 28 to 40 percent of computer programmers, and 10 to 15 percent of attorneys.[31] According to Greene, the Census Bureau data show that both ''men and women have lower wages in woman-dominated fields.'' He added that he believes that if more women enter male-dominated fields, the market would guarantee increased wages for those women in more traditional jobs.[32]

But while the gender gap in wages narrowed in journalism, the earning power of both men and women declined. As noted earlier, journalists in 1982–83 had a median income of about $7,000 less annual purchasing power than the journalists who were interviewed in 1971 by Johnstone, Slawski, and Bowman. A comparison of the incomes of men and women in the two studies illustrates this decline in purchasing power. In 1981 dollars, using the Consumer Price Index as a benchmark, only 4.7 percent of the men and 19.5 percent of the women made less than $9,359 in 1970. However, those percentages jumped to 22.2 percent for men and 33.7 percent for women by 1981.

In addition, the percentage of journalists in the highest income categories decreased between the two decades, with 6.6 percent of the women and 34.6 percent of the men earning the equivalent of $32,760 or more in 1970 and only 5.1 percent of the women and 13.5 percent of the men in that income bracket by 1981.

Table 7.4 Income of Journalists, 1970 and
1981, in 1981 Dollars
(Percentage in Each Income Category)

| | *1970* | | *1981* | |
Income	*Men*	*Women*	*Men*	*Women*
Below $9,359	4.7	19.5	22.2	33.7
$9,360–$14,039	5.0	15.7	16.3	26.6
$14,040–$18,719	8.9	17.8	14.2	14.5
$18,720–$23,399	15.4	15.3	11.8	8.9
$23,400–$28,079	17.0	15.5	13.2	7.1
$28,080–$32,759	14.3	9.6	8.8	4.1
$32,760–$37,439	12.1	4.8	4.8	2.7
$37,440–$42,119	6.0	0.9	3.2	0.0
$42,120–$46,798	3.5	0.2	1.4	1.5
$46,800–$51,479	3.7	0.5	2.4	.3
Above $51,480	9.3	0.2	1.7	.6

NOTE: The Consumer Price Index was used to compare the 1970 and 1981 earnings. The 1970 figures were calculated from Table 3.20 from William Bowman's Ph.D. dissertation, "Distaff Journalists: Women as a Minority Group in the News Media," University of Illinois at Chicago, 1974, p. 149.

One of the questions raised by this analysis is whether the influx of women into the field can be linked to the lower income of all journalists between the two decades. Some research suggests that the concentration of women in different occupations than men plays a crucial role in accounting for male-female earning differentials.[33] However, the decline in earning power experienced by journalists during the decade hit workers in other occupations as well.[34]

JOB TITLES

Job titles held by men and women in print and broadcast news organizations suggest women are more likely than men to be engaged in reporting. In print organizations, 46.3 percent of the women said they were employed in a reporting position, compared with 35.2 percent of the men.

Among broadcast journalists, 83.1 percent of the women indicated that they regularly undertook reporting assignments, compared with 63.7 percent of the men — a gap of about 20 percentage points. Only 1.4 percent

Table 7.5 Frequency of Reporting
by Journalists, 1982–83
(Percentage in Each Category)

Frequency	Print		Broadcast	
	Men (n = 489)	Women (n = 264)	Men (n = 168)	Women (n = 71)
Regularly	63.0	76.5	63.7	83.1
Occasionally	12.5	8.3	14.9	11.3
Seldom	13.3	8.7	13.1	4.2
Never	11.2	6.3	8.3	1.4

of the women broadcast journalists said they never reported stories, compared with 8.3 percent of the men.

Among print journalists, 76.5 percent of the women said they regularly reported, compared with 63 percent of the men — a significant gap of about 13 percentage points. A total of 6.3 percent of the women and 11.2 percent of the men in print organizations said they never undertook reporting assignments. One possible explanation for these gender differences is the greater frequency with which men hold higher-level supervisory or managerial positions — positions that often include heavy editing duties and fewer opportunities to write and report.

No significant differences exist in whether men and women print and broadcast journalists with regular reporting duties covered a specific beat or subject area, or usually wrote about a variety of topics. However, there were some differences in the kinds of beats that men and women journalists reported holding, even though the overall distribution of men and women in various beats appeared to be similar for both print and broadcast organizations. (The small number of persons representing certain beats makes such a generalization difficult to make with certainty, and it is also important to keep in mind that women more often than men were assigned as reporters.) In 1982–83, sports reporting continued to be a male bastion, as did sports editing, and women reporters were more likely than men reporters — particularly in the print sector — to cover human interest news. Among print reporters, 18 percent of the men and 2.7 percent of the women said they covered sports regularly. The percentages for broadcast sports reporters were 9.5 percent of the men and 3.3 percent of the women. A decade earlier, Bowman estimated that 2.1 percent of the sports reporters were women.[35]

This analysis also showed that 18.4 percent of the female print reporters covered human interest news, while only 6.6 percent of the men were assigned to this beat. A total of 9 percent of the female print journalists had the job title of lifestyle editor (a regular outlet for human interest stories), compared with 0.9 percent of the males. In addition, women print reporters were more likely than men to report that they covered local news (14.8 percent of the women and 8.3 percent of the men).

Women in broadcasting were more likely than men in the field to have jobs as anchors/announcers in the early 1980s (25.4 percent of the women and 11.9 percent of the men) or general assignment reporters (15.5 percent of the women and 3.6 percent of the men). Nearly 17 percent of the women in broadcasting reported that they were currently working as a reporter or writer, compared with 12.5 percent of the men.

THE POWER GAP AMONG REPORTERS

Job titles alone do not tell everything about sex segregation or gender-based power differences in the newsroom. This analysis also looked at some of those power differentials by comparing how often men and women with reporting duties were able to get subjects covered that they thought were important; how much freedom they had in selecting the stories on which they worked; how much editing their stories received; and how much freedom they had in deciding which aspects of a story should be emphasized.

Among broadcast journalists there was a statistically significant gender

Table 7.6 Frequencies of Being Able to Select Stories
Worked on, by Gender, 1982–83
(Percentage in Each Category)

Frequency	*Print*		*Broadcast*	
	Men (n = 370)	*Women* (n = 225)	*Men* (n = 132)	*Women* (n = 67)
Almost always	60.3	60.0	67.4	44.8
More often than not	27.3	26.2	23.5	28.4
Only occasionally	11.4	12.4	8.3	22.4
Don't make proposals	1.1	1.3	0.8	4.5

Table 7.7 Freedom to Select Story
Emphasis, by Gender, 1982–83
(Percentage in Each Category)

Amount of Freedom	*Print*		*Broadcast*	
	Men (n = 370)	*Women* (n = 225)	*Men* (n = 132)	*Women* (n = 67)
Almost complete	65.1	64.9	74.2	56.7
A great deal	24.3	25.3	22.0	40.3
Some	10.5	8.4	3.8	3.0
None at all	0.0	1.3	0.0	0.0

Table 7.8 Amount of Editing That Respondents'
Stories Receive, by Gender, 1982–83
(Percentage in Each Category)

Amount	*Print*		*Broadcast*	
	Men (n = 368)	*Women* (n = 223)	*Men* (n = 132)	*Women* (n = 67)
A great deal	13.3	9.0	3.8	6.0
Some	64.1	69.5	40.2	58.2
None at all	22.6	21.5	56.1	35.8

difference in the frequency of being able to get a story covered if the
journalist thought it was important, with 67.4 percent of the men as opposed to 44.8 percent of the women saying they could almost always get
such a story covered. For print journalists, however, no gender gap in
newsroom influence was found. About 60 percent of both male and female
print journalists said they could almost always select the stories they
worked on. (See table 7.6.)

The same pattern held true for having the freedom to select story emphasis; no significant differences were found among men and women print
journalists, but men in the broadcast industry are more likely than women
to say they have autonomy. (See table 7.7.)

No significant differences existed in the amount of editing the stories
of men and women reporters received. (See table 7.8.) The overwhelming
majority of print journalists said their stories received at least some editing

(77.4 percent of the men and 78.5 percent of the women), while only 22.6 percent of the men and 21.5 percent of the women said that their stories received none.

On the contrary, broadcast journalists reported receiving less editing than journalists working for print organizations, and male broadcast journalists in particular reported little editing. More than half of the men in broadcast journalism said their stories did not receive any editing. While women in broadcast journalism were also less likely to have their stories edited than women in the print media, female broadcast journalists were more likely than male broadcast journalists to have their work edited (64.2 percent compared with 44 percent).

In addition to having their stories edited more frequently than men, women in broadcast journalism also reported having less freedom than their male counterparts. While 74.2 percent of the men in the 1982–83 study reported having almost complete freedom in deciding the emphasis of their stories, only 56.7 percent of the women reported holding that amount of power. It is important to note, however, that 40.3 percent of the women reported that they had a great deal of freedom in deciding the emphasis of their stories. Less than 4 percent of the men and women broadcast journalists reported having only some freedom, and no one reporting having no freedom.

MANAGERIAL DUTIES

A 1977 study of women in newspaper management found that the daily newspaper industry appeared to be behind other employers in the propor-

Table 7.9 Freedom to Decide Story
Emphasis, by Gender, 1982–83
(Percentage in Each Category)

Amount of Freedom	Print		Broadcast	
	Men *(n = 370)*	*Women* *(n = 225)*	*Men* *(n = 132)*	*Women* *(n = 67)*
Almost complete	65.1	64.9	74.2	56.7
A great deal	24.3	25.3	22.0	40.3
Some	10.5	8.4	3.8	3.0
None at all	0.0	1.3	0.0	0.0

tion of women employed as managers, regardless of the size of the newspaper, with dailies employing an average of about one woman manager each.[36] The opportunities appeared better for women working for weekly newspapers, where one-third of the editors were women in 1977.[37]

Although journalists with managerial duties were still overwhelmingly male in the early 1980s, as noted earlier, there was an increase in the percentage of female managers during the two decades, from 12 to 28 percent.

Further analysis of the 1982–83 data showed that 39.3 percent of the women and 51 percent of the men reported that they carried out some managerial duties in their newsrooms. This analysis showed, too, that women in broadcasting were less likely to have managerial or supervisory responsibilities than women in print organizations. However, men in broadcasting were found to be more likely than their print counterparts to be assigned managerial or supervisory duties.

In a 1985 study, Jean Gaddy Wilson found that only 6 percent of the top media jobs and 25 percent of the middle management jobs were held by women.[38] In 1987, a survey by Vernon Stone found that 14.5 percent of U.S. television stations and 23.6 percent of U.S. radio stations employed women as news directors.[39]

THE GENDER GAP IN POWER AMONG NEWSROOM MANAGERS

Certainly, there is a wide range in the power wielded by individual managers. And it seemed likely that the findings of this study would be similar to those of Christine Ogan in her study of men and women newspaper managers, in which she found that women spent less time fulfilling managerial duties than men.[40] Better insight into the power differences between men and women managers came by looking in more depth at the answers to questions dealing with the amount of influence the respondents had in hiring and firing decisions, the frequency with which respondents met with reporters to discuss story ideas, the amount of editing the respondents did, and the amount of freedom they had in deciding how stories written by others would be used in print or in the broadcast.

A wide gap in the influence over hiring for men and women emerged in both the print and broadcast media, with men in management more likely than women to report that they had a say in hiring decisions. These differences were greater between men and women broadcast journalists

Table 7.10 Male and Female Newsroom Managers'
Influence on Hiring, 1982–83
(Percentage in Each Category)

Influence	Print		Broadcast	
	Men *(n = 242)*	*Women* *(n = 111)*	*Men* *(n = 96)*	*Women* *(n = 19)*
A great deal	47.1	27.0	37.5	10.5
Some	17.8	20.7	25.0	10.5
A little	12.8	16.2	12.5	26.3
None	22.3	36.0	25.0	52.6

than between those in print, although both differences were significant.
Meanwhile, there were only slight differences in the scope of responsibility
in hiring that men managers in the print and broadcast newsrooms experienced. (See table 7.10.)

Among the women broadcast supervisors surveyed in 1982–83, only 21
percent said they had some or a great deal of influence in the hiring and
firing of editorial employees, compared with 62.5 percent of the men.
More than half of the women broadcast supervisors (52.6 percent) said
they had no influence over such decisions, compared with only 25 percent
of the men. The gap was not quite as wide among men and women supervisors working for newspapers, magazines, and the news services, although it was still substantial. A total of 47.7 percent of the women print
managers said they had some or a great deal of influence over hiring and
firing decisions, compared with 64.9 percent of the men. A total of 36
percent of the female managers and 22.3 percent of the male managers in
print said they had no influence in such decisions.

Significant differences also exist between the frequencies with which
men and women broadcast newsroom managers met with individual reporters to discuss ideas for future stories, one measure of power in the
newsroom. (See table 7.11.) Men tended to meet with individual reporters
more frequently than women. Again, the differences were stronger for
broadcast journalists than print journalists, with women in broadcast management meeting with reporters less frequently than men in broadcast
management.

For men and women managers in both the print and broadcast sectors
there were no significant differences in the amount of editing performed.
(See table 7.12.) About three-fourths of both men and women said they

Table 7.11 Frequency of Meeting with Individual Reporters
to Discuss Story Ideas, 1982–83
(Percentage in Each Category)

Frequency	*Print*		*Broadcast*	
	Men (n = 490)	*Women* (n = 264)	*Men* (n = 189)	*Women* (n = 71)
Several times daily	8.6	3.4	8.5	7.0
Daily	12.0	10.2	23.8	15.5
Almost daily	3.1	1.5	4.2	0.0
Several times weekly	5.7	5.3	7.1	2.8
About weekly	10.2	11.0	7.1	1.4
Less than weekly	56.1	63.3	46.4	71.8
Never	4.3	5.3	2.4	1.4

Table 7.12 Amount of Editing Performed by Men
and Women Newsroom Managers, 1982–83
(Percentage in Each Category)

Amount	*Print*		*Broadcast*	
	Men (n = 489)	*Women* (n = 264)	*Men* (n = 168)	*Women* (n = 71)
A great deal	35.8	33.0	23.2	19.8
Some	36.0	34.4	51.2	56.3
None	28.2	32.6	25.6	23.9

did at least some editing, compared to about two-thirds of both male and female print journalists.

No significant differences exist in the amount of freedom that male and female print editors said they had in deciding how the stories written by others were to be used. (See table 7.13.) Among broadcast editors, more men than women said they had almost complete freedom to determine story use.

JOB SATISFACTION

Bowman's analysis of the 1971 survey showed that even though women in journalism received fewer financial rewards and were a minority group

Table 7.13 Amount of Freedom Men and Women with
Editing Duties Have in Deciding How
Stories Will Be Used, 1982–83
(Percentage in Each Category)

Amount	Print		Broadcast	
	Men (n = 350)	*Women* (n = 178)	*Men* (n = 126)	*Women* (n = 56)
Almost complete	42.3	34.8	49.2	37.5
A great deal	25.7	25.8	23.0	37.5
Some	21.7	23.0	23.0	12.5
None at all	10.3	16.3	4.8	12.5

within the profession, they were more likely than males to say that they were very satisfied with their work. He found that being female was a positive predictor of job satisfaction.

The higher degree of job satisfaction among women found in 1971 no longer existed by 1982–83. Women did not express any less satisfaction than men, even though women journalists still did not hold as many managerial or other upper-level positions as men and the pay of women journalists was still lower than that of men. Likewise, women and men in 1982–83 were equally committed to their jobs, with 84 percent of the women and 81.8 percent of the men saying that five years in the future they would still like to be working for a news organization.

There were some shifts in the ratings men and women journalists gave to various job dimensions between the two decades. Bowman saw the differences between men and women in the areas of pay, fringe benefits, and advancement opportunities as "consistent with the differential definition of work roles," which he believed to be influenced by the greater family responsibilities of women.[41] Men still placed more importance on pay in 1982–83, and women still placed more importance than men on the chance to develop a specialty. (See table 7.14.)

The most dramatic change between the two decades was the increase in the percentage of women and the decrease in the percentage of men who rated the chance to get ahead in the organization as very important. In 1971, 52.4 percent of the men and 38.7 percent of the women rated the opportunity for career advancement as very important. A decade later, 43.9 percent of the men and 52.8 percent of the women rated this dimension

Table 7.14 The Importance of Job Dimensions
for Journalists, 1971 and 1982–83
(Percentage Who Rated Each Dimension Very Important)

Dimension	1971		1982–83	
	Men	Women	Men	Women
Pay	28.7	15.3	24.5	18.9
Fringe benefits	25.6	23.3	25.8	25.1
A chance to get ahead in organization	52.4	38.7	43.9	52.8
Job security	50.9	52.5	56.6	57.7
Chance to develop a specialty	43.5	48.8	41.9	50.4
Chance to help people	65.0	73.1	56.6	68.9
Editorial policies of organization	48.9	62.3	54.1	62.3
Freedom from supervision	52.4	54.8	38.1	39.3
Amount of autonomy	55.4	54.9	50.1	51.1

as very important. Similarly, women in the 1980s, like the 1970s, also rated the chance to develop a specialty higher than did men.

The chance to help people became less important for both men and women between the two decades, although women in both surveys were more likely than men to say that this was a very important dimension of their job. Similarly, in both decades more women than men rated the editorial policies of the organization as "very important."

The importance of pay and fringe benefits showed less change. Pay was rated as "very important" for 15.3 percent of the women in 1971, 18.9 percent in 1982–83. Pay slightly declined in importance for men between the two decades, with a total of 28.7 percent in 1971 and 24.5 percent in 1982–83 rating pay as "very important." Roughly a quarter of men and women in both decades rated fringe benefits as "very important." Clearly, there were few differences in the importance men and women journalists placed on pay and fringe benefits, with neither group rating these tangible rewards and benefits as the most important aspects of their job.

PROFESSIONAL AFFILIATIONS

One of the significant developments for women between the two decades was their admittance into the Society of Professional Journalists, Sigma Delta Chi, the oldest and largest of the journalistic fraternities. When women began to look for membership in press clubs and associations in the latter part of the nineteenth century, they found that they had to organize themselves because they were not welcome in most of the existing organizations. The New England Women's Press Association and the Women's National Press Association were formed in 1885, with the latter group counting 300 women in its membership by the end of the decade.[42] (It was not until 1937 that several state organizations, including the Illinois group, joined together to form the National Federation of Press Women, Inc.[43])

Finally, in 1973, the Society of Professional Journalists, Sigma Delta Chi, opened its doors to women — a change that reflected a shift in attitudes that only a few years before had seemed entrenched — and other organizations soon followed suit. As late as 1965, media scholar William Rivers predicted that women were not likely ever to be admitted to the ''alcoholic camaraderie'' of another all-male bastion, the National Press Club.[44] But the barriers did break down, and today there are no professional journalism organizations that limit membership on the basis of gender.

Neither male nor female journalists, however, can be described as enthusiastic joiners of professional organizations. In fact, only 41 percent of the women and 39 percent of the men in the 1982–83 survey named a professional organization to which they belonged. As noted earlier, even the Society of Professional Journalists could claim only 17 percent of journalists on its membership rolls by 1983, and this analysis found that the percentages of women and men journalists who belonged to SPJ were not significantly different.

At the time Johnstone, Slawski, and Bowman did their study, women were not admitted to membership in SPJ. Given how quickly women flocked to the organization after 1973, it is interesting to speculate on changes in the roles played by women's groups such as Women in Communications, Inc. (WICI), and the National Federation of Press Women. Unfortunately, no figures are available on the percentage of women journalists who belonged to these groups in 1971, although it seems likely that they lost some of their influence among journalists after the Society of

Professional Journalists opened its doors to women. It is possible that a decline in the influence of these women's organizations might mean that women journalists were receiving a different type of socialization in the 1980s. As of 1982–83, however, those organizations for women were still playing an important role in the lives of women journalists, with 12.1 percent of the women who belonged to a professional organization reporting that they were members of WICI and 9.3 percent reporting membership in the National Federation of Press Women. No men surveyed in 1982–83 reported belonging to either of these groups, although both have membership policies that do not exclude men.

JOURNALISTIC ROLES AND ETHICS

Men and women responded in similar patterns to questions about the importance they placed on various journalistic roles. (See table 7.15.) Gender was a significant predictor only for questions about avoiding stories with unverified content and the importance of media's providing entertainment and relaxation. In 1982–83, women journalists were just as likely as men in the field to think it was extremely important to investigate government claims and get information to the public quickly, and were just as unlikely as men to place a great deal of importance on serving as an adversary of government or business. It is possible that the minor differences found here, however, may be a result of something other than gender.

Table 7.15 Importance Journalists
Assign to Various Mass Media Roles, 1982–83
(Percentage Who Rated Each Role Extremely Important)

Journalistic Role	*Men* (*n = 661*)	*Women* (*n = 338*)
Investigate government claims	64.0	68.6
Get information to public quickly	57.8	63.3
Avoid stories with unverified content	45.8	58.0
Provide analysis of complex problems	49.2	49.1
Discuss national policy	39.5	39.6
Develop intellectual/cultural interests	23.5	25.7
Provide entertainment, relaxation	18.2	23.1
Serve as an adversary of government	21.0	18.7
Serve as an adversary of business	15.1	16.0

CONCLUSIONS

A number of factors make the decade between the Johnstone, Slawski, and Bowman survey and the 1982–83 survey a particularly significant one for women journalists. The substantial increase in the number of women journalists coincided with growth in the work force as a whole and equal opportunity legislation that had an impact on the the broadcast industry in particular. In addition, the decade saw the opening to women of formerly all-male organizations such as the Society of Professional Journalists that provide women with collegial contacts for professional identification, acceptance, and networking.

This study shows that women were better represented in the journalistic work force as a whole, as well as in decision-making positions in news organizations, during the 1980s than the 1970s. But women still were not represented in newsrooms, and particularly in the upper echelons of newsroom hierarchies, in anything close to their proportions in the population as a whole. As of 1983, women still made up less than four-tenths of the newsroom population. Yet it seems likely, given that 60 percent of the students in U.S. college journalism programs are women, that women are on their way to becoming "a new majority" in the field.

This study found that female journalists differ from male journalists in ease of entry into the field, the income they earn, their representation in management, and in some values. It also found that women and men journalists were more similar than different, particularly in terms of their educational levels, overall job satisfaction, valued job characteristics, and attitudes about professionalism. Furthermore, the gender differences diminished between the time of this study (1982–83) and the 1971 study by Johnstone, Slawski, and Bowman. Some specific findings include these:

- Female and male journalists come from similar religious and ethnic backgrounds, although more women than men were African American, Latino, Asian American, or members of other racial minority groups.
- Women tended to be younger and less experienced than male journalists, but part of this difference can be attributed to the influx of large numbers of young women at the entry levels.
- Women were just as likely as male journalists to have received formal training in a college journalism program. This means that the educational gap of the 1970s — in which women were less likely

than men to be college educated — had disappeared by the early 1980s. All journalists are more formally educated now than ever before.

- Women and men in 1982–83 were equally satisfied with their jobs, equally committed to journalism, and just as likely to say that they would like to be working in journalism five years from now.

The status of women in journalism in many ways reflects the status of women in the workplace as a whole. Women have entered journalism in greater numbers at the same time they have increased their representation in the work force as a whole. Furthermore, the inequities that women face in salaries, promotion, and the challenges of balancing family and work roles are not unique to journalism.

Much of the progress of women made between the 1971 and 1982–83 studies was a result of a combination of favorable labor market conditions and equal opportunity legislation. The degree of progress in future years will depend on a commitment to anti-discrimination policies on the federal and state levels and a commitment on the part of employers to equal opportunity and other policies that make it easier for workers of both sexes to accommodate the dual demands of career and family responsibilities. Finally, the advancement of women in the field also depends on the activism of those who have a direct stake in the attainment of equal opportunity for women.

—8—

Television, Radio and Newspaper Journalists

As Americans report increasing reliance on television for their public affairs information,[1] critics continue to express concern about the quality of news it provides. Some of that concern is directed toward the journalists who work in the broadcast media. Edwin Diamond, for example, points out that the first generation of journalists to work in television news was trained in print.[2] Now he worries that television employs a generation of editorial people whose experience has been totally in broadcast, suggesting that they may "have keen eyes for format but no real ear for content."[3]

This concern about possible differences between print and broadcast journalists is not new, however. Ismach and Dennis surveyed newspaper and television reporters in the Minneapolis–St. Paul area and compared the two samples on a number of indicators of professionalism. They found that the television people held fewer college degrees, were younger, and belonged to fewer professional organizations than those working in print. The two groups were quite similar, though, in attitudes about their work roles.[4]

When Becker reanalyzed the results of a national survey by Johnstone et al.,[5] however, he found that broadcast reporters were more likely than newspaper reporters to reject the neutral role of the press. In addition,

Becker concluded that broadcast journalists from smaller organizations tended to be less professionally oriented than their print counterparts.[6]

Pollard used a scale developed by McLeod and Hawley[7] to measure the professionalism of a sample of Canadian journalists. When he compared the results across media (radio, television, and daily newspapers), Pollard found that some essential professional attributes — desires for autonomy, expression, growth, and influence — were shared widely. More significantly, the broadcast journalists were "relatively more professional" than their print colleagues.[8]

While these studies have provided insights into the demographic characteristics, attitudes, and values of broadcast journalists, most have used local samples, and the data in some cases are more than a decade old. Also, when both radio and television have been included in the data analysis, they have been lumped together, rather than analyzed separately. Yet, with the disparity in pay between the two and the tendency, observed in some broadcast journalism classes, for students to set their sights on a career in television rather than radio, one might expect these two groups to be quite distinct. This chapter draws a national profile of radio and television journalists and compares them, on several possible indicators of professionalism, with the people who work at daily newspapers.

This chapter is based primarily on the 119 radio, 121 television, and 465 daily newspaper journalists interviewed from the total of 1,001.

DEMOGRAPHICS

As would be expected, there is a large difference in editorial staff size when radio, television, and daily newspapers are compared. The median number of people on the radio news staff is three, contrasted with a figure of 22 for television and 42 for newspapers. As was the case in the Becker study,[9] staff size is used as a control variable. The median is the dividing line between small and large organizations.

The journalistic work force in all three media is predominately male. Twenty-six percent of those working in radio are women compared to 33 percent for television and 34 percent for daily newspapers. These are below the 1980 census figures for the percentage of women employed in the full-time U.S. labor force (43 percent),[10] but in general are higher than the proportion of women in some comparable professional groups.[11] The Johnstone et al. data listed 5 percent of those working in radio, 10 percent of

Table 8.1 Political Distribution
of Journalists by Medium
(Percentages)

	Television (n = 116)	Radio (n = 116)	Daily Newspaper (n = 455)	General Public[a]
Democrat	36	30	41	45
Republican	22	30	17	25
Independent	41	38	40	30
Other	1	2	2	—

Column totals may not add up to 100 percent because of rounding.

[a]From George H. Gallup, *The Gallup Poll: Public Opinion 1983*. Wilmington, Del.: Scholarly Resources Inc., 1984, p. 82.

the people working in television, and 22 percent of those in daily newspapers as female.[12]

Analysis of the age distribution for the sample shows that broadcast journalists as a group are younger than their print counterparts. The median newspaper worker is 33 years old compared to a median age of 28 years in radio and television.

There are significant differences also in the racial composition of the journalistic groups working for the three media. Nearly 8.5 percent of television journalists are Black compared to only 2 percent of newspaper journalists and 2.5 percent of the radio people. Less than one percent of the work force in each medium is Hispanic. The census figures for 1980 indicate that nearly 12 percent of the U.S. population is Black and 6.5 percent is Hispanic.[13]

In terms of political party identification, a plurality of the people in the sample labeled themselves as Independents. There were some slight differences by medium in 1982–83, however. There were more Republicans in radio than in television or daily newspapers and more Democrats in daily newspapers than in either broadcast medium. (See table 8.1.) Although the distribution of political party identification does not vary by organization size for the broadcast media, it does for newspapers. Forty-eight percent of the newspaper people in large organizations called themselves Democrats compared to 35 percent of those in small organizations, while 11 percent of the print people on large newspapers called themselves Republicans, compared to 23 percent at small papers.

WORKING PATTERNS

Because they have fewer people on staff, broadcast journalists are less likely to have responsibility for following a beat than those working for daily newspapers. Thirty-one percent of the television reporters, 35 percent of the radio journalists, and 60 percent of the daily newspaper people say they work a beat. Radio reporters are more likely to attend to traditional geographical beats such as city hall and the police department, indicating an emphasis on spot news coverage. Television, on the other hand, uses its beat reporters most frequently for consumer-oriented coverage. None of the television journalists in the sample listed state government as a beat.

Regardless of the beat system, journalists seem to feel that they have quite a lot of freedom to determine story coverage. When asked how often they are able to get a subject covered if they come up with a good idea for a story, 56 percent of the television people say "almost always" while 35 percent say "more often than not" and only 7 percent say "occasionally." No significant differences appear when television, radio, and daily newspapers are compared on this question.

There are some differences by medium, however, when journalists are asked how much freedom they usually have in selecting the stories on which they work. Seventy-one percent of those in radio news say they have "almost complete freedom." Some 60 percent of the daily newspaper people and 48 percent of the television journalists chose that response. Apparently because of the smaller staff size in radio, there is less supervision than in newspapers or television. Also, the logistical problems of shuffling television crews around a city probably keep much of the responsibility for story selection in the hands of assignment editors.

The same pattern appears when journalists are asked how much freedom they have in deciding "which aspects of a story should be emphasized." Seventy-three percent of the radio, 67 percent of the daily newspaper, and 64 percent of the television journalists say "almost complete freedom."

The broadcast media are quite different from print when it comes to the amount of editing stories receive. Nearly 56 percent of the radio people and 42 percent of the television journalists report that their stories receive

Table 8.2 The Most Commonly
Mentioned Faults in Stories
(Percentages)

	Television (n = 88)	Radio (n = 86)	Daily Newspaper (n = 310)
Grammar, syntax	17	26	21
Awkward writing	9	8	5
Repetition	8	7	7
Hasty writing	6	2	0
Poor broadcast style	6	5	0
Unclear writing	5	5	5
Poor production	4	1	0
Camera work	4	0	0
Spelling	2	11	18
Poor organization	2	5	5

Columns do not add up to 100 percent because all responses are not listed.

"no editing at all" from others in their organization. Only 18 percent of the daily newspaper responses fall into that category, while 68 percent of the print people say there is "some editing" and 14 percent say there is "a great deal."

In addition, journalists in all three media receive feedback from a number of other sources. Respondents are more likely to say they hear from members of the audience than from others in their own organizations. When organization size is controlled, there are some slight differences between print and television. More television employees in large organizations (60 percent) than TV journalists in small organizations (50 percent) report regular feedback from the audience. The reverse is true for newspaper employees, with 46 percent in large organizations and 55 percent on small papers saying they have regular contact with the audience.

When they edit stories, supervisors turn up a list of complaints familiar to most journalism professors. Table 8.2 shows that problems with grammar and syntax head the list, followed by spelling (for newspapers and radio), awkward writing, and repetition. The most commonly cited problems in broadcasting deal with writing rather than reporting or production.

ATTITUDES TOWARD THE JOB

The majority of the respondents say they are satisfied with their jobs, and there are no significant differences by type of medium. (See table 8.3.) Size of organization has no significant relationship with job satisfaction in broadcasting, but more print journalists who work for the larger firms report a high level of satisfaction than those who work for the smaller ones.

Table 8.3 Job Satisfaction
(Percentages)

	Television (n = 121)	Radio (n = 119)	Daily Newspaper (n = 463)
Very Satisfied	36	42	40
Fairly Satisfied	47	40	44
Somewhat Satisfied	16	16	15
Very Dissatisfied	2	2	1

Columns may not add up to 100 percent because of rounding.

Table 8.4 Factors Journalists Consider Very
Important for Judging Jobs
(Percentages)

	Television (n = 121)	Radio (n = 119)	Daily Newspaper (n = 463)
Pay	26	22	22
Benefits	27	28	26
Freedom from Supervision	31	37	40
Helping People	68	67	57
Editorial Policies	55	47	54
Autonomy	53	41	53
Job Security	48	71	57
Chance to Get Ahead	54	59	43
Chance to Develop a Specialty	58	48	44

A series of questions described in Chapter 4 also probed further to determine the factors journalists use to judge the attractiveness of jobs. Table 8.4 shows the percentages who rate these items "very important."

The figures indicate that money is not the major source of satisfaction for journalists. They are much more likely to stress the opportunity to help people. Small market broadcasters are more likely than small market newspaper workers to say this is very important, but this difference is not present in large organizations. The radio people are most concerned about job security, and radio and newspaper employees in small organizations are more likely than their counterparts in large organizations to rate job security as important. Also, radio journalists in large organizations are most likely to value a chance to get ahead.

Finally, more broadcast than print journalists say the opportunity to develop a specialty is very important. This difference probably reflects the fact that newspaper reporters are more likely to cover a beat, which forces one to develop a specialty.

Still another indication of job satisfaction is the future plans of those currently working in the field. Nearly 84 percent of the television journalists say they plan to be working as journalists five years from now, and only 12 percent hope to be elsewhere. The figures do not differ significantly for radio or daily newspapers.

Although most respondents want to continue to work as journalists, some would like to move to a different medium. Seventeen percent of those in radio would like to cross over to television, while only two percent of those in television would rather be in radio. There is little desire on the part of broadcast journalists to work in print, and vice versa.

If there is any one factor that could persuade the journalists to leave their chosen field, however, it is pay. Some 39 percent of the television people say they might be tempted to leave journalism for a higher paying job. Other factors that might tempt them to leave are a new challenge (8 percent), lack of freedom (7 percent), burnout (6 percent), and better job security (6 percent). Responses for radio and daily newspaper employees are not significantly different than those for television.

People who actually plan to leave journalism in five years list a number of fields as their alternative choices, including teaching, public relations, performing, production, self-employment, and retirement. Public relations is the most popular option. It is cited by 22 percent of the journalists who desire a change.

Table 8.5 Percentage of Journalists Who Agree
with Statements about the Audience

	Television (n = 121)	Radio (n = 119)	Daily Newspaper (n = 459)
Audience most interested in breaking news	85	83	75
Audience not interested in social problems	30	36	28
Audience is gullible	19	22	14

PERCEPTIONS OF AUDIENCE AND ROLE

One indication of a journalist's view of his or her function in society is the perception of audience interests. Respondents were given a series of three statements about the audience and asked to agree or disagree using a five-point scale.

Nearly 85 percent of the television journalists agree "somewhat" or "strongly" with the first statement, "Audience members are more interested in the day's breaking news than in analysis of long-term trends" (see table 8.5), and responses of the radio people do not differ significantly. Daily newspaper employees are less likely (75 percent) to agree. Those who work for small newspapers and radio stations are more likely than their peers who work for large organizations to endorse that opinion.

There are no significant differences by medium when surveyed journalists respond to the statement, "The majority of audience members have little interest in reading about social problems such as racial discrimination and poverty." Only about a third agree. Television journalists in the large organizations express stronger opposition to the statement than TV people in small stations.

Journalists in all three media express little support for the idea that the audience is gullible and easily fooled. Newspaper people in large organizations are more likely to say they strongly disagree than their peers who work for small firms. For radio employees, however, the strongest disagreement is in the smaller organizations.

Another series of questions described in chapter 5 asked about the importance of various roles that traditionally have been associated with the news media. Journalists were asked, for example, to indicate on a four-point scale how important they think it is for the news media to "Get information to the public quickly." Factor analysis of the responses indicated the existence of three main role types labeled "Adversary," "Disseminator," and "Interpreter." The adversaries say it is extremely important to be skeptical of public officials and business leaders. Interpreters say it is extremely important to investigate claims and statements made by the government, analyze complex problems, and discuss national policy. The disseminators, on the other hand, say it is important to get information out quickly and to concentrate on the widest possible audience.

There is a great deal of overlap among these roles, but differences do show up by medium and organization size. Regardless of organization size, newspaper journalists are more likely than the broadcast people to embrace the adversary role. Television employees who work for large organizations are about twice as likely as those who work for small firms to rate adversary behavior as extremely important. The disseminator role is supported strongly by radio journalists when compared with their television and print counterparts in large organizations. In smaller organizations, however, the figures are not significantly different. Newspaper journalists give strongest support to the interpretative role, followed by television and radio. These data seem to indicate that perceptions of journalistic role held by the television people are similar to those of their print counterparts, especially in large markets. Radio people, on the other hand, support a more passive view of the journalists' function. (See table 8.6.)

The television employees also express opinions similar to those voiced by newspaper people on the topic of ethics. Because some have criticized journalists, especially those who work for television, for a lack of ethics in reporting,[14] this study analyzed opinions about controversial reporting methods and compared them by medium and organization size. The respondents were asked to indicate on a three-point scale whether the following practices are justified on occasion: using confidential documents without authorization, using personal documents or photographs without authorization, and seeking employment with a firm in order to gather inside information. Answers to these questions were added to create an ethics scale. The patterns of responses are the same for both large and small organizations. About 20 percent of the television and newspaper people in small organizations say these practices are justified on occasion, but only two percent of the radio journalists approve of them. Journalists in

Table 8.6 Percentages of Journalists Who Strongly Endorse Various Journalistic Roles[1]

	Adversary	Disseminator	Interpretative
Large Organizations	Newspaper 26 Television 23 Radio 7	Radio 67 Television 46 Newspaper 44	Newspaper 78 Television 61 Radio 37
	a	b	c
Small Organizations	Newspaper 18 Television 11 Radio 11	Newspaper 61 Radio 62 Television 42	Newspaper 60 Television 44 Radio 31
	d	e	f

a. Cramer's $V = .21$, $p < .000$ d. Cramer's $V = .15$, $p < .006$
b. Cramer's $V = .14$, $p < .01$ e. Cramer's $V = .11$, $p < .10$
c. Cramer's $V = .25$, $p < .0000$ f. Cramer's $V = .18$, $p < .0002$

[1]This table shows the percentage of journalists who score in the top quartile of a scale for each role type created by adding the responses to questions associated with that role.

the larger organizations are somewhat more likely to voice approval, with 36 percent of the newspaper, 30 percent of the television, and 11 percent of the radio journalists saying they are justified.

OTHER INDICATORS OF PROFESSIONALISM

We also asked a number of questions about other variables that traditionally have been seen as indicators of professionalism in a field.[15] One is an individual's motivation for choosing a career. Encouragement from grade and high school teachers is listed most frequently by TV personnel, while a long-standing desire to enter the field was the single largest attraction for radio journalists. "Always liked to write" tops the list for the daily newspaper people.

The educational background of journalists in this study also varies by medium. Television personnel earned the most college degrees, followed by employees in daily newspapers and radio. Although organization size does not account for the percentage of college diplomas held by television

Table 8.7 Education Levels of Journalists
(Percentages)

	Television	Radio	Daily Newspaper
Some High School	0	3	0
Completed High School	0	13	7
One to Three Years College	20	32	18
College Graduate	62	40	57
Some Graduate School	11	5	7
Advanced Degree	7	8	10

Columns may not add up to 100 percent because of rounding.

people, it does so for radio — with more degrees in the larger organizations. Newspapers show the same pattern. (See table 8.7.)

As might be expected from the discussion of age at the beginning of this chapter, the typical newspaper journalist has more journalistic experience (13 years) than the typical radio (9 years) or television journalist (8 years).

In terms of keeping up with professional reading, the newspaper and television respondents are ahead of the radio journalists. Newspaper and television personnel read more newspapers, general magazines, and professional journals such as *Columbia Journalism Review, Quill*, and *Washington Journalism Review* than the radio people. There is no difference by medium, however, in the average number of professional organizations journalists have joined. The mean for each group is about six-tenths of one organization, indicating that journalists are not generally joiners of professional groups.

CONCLUSIONS

This comparison of U.S. television, radio, and daily newspaper journalists indicates that television journalists are strikingly more similar to daily newspaper journalists in size of editorial staff, political party affiliation, perceptions of journalistic roles and ethics, education levels, and professional reading patterns than they are to radio journalists, supporting the findings of earlier studies by Ismach and Dennis, and Pollard.[16] This suggests that the traditional "print-broadcast" distinction frequently made between journalists is often not valid.[17] The differences between radio and television journalists in the United States are substantial according to our national data from 1982–83. Because of these differences in some of the indicators of professionalism, scholars and practitioners of journalism should use care in categorizing journalists as either print or broadcast.

Our study also suggests that differences between the professionalism of newspaper and television journalists are less than those between television and radio journalists. We did find some differences between print and broadcast journalists, including age, racial composition, coverage of a beat, amount of editing of stories, and importance of developing a specialty, but these differences tended to be in demographics and working patterns rather than in indicators of professionalism such as perceived roles, ethics, education and professional reading habits.

—9—

Journalists' Best Work

What are the characteristics of stories selected by the journalists in our study as their best work? Are certain story categories more likely to be represented? How long are these stories? What kind of sources do journalists rely on for their best work? Are the stories based on news events or issues — or both? What news values are present in the best stories? Are they timely, unusual, full of conflict or great impact?

This chapter addresses these questions through content analysis of the stories we asked journalists to submit and their responses to our open-ended questions about their best work. It provides a descriptive summary and offers some insights into the correlates of content selected by journalists as their best.

HOW THE ANALYSIS WAS CONDUCTED

We asked journalists in our survey to answer three open-ended questions about a story that represented some of their best work and then encouraged them to send us a copy of the story they had discussed. Specifically, we asked them to tell us briefly about a story that represented some of their best work from the past year, what made the story particularly good, and what thoughts they had about their audience while working on the story.

The two persons who conducted the analysis considered the responses to all three questions together, because evidence for the several content categories could be found in any of the three.[1]

We also received actual stories from 13 percent of the journalists in our survey.[2] All but one of these were from journalists who worked in the print media (daily and weekly newspapers, primarily, with a handful of stories from magazine journalists and a single television script). We used only those stories submitted by newspaper journalists for the content analysis. Of the 131 stories considered in this analysis, the length ranged from one paragraph to 170 paragraphs. The average length was 35 paragraphs, and the median was 29 paragraphs. Although most journalists clipped their articles from newspapers, we ascertained that at least 45 percent of all the stories appeared on page one, and 34 percent were part of the on-going coverage of a single issue or event. Of the 131 newspaper journalists who submitted stories, 97 percent were employed by daily newspapers, with the rest from weekly newspapers.[3] All the newspaper stories were coded by the author.

Several content categories were used for this analysis, including general story topics, indicators of journalist role concepts, the presence of news values, and whether the story was based on events or issues. In the actual stories sent by journalists we also looked at source type and source frequency, although these could not be determined from the open-ended question responses.

GENERAL STORY TOPICS

News about state and local government and news about crime were the two most popular story topics cited by the journalists in our study. From a list of 19 possible story topics based on the newspaper story classification suggested by Burgoon et al.,[4] we found that about 14 percent of the stories and responses to the open-ended questions dealt with each of these two topics. The two leading topics were followed by stories of general human interest (9 percent of newspaper stories and 10 percent of question responses), social problems (8 percent of stories and 10 percent of question responses) and sports (5 percent of stories, 8 percent of responses). The remainder of the story topics were cited or submitted by fewer than 8 percent of journalists in our sample. (See table 9.1.)

While we didn't ask the journalists in our sample how important these topics were to readers, the journalists from eight newsrooms who partic-

Table 9.1 Story Topics of Journalists' Best Work

Story Topics	Percent of Best Work	
	Stories (n = 131)	Open-Ended Questions (n = 850)
State and local government news	14	15
Crime news	14	14
General human interest	9	10
Social problems	8	10
Sports	5	8
Business and finance	4	6
Accidents and disasters	3	5
Environment and energy	3	5
Economic news	2	5
National government news	4	4
Education and schools	5	4
Medical news	5	4
Celebrities and personalities	5	3
Arts, leisure and travel	5	2
International news	2	2
Religion	4	1
Consumer information and advice	5	1
Science, invention and space	1	0
Humor	3	—

ipated in the Burgoon study were asked to estimate what proportion of their readers were very interested in these topics.[5] We provide only the rankings based on these figures in table 9.2, because a comparison of the two helps to illustrate that some journalists' perceptions of what readers want do not necessarily correspond with what other journalists see as their own best work.

While one of the most-cited story topics by journalists in our study was state and local government news, journalists in the Burgoon study ranked that category 13th out of 18 on reader interest. News about crime was cited by 14 percent of the journalists in our study, and this category did finish fifth with the Burgoon journalists. The top three categories in the Burgoon study, however (sports, celebrities and personalities, and acci-

Table 9.2 Journalists' Best Work
Compared to Journalists'
Perceptions of Reader Interest

Story Topics	Rank of Topics Cited as Best Work[a]	Rank of Topics Readers Very Interested In[b]
State and local government news	1st	—
Crime news	2nd	5th
General human interest	3rd — tie	—
Social problems	3rd — tie	—
Sports	4th	1st
Business and finance	5th	—
Education and schools	—	—
Celebrities and personalities	—	2nd
Consumer information and advice	—	—
Medical news	—	—
Arts, leisure and travel	—	—
Religion	—	—
Accidents and disasters	—	3rd
Environment and energy	—	—
Humor	—	—
National government news	—	—
International news	—	—
Economic news	—	—
Defense and military	—	—
Science, invention and space	—	—
General local news	—	4th

[a]For best work, n = 850.
[b]For percent of readers thought to be very interested in topics, source: Burgoon, Judee K., Michael Burgoon, and Charles K. Atkin. *The World of the Working Journalist.* New York: Newspaper Advertising Bureau, 1982, p. 69.

dents and disasters), were represented by 8 percent or fewer of the stories discussed by journalists in our study. The Burgoon category of general local news (not used in the typology here) finished fourth, and may actually correspond more closely with our category of general human interest, represented by about 10 percent of the stories mentioned by journalists.

From this comparison we conclude that some journalists do not (or cannot, because of job constraints) use the same standards to determine excellence in their own work as they use to determine what readers will find of interest. It may be, too, that many journalists make a distinction between what readers ought to know and what readers will find of most interest.

MASS MEDIA ROLE PERCEPTIONS

The stories journalists submitted and the responses they gave about their best work were also coded for the presence of the three distinct media roles we identified in our factor analysis in chapter 5 — the disseminator, the interpretive, and the adversarial roles. While several scholars have categorized journalists according to their endorsement of a particular journalistic role,[6] few studies have looked for evidence of such roles in actual news content.

We also considered the seven roles which loaded heavily on the three factors as content categories themselves, and stories and responses to open-ended questions were coded for specific references to each of the seven roles in addition to being coded for the three more general role perceptions.[7]

We conducted the content analysis using these categories because we were particularly interested in comparing what journalists *said* about the importance of journalistic roles (based on our survey questionnaire) and whether their examples of best work actually displayed evidence of these roles. Our expectation was that "best" work would be more likely than routine stories to contain evidence of media roles that journalists deem important. We also believed that journalists who endorsed one of the media roles would be more likely to report as their best work stories that were characterized by that role.

A problem arose, however, when we found a discrepancy between what we learned from journalists' responses to our open-ended questions about best work and the actual examples submitted by the 131 newspaper journalists in our sample. (See table 9.3.) Specifically, the percentages for two of the three role orientations (disseminator and interpretive) and three of the seven media roles (appealing to a wide audience, analyzing complex problems and getting story to the public quickly) were significantly different for the two samples. We believe the reason lies in the coding of comments *about* best work versus the coding of actual stories selected by journalists as their best work.[8]

Table 9.3 General Media Roles in Stories and Question Answers

Media Roles	Percent of Best Work		Percent Who Endorse or Say Role Extremely Important[a]	
	Stories (n = 131)	Open-Ended Questions (n = 814)	Stories	Open-Ended Questions
Disseminator	37	61	51	51
Interpretive	46	25	77	62
Adversarial	13	12	19	17
Can't categorize	4	2	—	—

[a]Percentages of those who endorsed each role determined by number of journalists who scored in the top quartile on each role scale. Journalists can endorse more than one role so percentages do not sum to 100.

Because of this discrepancy, we give greater emphasis in reporting the results to the actual newspaper stories we analyzed. Our findings indicate that there were some similarities between the presence of mass media roles in stories representing best work and what journalists generally say about the importance of those media roles, and we found some evidence to suggest that journalists who believe a role is extremely important are more likely to include evidence of that role in their best work.

We considered first the three general role perceptions endorsed by the journalists in our study. The proportions of actual stories which were classified as either disseminator, interpretive, or adversarial are similar to the proportions of journalists who sent stories and who endorsed each particular role. While percentages are not exact, the greatest proportion of newspaper stories submitted to us were interpretive stories (46 percent) and the greatest proportion of journalists who sent stories were those who endorsed the interpretive role (77 percent). The smallest proportion of stories were adversarial in nature (13 percent) and only 19 percent of the newspaper journalists who sent stories endorsed the adversarial role. Another 37 percent of stories were disseminator stories, compared to 51 percent of those who sent stories who strongly identified with that role. This is a good indication that, *in general*, journalists tend to write stories with evidence of the three media roles in the same relative ranking as they endorse these media roles.

The proportions of all journalists in our study who endorsed the three roles are strikingly similar to the percentage of those who sent stories, suggesting that those who sent stories were typical of the larger group in their views about the importance of general roles for journalists. But most of the stories discussed in the open-ended questions were classified as disseminator stories (61 percent), with only 25 percent considered interpretive and 12 percent adversarial. Again, we attribute this difference to the difficulty in coding *discussion* of stories as opposed to actual content.

We also suspected that endorsing a particular role might be related to writing a story with characteristics of that particular role, and we found some indication to support this. Both for the stories we coded and for the responses to open-ended questions, we found a small but significant increase in the number of interpretive stories written when journalists endorsed the interpretive role.[9]

These results were true both for the stories submitted and those discussed. Of the 131 journalists who submitted stories and who endorsed the interpretive role, 50 percent wrote stories of that type; only 46 percent of all submitted stories were interpretive. This difference was significant at the .10 level. For the 814 stories discussed, 29 percent of the journalists who endorsed the interpretive role also wrote stories of this type. This was significantly greater than the 25 percent generally who discussed interpretive stories. (See table 9.4.)

The newspaper journalists who submitted stories for this study were more likely than the larger sample of all journalists to endorse the interpretive role (77 percent versus 62 percent). They were also more likely to submit interpretive stories than were journalists in the larger sample to discuss such stories. While we have already speculated that this results from our inability to correctly classify all discussion of stories of an interpretive nature, it also suggests that interpreters may be more likely to respond to a request to send a sample of their work. While we determined that our self-selected sample of journalists did not differ from the rest of our sample significantly on several variables, it may be that interpreters are not only more likely to write interpretive stories, but also to take pride in their work, or to want to share examples of it with others.

We also looked for evidence of the seven specific news media roles in the stories and responses to open-ended questions. We found similar proportions of newspaper journalists who said several of these roles were extremely important as compared with the proportions of those roles in their actual stories. This was true for the roles of adversary to government

Table 9.4 Journalists Who Endorsed the Three General Media Role Orientations and Wrote Stories Characterized by the Same Role

Role Endorsed by Journalists	Percent Who Wrote Stories of Each Type			Percent of All Stories of This Type
	Diss.	Interp.	Adver.	
Who Submitted Stories (n = 131)				
Disseminator (n = 67 or 51%)	40			37
Interpreter (n = 102 or 77%)		50[a]		46
Adversarial (n = 25 or 19%)			12	13
Who Responded to Open-Ended Questions (n = 814)				
Disseminator (n = 410 or 51%)	62			61
Interpreter (n = 499 or 62%)		29[b]		25
Adversarial (n = 133 or 17%)			14	12

[a]Significant at $p = .10$.
[b]Significant at $p = .01$.

and business, analysis and/or interpretation of complex problems, discussing policy as it is developed and getting a story to the public quickly.

However, not all roles display this similarity between what journalists say and what they do. Journalists were more likely to say that investigating government claims is an important media role than they were to present such investigation as their best work. Sixty-six percent of all journalists and 62 percent of those who submitted stories said the role was important, but only 13 percent of stories actually contained such investigation (and only 8 percent of question responses indicated this function). Slightly more

Table 9.5 Specific Media Roles in Stories and Question Answers

Media Role	Percent of Best Work		Percent Who Endorse or Say Role Extremely Important	
	Stories (n = 131)	Open-Ended Questions (n = 814)	Stories	Open-Ended Questions
Appeals to a wide audience	70	51	52	36
Analysis/ interpretation of complex problems	52	38	43	49
Gets story to the public quickly	47	15	69	60
Discusses policy as it is developed	21	23	36	38
Adversary to government	11	13	19	20
Investigates government claims	13	8	62	66
Adversary to business	9	6	14	15

than half (51 percent) of journalists who sent stories and 36 percent overall say that appealing to a wide audience is important, yet 70 percent of stories submitted include evidence of this role. (See table 9.5.)

While we have already attributed some differences to difficulty in coding the discussion of content versus actual content, these discrepancies cannot be so easily dismissed. We can speculate that most of the journalists in our study covered local and state government, and perhaps had fewer government claims to investigate. It's also possible that there simply was not enough time or money available for pursuit of these kinds of stories.

Journalists tell us that particular media roles and functions are important, yet those same journalists are not necessarily performing those functions in the creation of the work they consider to be their best. It may be that organizational constraints such as beat systems prohibit them from performing the roles they believe are most important. It's also possible that the discrepancy between what journalists say is most important and what they actually do may be contributing to dissatisfaction with their jobs in the media industries.

NEWS VALUES

In chapter 5 we analyzed how influential different factors were in determining what was newsworthy to journalists in their day-to-day work. There we noted that the most-cited factor was journalistic training. Because most college newswriting textbooks and reporting courses stress the traditional news values of conflict, unusualness, timeliness, proximity, prominence, and impact, we decided to look for evidence of these news values in the best work of journalists.

When we coded the newspaper stories for news values, we simply looked for the presence of each news value in each story. But we expected, in responses to our open-ended questions, that it would be unlikely for journalists to mention every news value present in their stories. We tried to devise a way to account for the "unmentioned," yet relevant, news values. Thus, when we coded the responses to open-ended questions we first recorded whether the respondent actually mentioned the news value; secondly, we recorded whether it was likely that the news value was present.

In response to our open-ended questions, for example, one journalist described a story involving a train derailment. Three cars ran off the track, millions of dollars in damage occurred, and it was necessary to evacuate residents of the area because of danger to their health. The journalist mentioned the interest that people in the area had in the subject and said the news organization's coverage provided an accurate picture of the situation.

This response was coded as follows: "mentioned" were the news values of proximity and impact; "likely" were the news values of unusualness and timeliness; "not mentioned nor likely to apply" were the news values of conflict and prominence.

Based on this coding scheme, we found that the news value evident in the most stories was proximity. Seventy-six percent of all the newspaper stories we received and 37 percent of the responses to our open-ended questions contained this value. We were not surprised, because these stories were written primarily by local journalists working for local news-

Table 9.6 Six Traditional News Values in Stories and Question Answers

News Value	Percent of Stories Containing This News Value			
	Newspaper Stories (n = 131)	Open-Ended Questions (n = 814)		
		Mentioned[a]	Likely[b]	Total
Proximity	76	37	39	76
Impact	62	35	27	62
Conflict	50	20	35	55
Unusualness	48	9	29	38
Timeliness	46	12	45	57
Prominence	21	14	11	25

[a]Respondent actually mentioned news value.
[b]Respondent did not mention news value, but presence of news value was likely.

papers. And our survey of story topics showed a large number of stories in the sample dealt with state and local government news, crime and general human interest — all topics that we would expect to be of value because of proximity.

Although proximity was not specifically mentioned, 39 percent of the stories discussed in the open-ended questions were also likely to contain this news value. By adding this to the 37 percent of journalists who did mention proximity, we found a total of 76 percent, which is identical to the percent of actual stories that emphasized proximity. (See table 9.6.)

Impact was the second most evident news value, a part of 62 percent of all stories. About half of all stories contained conflict (50 percent), unusualness (48 percent), and timeliness (46 percent). Only 21 percent contained evidence of the news value of prominence. This may be in part because of the small percentage of stories dealing with national government news and celebrities. A larger proportion of stories dealt with crime and general human interest, and with local and state government news where prominence may be of less consequence.

Responses to our open-ended questions about best work contained significantly smaller percentages of these news values when only the values that were actually mentioned are counted. When the "mentioned" news value percentages are added to the "likely" news values present, however, the totals are strikingly similar to the presence of these news values in the stories we received. In addition to providing a measure of the presence of these news values in the best work of U.S. journalists, our analysis of these stories and open-ended questions also allowed us to speculate about the weight that journalists place on the traditional news values themselves. Three-quarters of the stories submitted or discussed contained (or were likely to contain) the news value of proximity. Thus, the local journalists in our study suggested that their best work is generated when local issues or events are the focus of their stories. Not surprisingly, few would claim their best work came from editing a wire service story on a distant earthquake or other disaster, for example.

Impact also figured prominently in more than 60 percent of stories submitted or discussed. This finding is encouraging because it suggests that the best work of journalists is significant and influential in the lives of readers.

When we considered only the news values actually present in the responses to our open-ended questions, however, the percentage of journalists who *mentioned* the six traditional news values in the open-ended questions was considerably less than the percentage of stories that actually contained that news value. And for two of the news values — unusualness and timeliness — journalists mentioned these only about one-fourth as often as they were present in stories. While journalists mentioned proximity and impact about half as often as these actually occurred in stories, journalists mentioned prominence two-thirds of the time it was included in stories — even though prominence was evident in fewer than 25 percent of stories.

This leads us to conclude that journalists place a greater value on stories that deal with local issues, those with significant impact on the community, and — when they write them — stories that deal with prominent people. The values of unusualness and timeliness, while they appear in about half of all the stories written, might represent the minimum requirement for a story to be considered "news." That is, most of what gets presented as news in the media is, by definition, timely and out of the ordinary. It takes something more for a story to take on the qualities of the journalists' "best work," and this "something else" may well be the value the story has in terms of proximity, impact and, to some extent, prominence.

STORY ORIENTATION

Another area of interest to us was the event and issue orientation of the stories submitted and discussed as best work by the journalists. Tuchman's

Table 9.7 Events and Issues in Stories and Question Answers

| | Story Based on: | | | | For Event Stories Only: | | |
	Event	Issue	Both	Neither/ Can't Tell	Anti- cipated	Unex- pected	Can't Tell
Percent of Open-Ended Questions (n = 814)[a]	37	41	19	3	43	51	6
Percent of Newspaper Stories (n = 131)[b]	34	48	12	6	39	48	13

[a]For open-ended question responses that are event-oriented, n = 465.
[b]For newspaper stories that are event-oriented, n = 64.

suggestion of a "news net" in which reporters rely on institutional sources and events over issues for the bulk of their information led us to wonder if the best work of journalists would also rely heavily on events.[10]

Our analysis indicated that about 60 percent of the stories either submitted or discussed by journalists dealt with issues; 48 percent of the newspaper stories submitted and 41 percent of the responses to open-ended questions dealt with issues alone, while 12 percent of stories and 19 percent of responses were about both issues and events. About 34 percent of all stories and 37 percent of the responses to open-ended questions were exclusively about events.

We also coded all event stories and question responses according to whether the event was anticipated or unexpected. Of the 64 newspaper stories that covered events, 39 percent of those stories were about an anticipated event, while 48 percent dealt with unexpected events. In the responses to open-ended questions about events, 43 percent of the 465 responses were anticipated and 51 percent were unexpected.

These results suggest that U.S. journalists are more likely to select stories dealing with issues than with events when asked to cite examples of their best work. This may be a kind of acknowledgment by journalists that stories with an issue orientation have greater value than those that rely exclusively on events. For those journalists who do cite event stories, a greater proportion of them deal with unexpected events — the kind of spot news coverage which is the bread and butter of the news business. These findings suggest that journalists are least likely to find scheduled, planned, or announced events to result in work that they consider their best.

SOURCES

The newspaper stories submitted by journalists were also content analyzed according to several source categories. We wanted to know what proportion of sources used were identified or anonymous, institutional or non-institutional, documentary or human, and male or female.

Table 9.8 illustrates the means and percentages for these various source categories in the newspaper stories only. (Responses to open-ended questions were not detailed enough to support this analysis.) The number of sources per story ranged from 11 stories with no source at all (several submissions were editorials or columns that did not rely on sources) to one story with 40! The mean number of sources for the 120 stories with one source or more was 5.3.

Of all the sources used in the 120 stories analyzed, 89 percent of them were identified. Ninety-eight percent of all the stories contained identified sources, and the average number of identified sources per story was 4.6.

About 9 percent of all the sources used were anonymous, and 30 percent of all the stories contained at least one anonymous source. The average number of anonymous sources per story was less than one (0.6). This finding contradicts the conventional wisdom about journalists' frequent use of anonymous sources, because 70 percent of the stories contained only identified sources.

Seventy percent of all the sources used in the 120 stories we analyzed were institutional, and only 26 percent were non-institutional. While 89 percent of the stories contained institutional sources, 51 percent of the stories had at least one non-institutional source. The average number of institutional sources per story was 3.9 while the average for non-institutional sources per story was 1.2. This is a confirmation of other studies that have established the importance of institutional sources in journalism, such as the police, courts, welfare departments and other government agencies.

Special interest group sources comprised the smallest source category. Only 4 percent of all sources were of this type, and only 14 percent of all the stories written contained special interest group sources of any kind.

When sources were coded for gender, only 15 percent of all sources

Table 9.8 Sources in Newspaper Stories
(n = 120)[a]

Source Category	Percent of All Sources	Percent of Stories with This Type of Source	Mean Number per Story[b]
Identification of Sources			
Identified	89	98	4.6
Anonymous	9	30	.6
Institutional Nature of Sources			
Institutional	70	89	3.9
Non-institutional	26	51	1.2
Special interest group	4	14	.3
Nature of Sources			
Female	15	41	.9
Male	71	94	3.6
Documentary	8	30	.5

[a]Eleven stories contained no sources, thus of 131 stories submitted only 120 are used for this analysis.
[b]Mean number of sources per story = 5.3.

were women, again consistent with the findings of other studies. Of all stories, 41 percent contained at least one source who was a woman, yet the average number of female sources per story was just under 1 (0.9). Seventy-one percent of all sources were male, and 94 percent of all the stories analyzed contained at least one male source. The average number of male sources per story was 3.6.

In the final category, documentary sources, 8 percent of the total sources were of this type, with 30 percent of stories containing at least one documentary source; the average number of documentary sources per story was less than one (0.5 sources), confirming again the importance of the personal interview as the journalist's primary source of information.

There are few surprises in the summary of sources used in these stories, although perhaps some disappointment. Few of the sources used in these examples of best work move beyond the "news net," with journalists relying almost exclusively on institutional and male sources. Very few women are represented as sources, although this in part reflects the preponderance of men as newsmakers in government and business. And very few sources come from the category of special interest groups or documents either.

SUMMARY AND CONCLUSIONS

Our results suggest several important conclusions. First, journalists do not limit the topics of their best stories to one or two categories, even though we found most examples of best work fell into the state and local government news or crime categories. Each of the many topics we coded were found in someone's example of best work. We also discovered that some journalists do not rank the interest that readers have for story topics in the same order as they choose their own examples of best work, creating dual standards to judge the value of stories.

In general, the media roles that journalists endorse are also present in similar proportions in the stories they suggest as their best work. But only interpreters are more likely (than disseminators or adversarial journalists) to actually write stories that reflect their views on the importance of this media role. The differences we found for interpretive journalists suggest these journalists may be of a different breed, and we encourage greater emphasis in future studies on these journalists.

Another significant finding of this study is that journalists place great value on the investigation of government claims, and yet very few of them report such stories as their best work. We speculated about why this might occur and suggested that external constraints, such as beat systems and economics, may be involved. But we need to know more about such constraints.

When we considered the presence of traditional news values in the best work of U.S. journalists, we found we were also measuring the priority that journalists place on those news values. Because we could compare journalists' responses about best work with stories submitted that actually contained these values, we concluded that the news values of proximity, impact, and prominence are more salient to journalists than other values. The values of unusualness and timeliness are a given in most news stories — thus, news is, by definition, timely and out of the ordinary. For stories to be singled out as examples of a journalist's "best work," they often must have value in terms of proximity, impact, and, to some extent, prominence.

We also discovered the greater emphasis that journalists place on stories about issues over stories about events, although when event stories are suggested as their best work, journalists tend to choose those that deal with unexpected events over pre-scheduled ones. We see this as an indication again of the value journalists place on stories that go beyond concrete events to stories that deal with abstract issues and ideas. While all news stories written may not have this orientation, journalists themselves place a greater value on these kinds of stories because they are more likely to cite them as examples of their best work.

Finally, our conclusions about sources suggest areas where journalists can move beyond the routine. We found a predominance of institutional and male sources to the exclusion of women and non-traditional sources, such as documents or special interest groups. Even though these examples of best work indicate relatively little reliance on anonymous sources, we still found evidence for routine reliance on institutional sources.

This portion of our study is a first attempt at adding one new piece to the mosaic depicting the working journalist, moving beyond survey research and interviews to describe and classify the work that journalists select as their best. While our findings provide a fairly detailed description of the work that journalists select as their best, they also suggest some conclusions about journalists' beliefs as they are translated into the stories that journalists produce. A more detailed analysis of these stories might yield even more insights into how journalists think and work.

— 10 —

Conclusions

Despite the fascination of many in our society for the news media and those who work in them, there have been far fewer systematic studies of journalists than of the effects of their work on the public and the uses made of media content by various kinds of audience members.[1] This present study has been concerned with the historical and social origins of U.S. journalists, as well as their education and training, professional values and ethics, job conditions, and the impact of new technologies on them. Like Johnstone and his colleagues in 1971, we have focused on individual journalists, but we do not mean to downplay the importance of the economic and social structures of the news industry. Indeed, we have tried to relate these structures to our data from individual journalists by including measures of organizational feedback, perceived autonomy, organizational memberships, type and size of news organization, and type of ownership of news organization in our analyses. And we have emphasized the importance of organizational setting in shaping journalists' professional values, ethics, and practices.

Although we agree with Johnstone, Slawski, and Bowman that journalists cannot be viewed simply as individual communicators,[2] we find considerable diversity among journalists working for organizations similar in kind and size, type of ownership, and geographic location. And we find this diversity reflected in the pluralism of professional roles (both interpretive and disseminator) endorsed by journalists, regardless of size or location of their news media, and regardless of job title. Whether this pluralism in role perceptions is reflected in the news content of the various media is mostly beyond the scope of this study, although we do have some evidence that this pluralism is reflected in the news. We asked the journalists interviewed to tell us about some of the best stories they had been involved in during the previous year. The range of stories, the approaches, and the implied journalistic roles served by them reflected the pluralism of roles detected in the overall analysis. About a third of the stories appeared to deal with what Pulitzer would have called the "original, distinctive, dramatic, romantic"[3] aspects of public issues in the journalists' communities. Few journalists described adversarial stories, although disclosure of official or business malfeasance was an occasional theme. Human-interest stories were frequent, usually emphasizing an unusual personality. Event-oriented stories, such as accidents, provided a sprinkling of mentions. There was even the occasional mention of a story that portrayed the difficulty of being a public official. And there is evidence that journalists' conceptions of their best stories vary tremendously, even within the same kind of news organizations.

But we also find many signs of decreased diversity among American journalists in 1983, as compared to those studied in 1971 by Johnstone and his associates. Some of these areas of decreased differences seem to be related directly to current practices in journalism education and in the news media themselves.

We find, for example, that U.S. journalists in 1982-83 are younger than in 1971, that more leave the field after age forty-five, that there are proportionately no more blacks and Hispanics than in 1971, that more journalists place themselves in the middle of the political spectrum, and that there is much less difference in the political leanings of journalists working for prominent and nonprominent organizations. We also find that differences in educational backgrounds are less pronounced than in 1971, that all news media except news magazines are relying more on journalism schools for recruiting new employees, that the majority of journalists work in the same region of the country where they attended college, and that fewer journalists in 1983 than in 1971 say they have the freedom to determine story emphasis.

We do not interpret all of these signs of decreased diversity as detrimental to the quality of journalism in the United States. In fact, it can be argued that fewer differences in educational backgrounds and more hiring of those educated in schools of journalism are positive. But there are some worrisome changes in the U.S. journalistic workforce during the past dozen years.

These changes include the exodus of experienced journalists from the field during middle age and beyond, the lack of effectiveness of minority recruitment programs, the drop in perceived autonomy among reporters, the drop in proportions of those who are very satisfied with their work, the increase in proportions of those journalists who say they plan to leave the field during the next five years (especially those most highly educated and those who have the strongest feelings about the role of journalism in society), and the drop in real median income. We also find a decrease in the percentage of journalists belonging to any professional organization, a decrease in the proportions of journalists endorsing a more analytical role for the media, and a possible decrease in longer, more analytical articles because of the increased speed and efficiency of new technological devices.

Some of these changes are ironic, given the increased size and profitability of many media organizations, especially the larger media groups, and given the advances in technology that are supposed to make the work of journalists easier. But one managing editor from a major metropolitan newspaper in the Midwest who looked at the results of our research said there was disillusionment among some journalists because they came into the field hoping they could change the world. They have discovered that they cannot do very much to change things, but more important, some of the national leaders in journalism are discouraging reformist attitudes. The editor said that one of his experienced reporters had just decided to go into public relations:

> Here's a guy who's been through the mill. He hadn't ever made a lot of money. He had never stored away any money for his kids to go to school, and it just suddenly occurred to him, "It's not worth it! I've been beaten around, battered around, and we haven't accomplished anything much, and I'm going to give it up and make some money."[4]

This editor suggested that perhaps many journalists cite lack of money as a reason for intending to leave journalism when the real reason is dissatisfaction with the constraints placed on them by their news organizations and by the professional values of objectivity. He said money is "an easy and safe reason" to cite, because it is "tougher to admit openly that you're frustrated about your ambitions to change the world . . . When you become alienated from your calling, that's a really severe problem."[5]

This question of retaining seasoned journalists beyond middle age was raised on the final page of the 1971 Johnstone study. The authors concluded that there was little doubt that the qualifications of those entering journalism were higher than in the past, but they expressed concern over whether the news media as presently constituted would be able to hold their most promising recruits. Johnstone and his colleagues speculated that many U.S. news organizations would need to reassess how they control newswork and eventually to grant greater editorial autonomy to those who do news gathering, writing, and reporting.[6]

Our 1983 study suggests that just the opposite has occurred. About two-thirds of the journalists we interviewed said they had "complete freedom" to determine news story emphasis, compared to 77 percent a dozen years ago. This tendency to perceive less freedom is especially true among journalists who work in the largest news organizations, which reinforces Johnstone's conclusion that there is more perceived autonomy in smaller organizations, and underscores a paradox inherent in journalistic work — that while most journalists perceive more editorial autonomy in smaller organizations, most want to work for larger organizations because of increased prestige and higher pay.[7]

Thus, the challenge of retaining the best and brightest in journalism involves not only better pay and benefits but also increased autonomy, especially in the larger news organizations, where the work is likely to be more fragmented and to involve more dependence on others. Johnstone and his colleagues note that this situation is not unique to journalism. In fact, it is similar to the familiar industrial dilemma of how to maximize productivity and efficiency without alienating workers from their jobs. The sociological answer to this dilemma has been to decentralize authority and to create smaller and more autonomous work units.[8] That is difficult to do, however, in news organizations that subscribe to the popular view of a total organization where no department has too much autonomy and all departments (including editorial) are expected to work toward the common goal of increased profitability.[9]

It is also difficult to grant increased autonomy to journalists in a climate that nurtures a passive, neutral approach to reporting the news. Some editors claim that the widely discussed farewell address by Michael

J. O'Neill to the May 1982 meeting of the American Society of Newspaper Editors has "crystallized a feeling among major editors" that investigative reporting that sought change was compromising press credibility.[10] O'Neill said, "Muckraking has been overemphasized, tending to crowd out other more significant kinds of reporting." He concluded, "If we had not been so busy chasing corrupt officials, we might not be guilty of having missed some of the biggest stories of the last half century."[11]

David Hawpe, managing editor of the *Courier-Journal* in Louisville, Kentucky, disagrees with O'Neill. Hawpe said his organization's focus-group research revealed that readers give "really high marks" to *Courier-Journal* investigative series that attack problems and suggest solutions. He added, "It's just not true that we harm ourselves by taking an active view of what we ought to be doing." Some of journalism's vocal leaders, though, claim that such an approach threatens the "tenuous" hold the news media, particularly newspapers, have on their audiences. These leaders, Hawpe argued, "scare these young journalists to death."[12]

The finding that fewer U.S. journalists now think they have complete freedom to determine story emphasis compared to a dozen years ago hints at a "retrenchment," Hawpe said. He added:

> I think that's just another part of this whole tightening process. Moving away from adversarial situations, moving away from confrontation, moving away from that whole range of activities. Another part of that is that editors sort of tighten down, asserting their control. . . .[13]

Hawpe did perceive a distinction between the roles of interpreter and adversary, however, and was not surprised that we found journalists sharply differentiating the two in their answers to our questions on journalistic roles. He said, "Investigating government claims anticipates a role that people understand. . . . It's a role that is performed on behalf of readers." Being an adversary, on the other hand, is an active role. "Not only does the adversary investigate, but the adversary opposes — takes a position," Hawpe concluded.[14]

Lawrence "Bo" Connor, managing editor of the *Indianapolis Star*, agreed that not many journalists think of themselves as adversaries. He argued that journalists' primary duty is "finding out what's going on" and not "to see that business behaves and government behaves." He called the adversary role "presumptuous" and added: "We're looking for stories. . . . If we see something that's out of line, we think, well, that makes a good story. . . . We think, let's get on this and find out what's going on."[15]

Connor argued that newspapers often discourage adversary and analytical journalism, because they are more interested in their reporters' getting all the facts and playing them in an interesting and informative manner, especially with local news. He acknowledged that his paper carries more syndicated analysis pieces that deal with national and international happenings and trends, but "when you're in your own territory, you just have to tell them what's going on."

A CONCLUDING NOTE

Our study does not provide ready solutions for most of the problems and questions raised in this book, but it does suggest positive developments in a number of areas.

Journalism as an occupation in the United States has grown dramatically during the 1970s, especially in the number of women employed; more younger people are in management positions than ever before; more journalists belong to a national professional organization than in 1971; a large majority of journalists see their role in society as pluralistic; and American journalists are less willing to endorse questionable reporting practices than are their British counterparts, and are quite idealistic about the role of public opinion in American government. In addition, American journalists are more highly educated than ever before, are much heavier users of other news media than are members of the general public, and are mostly positive about the effects of computers and other new technologies on their work. Even though there has been a decline in the percentage of journalists perceiving the freedom to determine story emphasis, most journalists still perceive substantial autonomy in their work, with a large majority feeling they have the ability to get important stories reported. Altruism and autonomy remain important elements in how journalists evaluate their jobs.

This portrait of American journalists diverges somewhat from the prevailing, popular view. The image projected from many of the most vocal critics — that journalists are elitists, adversarial, and materialistic — is not given much support in our data, even among respondents from the prestige media in the United States. It is true, and certainly desirable, that the educational levels of journalists now put them among the elite of the society. Journalism is and should be an intellectual occupation that requires research and analytical skills. It is also true that journalism increasingly is becoming a young person's profession at a time when the society has larger proportions of the elderly. But we are less concerned that the younger journalist will be insensitive to news of importance to the elderly than that the most skilled, experienced persons are leaving journalism in their prime.

Women have made great strides in the field over the decade. Their numbers have gone up by 65 percent, and the salaries of beginning women journalists are now equal to men's salaries. Women also are much more likely to hold management positions than they were a decade ago. And, more significant, some veteran newsmen have told us the presence of women in newsrooms has increased sensitivity to news that is of special concern to women and children.

The political cleavages some see between journalists and the larger society appear to be less severe than the critics maintain. Our research suggests a significant shift toward middle-of-the-road political views. The general centrist mood among journalists is not consistent with the predictions by many critics, and even journalists from the most prominent media organizations appear much less left of center than their popular image would indicate.

In religious backgrounds and affiliations, journalists reflect the larger society almost exactly. And, the Northeast is no longer dominant in terms of sheer numbers, with the journalists in each region now proportionately closer to actual population figures than was the case a decade ago.

As we emphasized above, professional values of journalists still are typified by a sense of altruism and desire for autonomy. The extent of perceived autonomy is down, compared to that a dozen years ago, which no doubt reflects the field's concern about the blemishes on credibility resulting from an occasional fabrication of news and the public criticism of journalistic practices. But the critics' claim of an adversarial mentality clearly is not reflected in the journalists' view of themselves. Nor is this role manifested in what they chose for us as their finest work.

The claim of a materialistic bent among journalists seems far-fetched in the light of the dismal salary data accumulated here. Young journalists cannot seriously aspire to becoming rich, because their salaries are somewhat less than what they could earn in other comparable careers. And, although job security is of greater concern now than a decade ago, it is altruistic public service that journalists say they see as the dominant lure of the news business.

In short, our findings suggest that American journalists are more reflective of the pluralistic society in which they work than the popular rhetoric concedes.

Thus not all is gloomy in American journalism by any means. It is still considered a fascinating, exciting, fulfilling occupation by thousands of people throughout the country. As in 1971, it is still an extremely diverse occupation that requires a large variety of skills and training, and it is an occupation beset with serious problems in fairly compensating and retaining the best people and in recruiting minorities. But, as did Johnstone and his colleagues in 1971, we conclude with both optimism and concern — optimism about the qualifications of young people entering the field, and concern about whether the news media will be able to hold these promising recruits.

One thing seems sure, though — journalism in the United States has many more standards of work, duty, and ethics than it did when Henry Watterson wrote at the beginning of this century that its "moral destination" was "confused." Even so, American journalists are unlikely ever to assume a formal professional status.[16] Perhaps the skepticism of the institutional forms of professionalism among U.S. journalists revealed in this study is the most convincing evidence against the claim that they are elitists and are isolated from the society at large.

Appendix I

METHODOLOGY

Because this study was intended to be a partial replication of the 1971 national survey of 1,328 journalists by John Johnstone and his colleagues,[1] we followed both the definition of a journalist used by these researchers and their sampling plan, as closely as possible, to be able to compare our results directly with theirs. We also used many of the same questions used by Johnstone, worded in the same way, as well as some questions from a study of 489 journalists for eight U.S. daily newspapers conducted by Judee and Michael Burgoon and Charles Atkin.[2] And for comparative purposes, we included a few questions from a joint national survey of British and West German journalists done in 1980.

Population. As in the Johnstone study of 1971, the population under study in our survey may be defined as "the full-time editorial manpower responsible for the information content of English-language mass communications in the United States."[3] In other words, we are concerned in this study only with journalists who work for *public* communications media targeted at general audiences rather than special-interest groups. For purposes of this study, we defined such media as daily and weekly newspapers, news magazines, radio and television stations, and general news agencies (such as the Associated Press) circulating in the United States.

As with the Johnstone study, our focus was on persons who produce news, information, and opinion rather than those who produce fiction, drama, art, or other content. Thus, the universe for our study is all salaried full-time editorial personnel employed by daily and weekly newspapers, news magazines, the news services, and the news departments of radio and television stations. This universe includes only those news media which transmit information more frequently than once a month, as was true in the Johnstone study. Thus, no monthly (or less frequently published) periodicals are included.

Definition of Journalist. Following Johnstone, we defined journalists as those who have editorial responsibility for the preparation or transmission of news stories or other information — all full-time reporters, writers, correspondents, columnists, newsmen, and editors. In broadcast organizations, only editorial staff in news and public affairs were included. Our definition, like Johnstone's, includes editorial cartoonists but *not* comic-strip cartoonists, and does *not* include photographers who are not also reporters, librarians, camera operators, and audio technicians. Johnstone's reasoning, and ours, is that people defined as journalists should have direct editorial responsibility for the information they communicate. Because full-time photographers, librarians, camera operators, and technicians usually are directed by reporters and editors (or assist them in carrying out their work), we did not classify them as journalists.

Sampling. We used a three-stage sampling plan similar to that used by Johnstone and his colleagues in 1971 to draw our national sample of journalists:

1. The first task was to compile lists of daily and weekly newspapers, news magazines, news services, and radio and television stations in the United States. We used the 1982 *Editor & Publisher International Year Book* for our lists of daily and weekly newspapers and news services, the 1982 *Broadcasting-Cablecasting Yearbook* for our lists of radio and television stations, and the 1982 *Ayer Directory of Publications* for our lists of news magazines. The lists of daily and weekly newspapers and radio and television stations involved no judgment on our part — we simply used what was provided. But the lists of news services and news magazines did require decisions as to what constituted legitimate *news* services (as opposed to purely picture and entertainment services, which are also listed with news and press services in the *Editor & Publisher International Year Book*), and what magazines were bona fide *news* magazines (since there is no such category in the *Ayer Directory of Publications*). We did not include what appeared to be purely photographic, entertainment, or feature services in our list of news services, and we included only general-interest magazines published more than once a month in our list of news magazines, as did Johnstone and his colleagues.

From the sources noted above, we used systematic random sampling to compile a list of 151 daily newspapers (stratified by size of circulation so that we drew roughly 10 percent of the number of papers in each circulation category at random), 153 weekly newspapers (every fiftieth paper), 24 news magazines (all of them), 63 news service bureaus (every fifth one), 91 radio stations (every hundredth one), and 104 television stations (every tenth one). In all, our random sample of organizations included 586 separate news operations from a total of 19,869 in the country.

2. The second task was to obtain lists of all journalists working for the 586 organizations in our sample. That was done in three steps: In September 1982, we sent a letter to all editors or news directors of these 586 organizations, explaining our study and requesting the total number of editorial personnel working in their news organizations, as well as the names and positions of these journalists. We carefully defined in our letter what we meant by editorial personnel, and we audited the lists of employees we received. In October 1982, we sent a follow-up letter to all who had not responded, asking for the same information. We waited two weeks for a reply, then followed up these letters with telephone calls. In all, we were able to obtain numbers of editorial personnel from 523 of the 586 organizations in our sample, a response rate of 89.2 percent. The best response was from radio stations (95.6 percent), and the worst was from news services (74.6 percent).

3. The third task was to draw a representative sample of individual journalists from the lists of names and positions we collected in step 2. We used the total number of journalists working for the organizations that responded to estimate the total number of journalists working for news media throughout the United States. We did that by calculating the percentage of each kind of news organization responding with a list of employees (by dividing the number of organizations responding by the total number of organizations in the population), then multiplying the total number of persons listed as working for each kind of medium by 100 divided by the percentage in our sample.

Thus, for daily newspapers, we obtained lists of employees from 139, or 8 percent, of all 1,730 papers, stratified by circulation size. These lists indicated that 4,132 journalists worked for these papers. We divided 100 percent by 8 percent and obtained a multiplier of 12.5. Multiplying 4,132 by 12.5 gave us an estimated total number of journalists (as we defined them) of 51,650 for daily newspapers in the United States. The same procedure was used to estimate the total number of journalists working for weekly newspapers, news magazines, television and radio stations, and news services.

Once we had estimated the total number of journalists working for each kind of news organization, we calculated the percentages of all journalists working for the various media. We then used these percentages to determine how many journalists from daily and weekly newspapers, news magazines, radio and television stations, and news agencies should be included in a total sample of 1,250 journalists (comparable to Johnstone's sample of about 1,300 and limited to this number by the cost of interviews).

After going through this procedure, we found that using strict percentages of total estimated U.S. journalistic workforce would result in only 14 news magazine journalists and 16 news service journalists in our sample of 1,251. Because we wanted to be able to analyze each kind of journalist separately, we increased the sample of news magazine journalists from 14 to 109 (from 1.15 percent of the sample to 8.7 percent), and we increased the number of news service journalists from 16 to 61 (from 1.25 percent of the sample to 4.9 percent). This oversampling of these journalists meant, of course, that we slightly *undersampled* some other kinds of journalists, but we still ended up with 67.4 percent of the sample being print journalists (daily and weekly newspapers, and news magazines), as compared to 67.7 percent called for in the original sample. Broadcast journalists constituted 27.7 percent of our sample, as compared to 31.1 percent called for in the original sample. The most undersampled group of journalists was from weekly newspapers. We included 15.0 percent of such journalists in our sample, as compared to 20.5 percent called for by the total employment percentages.

In short, then, the final sample slightly oversampled news magazine and news agency journalists to ensure enough of them to analyze separately, and slightly undersampled daily and weekly newspaper and radio journalists. But no group of journalists was undersampled by more than six percentage points from the original percentages based on total estimated journalists in all U.S. news media.

Interviewing. From this systematic random sample of 1,251 U.S. journalists, telephone interviews were completed with 1,001 of them, for an overall response rate of 80.0 percent for individual journalists. We requested three callbacks for each journalist, but up to thirteen callbacks were made for some journalists. Before these interviews were conducted by Market Interviews (a subsidiary of Market Opinion Research in Detroit, Michigan) in December 1982 and January and February 1983, we sent a letter to each of the 1,251 journalists in our systematic random sample in November 1982, telling them about the study and how they were selected into the sample, and urging them to participate when called for a half-hour interview.

The interviewers employed by Market Interviews were instructed to call each journalist (we provided names and telephone numbers) and to ask for a convenient time to interview him or her. They were instructed to refer to the letter we had sent in November, and they were told not to make any substitutions unless the journalist refused or had left the job. If either of these conditions had occurred, the interviewer was allowed to make substitutions *if* the interview was conducted with another person holding the *same job title* as the original respondent (reporter, city editor, etc.), but only after all names for that kind of news organization had been called. Near the end of the interviewing, we provided about 50 additional randomly selected names of journalists from our original lists to enable the interviewers to reach at least 1,000 repondents.

We are confident, however, that at least 90 percent of the 1,001 journalists interviewed came from our original systematic random sample.

Almost all interviews ranged from twenty to forty minutes in length.

Appendix II

JOURNALISTS' SURVEY QUESTIONNAIRE

Market Interviews
17320 W. Twelve Mile
Southfield, MI 48076
(313) 552-1999

(INTERVIEWER: initial
above when complete)

Questionnaire #

Study Name

Indiana University Journalists Survey Date November 1982

Sample: 1000

Comp. Male (CM)	[ ]1								16-34
Comp. Female (CF)	[ ]1								
No Answ./Busy (NA/B)	[ ]1	[ ]2	[ ]3	[ ]4	[ ]5	[ ]6	[ ]7	[ ]8	[ ]9
No answ./Busy (NA/B)	[ ]1	[ ]2	[ ]3	[ ]4	[ ]5	[ ]6	[ ]7	[ ]8	[ ]9

Designated Person Not in Now/
No Time Now/Call Back

(DPNI/NTN/CB)	[ ]1	[ ]2	[ ]3	[ ]4	[ ]5	[ ]6	[ ]7	[ ]8	[ ]9
Refusal (REF)	[ ]1	[ ]2	[ ]3	[ ]4	[ ]5	[ ]6	[ ]7	[ ]8	[ ]9
Respondent Term.(R-Term.)	[ ]1	[ ]2	[ ]3	[ ]4	[ ]5	[ ]6	[ ]7	[ ]8	[ ]9
MI Term. (M-Term)	[ ]1	[ ]2	[ ]3	[ ]4	[ ]5	[ ]6	[ ]7	[ ]8	[ ]9
Business Numb. (BUS)	[ ]1	[ ]2	[ ]3	[ ]4	[ ]5	[ ]6	[ ]7	[ ]8	[ ]9
Non-Working #(DISC/NIS/CHNG)	[ ]1	[ ]2	[ ]3	[ ]4	[ ]5	[ ]6	[ ]7	[ ]8	[ ]9
Non-Working #	[ ]1	[ ]2	[ ]3	[ ]4	[ ]5	[ ]6	[ ]7	[ ]8	[ ]9
Geographic F.O. (G-F.O.)	[ ]1	[ ]2	[ ]3	[ ]4	[ ]5	[ ]6	[ ]7	[ ]8	[ ]9
Non-Register Voter F.O. (V-F.O)	[ ]1	[ ]2	[ ]3	[ ]4	[ ]5	[ ]6	[ ]7	[ ]8	[ ]9
No Male in household (NM)	[ ]1	[ ]2	[ ]3	[ ]4	[ ]5	[ ]6	[ ]7	[ ]8	[ ]9
No Female in household (NF) .	[ ]1	[ ]2	[ ]3	[ ]4	[ ]5	[ ]6	[ ]7	[ ]8	[ ]9
OPEN	[ ]1	[ ]2	[ ]3	[ ]4	[ ]5	[ ]6	[ ]7	[ ]8	[ ]9
OPEN	[ ]1	[ ]2	[ ]3	[ ]4	[ ]5	[ ]6	[ ]7	[ ]8	[ ]9
Other Disp. (write in)	[ ]1	[ ]2	[ ]3	[ ]4	[ ]5	[ ]6	[ ]7	[ ]8	[ ]9
(No Eng., Deaf, etc.)	[ ]1	[ ]2	[ ]3	[ ]4	[ ]5	[ ]6	[ ]7	[ ]8	[ ]9

DESIGNATED NUMBER	DATE	TIME	Circle Disposi-tion One	NUMBER	DATE	TIME	Circle Disposition One
01.	/	:	AM/PM	10._____	/	:	AM/PM ____
Original Call							
02.	/	:	AM/PM	11._____	/	:	AM/PM ____
Call Back							
03.	/	:	AM/PM	12._____	/	:	AM/PM ____
Call Back							
04.	/	:	AM/PM	13._____	/	:	AM/PM ____
Call Back							
05.	/	:	AM/PM	14._____	/	:	AM/PM ____
Substitute							
06	/	:	AM/PM	15._____	/	:	AM/PM ____
Substitute							
07.	/	:	AM/PM	16._____	/	:	AM/PM ____
Substitute							
08.	/	:	AM/PM	17._____	/	:	AM/PM ____
Substitute							
09._____	/	:	AM/PM	18._____	/	:	AM/PM ____

35-36

224

-1-

1. What is your exact job title at (NAME OF ORGANIZATION) and main responsibility?

JOB TITLE:_____   5-6_____

RESPONSIBILITY:_____

2. In what year did you begin working for (NAME OF ORGANIZATION)?   7-8_____

YEAR:_____

3. What other job titles have you had since you have worked for (NAME OF ORGANIZATION)?

PREVIOUS JOB TITLES:

1. _____   9-10_____
2. _____   11-12_____
3. _____   13-14_____
4. _____   15-16_____
None 99

4. Before coming to work for (NAME OF ORGANIZATION), did you hold any other jobs in journalism?   17_____

Yes (ASK A) 3
No 1

A. (IF YES) What were they — from the first to the most recent?

PREVIOUS JOURNALISM JOBS:

1. _____   18-19_____
2. _____   20-21_____
3. _____   22-23_____
4. _____   24-25_____

5. How long have you worked in journalism?   26-27_____

YEARS:_____

6. In looking back, what persons or circumstances motivated you to become a journalist?
(PROBE FULLY AND RECORD VERBATIM)   28-29_____

_____

_____

_____

7. Where would you most like to be working in five years — in the news media, or somewhere else?

In news media (ASK B) 3   30_____
Somewhere else (ASK C) 1
Don't know 9

-2-

B. (IF NEWS MEDIA) In which of the news media — newspapers, magazines, radio, television, or news services?

Newspapers 1
Magazines 3
Radio 5
Television 7
News services 2
Don't know 9
Other (SPECIFY BELOW) 4

31_____

C. (IF SOMEWHERE ELSE) Where is that? Why?

32-33_____
34-35_____

8. Which of the following do you think is most true of the effects of frequent turnover on a newsroom's performance? (CIRCLE ONLY ONE)

A. It benefits the newsroom by bringing in
new perspectives and skills 1
B. It harms the newsroom by reducing the
journalists familiarity with the
community and the ability to establish
solid sources 3
C. It both harms and helps, but the benefits
outweigh the disadvantages 5
D. It both harms and helps, but the disadvantages
outweigh the benefits 7
E. It has negligible impact on newsgathering and reporting 8
F. Don't know (DON'T SUGGEST) 9

36_____

9. I'd like to find out how important a number of things are to you in judging jobs in your field — not just your job but any job. For instance, how much difference does the pay make in how you rate a job in your field — is pay very important, fairly important, or not too important?

	VERY IMPORTANT	FAIRLY IMPORTANT	NOT TOO IMPORTANT	
A. the pay?	5	3	1	37_____
B. fringe benefits?	5	3	1	38_____
C. freedom from supervision?	5	3	1	39_____
D. the chance to help people?	5	3	1	40_____
E. the editorial policies of the organization?	5	3	1	41_____
F. job security?	5	3	1	42_____
G. the chance to develop a specialty?	5	3	1	43_____
H. the amount of autonomy you have?	5	3	1	44_____
I. the chance to get ahead in the organization?	5	3	1	45._____

10. All things considered, how satisfied are you with your present job — would you say very satisfied, fairly satisfied, somewhat dissatisfied, or very dissatisfied?

Very satisfied 7
Fairly satisfied 5
Somewhat dissatisfied 3
Very dissatisfied 1
Don't know 9

46_____

-3-

11. Some observers fear journalism is not holding its most talented persons. Others disagree. What factors,
if any, could you imagine leading you to leave journalism for a job in another field?
(RECORD RESPONDENT'S ANSWER VERBATIM)
(PROBE IF RESPONDENT CANNOT THINK OF REASONS:
pay?
freedom?
boredom?
stress?
editorial policies?
chance to advance?)

47-48 _____
49-50 _____
51-52 _____

12. What are your thoughts, if any, on how new technologies such as VDTs and electronic news gathering
have affected your job?

(PROBE FOR DETAILS AND RECORD VERBATIM — IF RESPONDENT CAN'T THINK OF ANSWERS,
MENTION SUCH THINGS AS JOB SKILLS, ABILITY TO COMPLETE A WHOLE PIECE OF WORK,
AUTONOMY, FEEDBACK FROM OTHERS, ROUTINES, NEWS VALUES, NEWS SOURCES.)

_____

_____

_____

_____

53-54 _____
55-56 _____
57-58 _____

13. A. How often do you get reactions or comments on your work from people who are above you in your
organization — would you say regularly, occasionally, seldom or never?
(CODE IN COLUMN A BELOW)

B. How often do you get reactions or comments on your work from people at about your level in your
organization — would you say regularly, occasionally, seldom or never?
(CODE IN COLUMN B BELOW)

C. How often do you get reactions or comments on your work from people in other organizations who
do the same kind of work you do — would you say regularly, occasionally, seldom or never?
(CODE IN COLUMN C BELOW)

D. How often do you get reactions or comments on your work from news sources — regularly, occasionally, seldom or never?
(CODE IN COLUMN D BELOW)

E. How often do you get reactions or comments from readers, listeners, or viewers — regularly, occasionally, seldom or never?
(CODE IN COLUMN E BELOW)

	A. (people above)	B. (people at same level)	C. (people in other orgs)	D. (news sources)	E. (readers, viewers)	
Regularly	7	7	7	7	7	A. 59 _____
Occasionally	5	5	5	5	5	B. 60 _____
Seldom	3	3	3	3	3	C. 61 _____
Never	1	1	1	1	1	D. 62 _____
Not applicable	0	0	0	0	0	E. 63 _____

-4-

14. Do you have any managerial responsibilities, or do you supervise any editorial employees?

    Yes (ASK Q. 15) 3
    No (SKIP TO Q. 17) 1

    64_____

15. About how often do you meet with individual reporters to discuss ideas for future stories — would you say several times a day, daily, almost daily, several times a week, about weekly, or less often than that?

    Several times a day 9
    Daily........................ 7
    Almost daily 5
    Several times a week 3
    About weekly 1
    Less often than that 0
    Don't meet with reporters 8

    65_____

16. How much influence do you have in decisions on hiring and firing editorial employees — a great deal. some. a little, or none at all?

    A great deal 7
    Some....................... 5
    A little...................... 3
    None at all 1

    66_____

17. How much editing or processing of other people's work do you do — a great deal, some, or none at all?

    A great deal (ASK Q. 18) 5
    Some (ASK Q. 18) 3
    None at all (SKIP TO Q. 20) 1

    67_____

18. What faults would you say are most common in the work you edit or process?
    (RECORD ANSWER VERBATIM)

    _____

    _____

    68-69_____

    _____

    70-71_____

    (Anything in addition to spelling, grammar, and style?)_____

    72-73_____

    _____

19. How much freedom do you usually have in deciding how the stories written by others will be used in print or in the broadcast — almost complete freedom, a great deal, some, or none at all?

    Almost complete freedom 7
    A great deal 5
    Some....................... 3
    None at all 1

    74_____

20. How often do you do reporting — regularly, occasionally, seldom, or never?

    Regularly (ASK Q. 21) 7
    Occasionally (ASK Q. 21) 5
    Seldom (SKIP TO Q. 26) 3
    Never (SKIP TO Q. 26) 1

    75_____

-5-

21. Do you usually cover a specific "beat" or subject area, or do you usually cover different things?

    Cover a specific "beat" (ASK A) .. 3
    Cover different things (ASK B) ... 1

76_____

    A. (IF SPECIFIC BEAT) Which beat(s) or area(s)?

       BEAT: _____

77-78_____

    B. (IF DIFFERENT THINGS) What type(s) of news do you cover most often?

79 - BLANK
80 - "1"
CARD 2
1-4 (ID)_____

       TYPE OF NEWS: _____

5-6_____

22. If you have a good idea for a subject which you think is important and should be followed up, how often are you able to get the subject covered — almost always, more often than not, or only occasionally?

    Almost always 5
    More often than not 3
    Only occasionally 1
    Don't make such proposals 9

7_____

23. How much editing do your stories get from others in your organization — would you say a great deal, some, or none at all?

    A great deal 5
    Some 3
    None at all 1

8_____

24. How much freedom do you usually have in selecting the stories you work on — would you say almost complete freedom, a great deal, some or none at all?

    Almost complete freedom 7
    A great deal 5
    Some 3
    None at all 1

9_____

25. How much freedom do you usually have in deciding which aspects of a story should be emphasized — would you say almost complete freedom, a great deal, some, or none at all?

    Almost complete freedom 7
    A great deal 5
    Some 3
    None at all 1

10_____

26. Do the editorial employees working for your news organization belong to a union?

    Yes, belong to union 3
    No, don't belong to a union 1
    Don't know 9

11_____

27. Does your news organization employ someone either full or parttime as the following:

    A. Ombudsman?
        Yes 3
        No 1
        Don't know 9

    12_____

    B. Writing coach?
        Yes 3
        No 1
        Don't know 9

    13_____

28. Here are some statements about your audience members. Please indicate whether you strongly disagree, somewhat disagree, are neutral, somewhat agree, or strongly agree with each statement.

	Strongly disagree	Somewhat disagree	Neutral	Somewhat agree	Strongly agree	
A. Audience members are more interested in the day's breaking news than in analysis of long-term trends	1	2	3	4	5	14_____
B. The majority of audience members have little interest in reading about social problems such as racial discrimination and poverty	1	2	3	4	5	15_____
C. Audience members are gullible and easily fooled	1	2	3	4	5	16_____

29. How strong do you think the influence of the media is on the formation of public opinion? Please pick a number from zero to ten, where zero means no influence and ten means very great influence.

No influence   Very great influence
0   1   2   3   4   5   6   7   8   9   10

    17-18_____

Don't know 99

30. And how strong do you think the influence of the media should be on public opinion? Again, please pick a number from zero to ten, where zero means no influence and ten means very great influence.

No influence   Very great influence
0   1   2   3   4   5   6   7   8   9   10

    19-20_____

Don't know 99

-7-

31. Generally how strong do you think the influence of public opinion should be on governments? Again, please pick a number from zero to ten where zero means no influence and ten means very great influence.

No influence   Very great influence
0   1   2   3   4   5   6   7   8   9   10

21-22_____

Don't know 99

32. Journalists have to use various methods to get information. Given an important story, which of the following methods do you think may be justified on occasion and which would you not approve under any circumstances?

	May be justified	Would not approve	Unsure	
A. Paying people for confidential information	3	1	9	23_____
B. Using confidential business or government documents without authorization	3	1	9	24_____
C. Claiming to be somebody else	3	1	9	25_____
D. Agreeing to protect confidentiality and not doing so.	3	1	9	26_____
E. Badgering unwilling informants to get a story	3	1	9	27_____
F. Making use of personal documents such as letters and photographs without permission	3	1	9	28_____
G. Getting employed in a firm or organization to gain inside information	3	1	9	29_____

33. I'd like now to ask you how important you think a number of things are that the media do or try to do today. For example, how important is it for the news media to . . .

A. Get information to the public as quickly as possible — is that extremely important, quite important, somewhat important, or not really important at all? (CODE IN A BELOW)

(THEN ASK B - J: How important is it for the news media to . . . ?)

	Extremely Important	Quite Important	Some- what	Not Really	No Opinion	
A. Get information to the public quickly?	7	5	3	1	9	30_____
B. Provide analysis and interpretation of complex problems?	7	5	3	1	9	31_____
C. Provide entertainment and relaxation?	7	5	3	1	9	32_____
D. Investigate claims and statements made by the government?	7	5	3	1	9	33_____

-8-

E. Stay away from stories where factual content cannot be verified?	7	5	3	1	9	34_____
F. Concentrate on news which is of interest to the widest possible public?	7	5	3	1	9	35_____
G. Discuss national policy while it is still being developed?	7	5	3	1	9	36_____
H. Develop intellectual and cultural interests of the public?	7	5	3	1	9	37_____
I. Be an adversary of public officials by being constantly skeptical of their actions?	7	5	3	1	9	38_____
J. Be an adversary of businesses by being constantly skeptical of their actions?	7	5	3	1	9	39_____

34. Assume that you were covering the annual meeting of a major political organization and you found the policy of this organization dangerous. Would you simply report the discussions and decisions and leave your readers to see the danger for themselves, or would you select and emphasize the dangerous aspects so that your readers would be in no doubt that you were giving them a warning?

Would simply report the discussions and decisions 3
Would select and emphasize the dangerous aspects 1
Other (RECORD BELOW) 7
Not sure/don't know 9

                                                               40_____

OTHER:

35. How influential have the following been in shaping your ideas in matters of journalism ethics? Would you say they have been extremely influential, quite influential, somewhat influential, or not very influential in developing your ideas about what's right and wrong in journalism?

	Extremely influential	Quite Infl.	Somewhat Infl.	Not Very Infl.	No Opinion	
A. High school teachers?	7	5	3	1	9	41_____
B. University teachers?	7	5	3	1	9	42_____
C. Journalism teachers?	7	5	3	1	9	43_____
D. Family upbringing?	7	5	3	1	9	44_____
E. Religious training?	7	5	3	1	9	45_____
F. Day-by-day newsroom learning?	7	5	3	1	9	46_____
G. A senior reporter?	7	5	3	1	9	47_____
H. A senior editor?	7	5	3	1	9	48_____
I. Publishers or general managers?	7	5	3	1	9	49_____
J. Your co-workers or peers?	7	5	3	1	9	50_____
K. Other'(SPECIFY BELOW)	7	5	3	1	9	51_____

36. In your day-to-day job, how influential is each of the following on your concept of what is newsworthy, on a scale from one to five, where one means not at all influential and five means very influential? (CIRCLE ONE NUMBER FOR EACH ITEM)

	NOT AT ALL INFLUENTIAL			VERY INFLUENTIAL		NO OPINION	
A. Your peers on the staff?	1	2	3	4	5	9	52_____
B. Your supervisors?	1	2	3	4	5	9	53_____
C. Your friends and acquaintances?	1	2	3	4	5	9	54_____
D. Your journalistic training?	1	2	3	4	5	9	55_____
E. Findings of readership or audience research?	1	2	3	4	5	9	56_____
F. News sources?	1	2	3	4	5	9	57_____
G. Priorities of network news and prestige newspapers?	1	2	3	4	5	9	58_____
H. Local competing news media?	1	2	3	4	5	9	59_____
I. Wire service budgets?	1	2	3	4	5	9	60_____

37. How good a job of informing the public do you think your own news organization is doing — outstanding, very good, good, fair or poor?

Outstanding 8
Very good 6
Good 4
Fair 2
Poor 0
No opinion/don't know 9

61_____

38. The media are often classified politically in terms of left, right and center. On a scale from zero (meaning extreme left) to one hundred (meaning extreme right), where would you place the editorial policy of the organization for which you work?

RECORD POSITION:_____

62-63_____

39. And where on this scale would you place yourself, keeping in mind that zero means extreme left and one hundred means extreme right?

RECORD POSITION;_____

64-65_____

40. (a) I'd like to talk with you about a story you think represents some of your best work. Can you pick one of the best stories you've been involved in during the past year and tell me briefly what it was about?

66-67_____

(b) Why do you think that this story is particularly good? Any other reasons? (PROBE)

68-69_____

70-71_____

(c) While working on this story what thoughts, if any, did you have about your audience? (RECORD ANSWER VERBATIM AND IN FULL)

72-73_____

74-75_____

-10-

(d) Could you send a copy of this story to Prof. Weaver at Indiana University?

41. Which of the following publications do you read regularly (that is, almost every issue)? (CIRCLE ONE NUMBER FOR EACH)

	Read	Read Sometimes	Don't Read
ANPA News Research Report	3	2	1
ASNE Bulletin	3	2	1
Columbia Journalism Review	3	2	1
Editor and Publisher	3	2	1
Editor's Exchange	3	2	1
Gannetteer	3	2	1
Journalism Quarterly	3	2	1
Wirewatch	3	2	1
Masthead	3	2	1
Newspaper Research Journal	3	2	1
Journal of Broadcasting	3	2	1
Journal of Communication	3	2	1
Nieman Reports	3	2	1
Presstime	3	2	1
The Quill	3	2	1
APME News	3	2	1
Washington Journalism Review	3	2	1
Public opinion poll reports in newspapers and magazines (such as those fromm Gallup, Harris and Yankelovitch)	3	2	1

42. Which newspapers do you read regularly (at least once a week)? (LIST EACH PAPER — FULL NAME, CITY AND STATE OF PUBLICATION)

_____

_____

_____

43. How many days a week do you watch the early evening network newscasts on TV?

0   1   2   3   4   5   6   7   DAYS

44. How many days a week do you watch local newscasts on TV?

0   1   2   3   4   5   6   7   DAYS

45. Please list the magazines you read regularly (that is, almost every issue). (LIST FULL NAMES OF ALL MAGAZINES)

_____

_____

_____

Office Use Only

76_____
77_____
78_____
79 - BLANK   80 "2"
1-4 (ID) _____ _ _ _
5_____
6_____
7_____

8_____
9_____
10_____

11_____
12_____
13_____

14_____
15_____
16_____

17_____
18_____

19_____

20-21_____
22-23_____
24-25_____

26_____

27_____

28-29_____
30-31_____
32-33_____
34-35 _ _ _ _ _ _

-11-

46. Now a few questions about your background and we'll be through. First, what is the highest grade you completed in school?

Some high school or less 1
Completed high school 2
1-3 years of college 3
Graduated from college (ASK A-D) 4
Some graduate work, no degree (ASK A-E) 5
Advanced degree(s) (ASK A-G) 6

36_____

(IF GRADUATED FROM COLLEGE OR MORE)

A. From which college or university did you graduate?

37-39_____

B. What was your undergraduate major (or majors)?

40-41_____

C. What was your undergraduate minor (or minors)?

42-43_____

D. (IF DID NOT MAJOR OR MINOR IN JOURNALISM) How many courses, if any, have you taken in journalism or media studies?

44_____

(IF GRADUATE WORK OR MORE)

E. What field were you in in graduate or professional school?

45-46_____

(IF GRADUATE DEGREES)

F. Which graduate degrees do you hold? (RECORD BELOW)
G. From which university(ies) did you obtain it (them)? (RECORD BELOW)

47_____
48_____
49_____

DEGREE: _____   UNIVERSITY: _____
_____   _____
_____   _____

50-51_____
52-53_____
54-55_____

47. Would you like additional training in journalism or other subjects?

Yes (ASK A) 3
No 1

56_____

A. (IF YES) What kind of training would you want?
(RECORD ANSWER VERBATIM)

_____
_____
_____

57-58_____
59-60_____
61-62_____

48. Altogether, about what percentage of the people you see socially are connected in some way with journalism or the communications field?

PERCENTAGE: _____

63-64_____

49. What is your age? _____ years old

    Refused 99   65-66_____

50. In which of the following groups would you place yourself?

    White (Caucasian) 1
    Black/Negro 3
    Spanish/Latino 5   67_____
    Oriental (Japanese, Chinese) 7
    Other (SPECIFY BELOW) 8
    Refused 9

51. In which church, if any, were you brought up?

    CHURCH: 68-69_____ _

    Refused 99
    None 98

52. What is your marital status?

    Married (ASK A) 7
    Divorced or separated (ASK A) . . . 5
    Widowed (ASK A) 3   70_____
    Single: never married 1
    Refused 9

    A. (IF EVER MARRIED) Do you have any children?

        Yes 3
        No 1   71_____
        Refused 9

53. As of today, are you a Democrat, a Republican, or what?

    Democrat 1
    Republican 3
    Independent/no party (ASK A) . . . 5   72_____
    Other (SPECIFY BELOW) 7
    Refused 9
    OTHER:

    A. (IF INDEPENDENT OR NO PARTY) Which of the following best describes your political leanings?

        Lean toward the Republican party 3
        Lean toward the Democratic party 1
        Lean toward neither major party 5   73_____
        Others (SPECIFY BELOW) 7
        Refused 9
        OTHER:

-13-

54. Do you belong to any organizations or associations that are primarily for people in journalism or the communications field?

Yes (ASK A) 3
No 1

74_____

A. (IF YES) Which ones? (RECORD BELOW) Any others?

NAME OF ORGANIZATION

1. _____
2. _____
3. _____
4. _____

5-6_____
7-8_____
9-10_____
11-12_____

55. Finally, I'd like to ask you for some financial information. I'd like to mention once again that all information you give us will be treated in strict confidence, and neither you nor your organization will ever be reported by name.

Would you please tell me what your total personal income was, before taxes, from your work in the communications field during 1981?

1981 INCOME: $
Refused (ASK A) 9

13-18_____

A. (IF REFUSED) Well, would you tell me which category your income fell in last year — was it:

Below $10,000 01
Between $10,000 and $15,000 03
Between $15,000 and $20,000 05

Between $20,000 and $25,000 07
Between $25,000 and $30,000 09
Between $30,000 and $35,000 11

Between $35,000 and $40,000 13
Between $40,000 and $45,000 15
Between $45,000 and $50,000 17

19-20_____

Between $50,000 and $55,000 19
Between $55,000 and $60,000 21
Between $60,000 and $65,000 23

Between $65,000 and $70,000 25
Between $70,000 and $75,000 27
Over $75,000 29
Still refused 99

56. RECORD RESPONDENT'S SEX

Male 1
Female 3

21_____

57. RECORD THE NUMBER OF EDITORIAL, OR NEWS, PEOPLE EMPLOYED AT THIS ORGANIZATION.

NUMBER OF EDITORIAL PEOPLE: _____   22-24_____
Don't know 000

58. RECORD WHETHER NEWS ORGANIZATION IS LOCALLY OR INDEPENDENTLY OWNED, OR IS OWNED BY A LARGER CORPORATION OR GROUP.

Locally or independently owned 1
Group owned (ASK A) 3
Other (SPECIFY BELOW) 5   25_____
Don't know 9
OTHER:

A. (IF GROUP OWNED) which group or corporation is that?

NAME:_____   26-28_____
Don't know 999

Thank you very much for participating in this study. The School of Journalism at Indiana University hopes to have a report on the major findings completed by next summer. If you would like a copy of this report, please write to Professor Dave Weaver at Indiana University's School of Journalism, Bloomington, Indiana, 47405. And please remember to send a copy of the story you discussed to him.

Record type of news organization:
Daily newspaper 1
Weekly newspaper 3
News magazine 5
News agency (wire service) 7   29_____
TV station 9
Radio station 2

Record state of country:

Ala 01	Ky 35	N. Dak 69
Alaska 03	La 37	Ohio 71
Ariz 05	Maine 39	Okla 73
Ark 07	Md 41	Oreg 75
Calif 09	Mass 43	Pa 77
Colo 11	Mich 45	R.I. 79
Conn 13	Minn 47	S.C. 81
Del 15	Mass 49	S. Dak 83
D.C. 17	Mo 51	Tenn 85	30-31_____
Fla 19	Mont 53	Tex 87
Ga 21	Nebr 55	Utah 89
Hawaii 23	Nev 57	Vt 91
Idaho 25	N.H. 59	Va 93
Ill 27	N.J. 61	Wash 95
Ind 29	N. Mex 63	W. Va 97
Iowa 31	N.Y. 65	Wis 99
Kans 33	N.C. 67	Wyo 02

-15-

THANK YOU FOR YOUR TIME

FILL OUT AFTER COMPLETION OF INTERVIEW

AREA CODE

NAME:_____ TELEPHONE NUMBER:_____

ADDRESS:_____ COUNTY:_____ ____

CITY:_____ STATE_____ ZIP CODE_____

	LENGTH OF		TIME		DATE OF	

(V15) INTERVIEW:_____ ENDED:_____ INTERVIEW _____

32-33 MONTH

INTERVIEWER'S NAME:_____ LENG. 68-69   (V16)   34-35 DAY

INTERVIEWER, PLEASE READ AND SIGN.

I have reread this completed questionnaire and certify that all questions requiring
answers have been recorded in the respondent's exact words, and that all boxes and
spaces requiring an "X," a number, or a letter are filled in. This bona fide interview has been obtained according to quota and all interviewing specifications. I
agree to keep the content of questions, respondent's answers, and the subject of
this interview confidential.

INTERVIEWER'S SIGNATURE:_____

SUPERVISOR'S NAME:_____ DATE:_____

<u>INTERVIEWER</u>

Were there any special circumstances or conditions under which this interview was
conducted?
If so, please explain in detail:

_____

_____

_____

_____

If Phone: Dearborn. . . . .1 PHONE
                                       74
                  Detroit 2
                  Southfield. . . .3
                  No answer 9

                      75-76 = EXTRA
                      77=80 JOB NO

NOTES

1. A Historical View of the Journalist

1. Some twenty years after his death, the July 21, 1934 *Editor & Publisher* disclosed results of a poll of newspapermen that found Joseph Pulitzer to be considered the greatest American editor of all time.

2. Joseph Pulitzer, "The College of Journalism," *North American Review*, May 1904, p. 649.

3. Frank Luther Mott, *American Journalism; A History: 1690-1960*, 3d ed. (New York: Macmillan Co., 1962), p. 489.

4. Mott, *American Journalism*, p. 604.

5. Ibid., p. 605. Pulitzer agreed to endow the school in 1903. The school did not open until 1912.

6. Talcott Williams, *The Newspaperman* (New York: Charles Scribner's Sons, 1922), p. 123.

7. Alexis de Tocqueville, *Democracy in America* (New York: Alfred A. Knopf, 1948), p. 211.

8. For an interesting discussion of the role colonial journalists played leading up to independence, see Arthur Schlesinger, *Prelude to Independence* (New York: Knopf, 1958).

9. Not only were correspondents not paid, but evidence suggests that some of them might have paid for space. Benjamin Franklin wrote that "a Newspaper was like a stage coach in which any one who would pay had a Right to a Place." See Benjamin Franklin, *The Autobiography of Benjamin Franklin*, ed. Leonard W. Labaree (New Haven: Yale University Press, 1964), p. 165.

10. See the *Pennsylvania Gazette*, September 25 to October 2, 1729, no. 40, p. 1.

11. Isaiah Thomas, *The History of Printing in America*, vol. 1. (New York: Burt Franklin, 1874), p. 146; William Coolidge Lane, "The Printer of the Harvard Theses of 1771," *Publications of the Colonial Society of Massachusetts* 26, Transactions; 1924-1926, p. 9.

12. "Advertisements," the *Boston News-Letter*, February 28-March 7, 1723, no. 997, p. 2.

13. For a comparison to wages of the day laborer, see Lawrence C. Wroth, *The Colonial Printer* (Charlottesville, Va.: Dominion Books, 1964), p. 164.

14. Alexander Hamilton, who attended King's College (which later became Columbia University), sponsored and supported the *Gazette of the United States*; Noah Webster, a graduate of Yale, was editor of the Federalist *Minerva*; and Phillip Freneau, a graduate of Princeton, was editor of the Jeffersonian paper *National Gazette*.

15. Henry King, *American Journalism* (New York: Arno Press, 1970), p. 6.

16. Alfred McClung Lee, *The Daily Newspaper in America* (New York: Macmillan Co., 1937), p. 718; also Mott, *American Journalism*, p. 216.

17. *New York Sun*, September 3, 1833, p. 1. See also Mott, *American Journalism*, pp. 221-23.

18. Frederic Hudson, *Journalism in the United States, 1690-1872* (New York: Harper and Brothers, 1873), p. 418.

19. Edwin Emery and Michael Emery, *The Press in America*, 5th ed. (Englewood Cliffs, N.J.: Prentice-Hall, 1978), p. 140.

20. Michael Schudson, *Discovering the News* (New York: Basic Books, 1978), p. 24.

21. *New York Transcript*, June 23, 1834, cited in Willard G. Bleyer, *Main Currents in the History of American Journalism* (Boston: Houghton Mifflin, 1927), p. 165.

22. Lee, *Daily Newspaper*, p. 608.

23. James Parton, *The Life of Horace Greeley* (Boston: J. R. Osgood and Co., 1872), p. 396.

24. Peter Marzio, *The Men and Machines of American Journalism* (Washington, D.C.: Smithsonian Institution, 1973), p. 49.

25. Anthony Smith, "The Long Road to Objectivity and Back Again," in George Boyce, ed., *Newspaper History from the Seventeenth Century to the Present Day* (Beverly Hills, Calif.: Sage Publications, 1978), p. 167.

26. Emery and Emery, *Press in America*, pp. 197, 202.

27. Mott, *American Journalism*, p. 236.

28. Ibid., p. 227.

29. Schudson, *Discovering the News*, p. 68.

30. Mott, *American Journalism*, p. 338.

31. Monthly pay cited in Henry King, "The Pay and Rank of Journalists," *Forum* 18 (January 1895): 589. Greeley's and city editor's incomes cited in Mott, *American Journalism*, vol. 2, p. 24. Reporter pay cited in Ted Curtis Smythe, "The Reporter, 1880-1900," *Journalism History* 7, no. 1 (Spring 1980): 2, 6. Writer's rates cited in Mott, *American Journalism*, vol. 4, pp. 34, 39.

32. Mott, *American Journalism*, p. 489.

33. Ibid.

34. Ibid., p. 490.

35. Ibid., p. 489.

36. Ibid.

37. Ibid., p. 488.

38. Michael Kirkhorn, "The Curious Existence: Journalistic Identity in the Interwar Period," in Catherine L. Covert and John D. Stevens, eds., *Mass Media between the Wars* (Syracuse, N.Y.: Syracuse University Press, 1984), pp. 127-55.

39. Lincoln Steffens, "Tweed Days in St. Louis" and "The Shamelessness of St. Louis," in *The Shame of the Cities* (New York: Hill and Wang, 1957), p. 98.

40. David Paul Nord, *Newspapers and New Politics: Midwestern Municipal Reform, 1890-1900* (Ann Arbor, Mich.: UMI Research Press, 1981), p. 1.

41. Ibid.

42. Ibid., p. 129.

43. Talcott Williams, *The Newspaperman*, p. 16.

44. Ibid., p. 19.

45. Mott, *American Journalism*, p. 457.

46. Tiffany Blake, "The Editorial, Past, Present, and Future," *Collier's* 48 (September 23, 1911): 35.

47. Upton Sinclair, *The Brass Check* (Pasadena, Calif.: Author, 1920), p. 436.

48. Nelson Antrim Crawford, *The Ethics of Journalism* (New York: Alfred A. Knopf, 1924), p. 72.

49. L. G. Salter, "Edgar Guest Longs for 'Good Old Days,' " *Editor & Publisher* 64, no. 26 (November 14, 1931): 9.

50. George Britt, *Forty Years — Forty Millions* (New York: Farrar and Rinehart, 1935), p. 25.

51. Ronald Steel, *Walter Lippmann and the American Century* (New York: Vintage Books, Random House, 1980), pp. 36-37.

52. Walter Lippmann and Charles Merz, "A Test of the News," supplement to the *New Republic*, August 4, 1920, p. 3, as quoted in Crawford, *Ethics*, pp. 90-91, and in Steel, *Walter Lippmann*, p. 172.

53. Walter Lippmann, *Liberty and the News* (New York: Harcourt, Brace and Howe, 1920), p. 79, 47.

54. Walter Lippmann, *Public Opinion* (New York: Harcourt, Brace and Co., 1922), pp. 226-27, 247; Lippmann, *Liberty and the News*, p. 88.

55. Lippmann, *Liberty and the News*, p. 11.

56. Mott, *American Journalism*, p. 797.

57. Commission on Freedom of the Press, *A Free and Responsible Press* (Chicago: University of Chicago Press, 1947). See also Margaret A. Blanchard, "The Hutchins Commission, The Press, and the Responsibility Concept," *Journalism Monographs* (May 1977); and Lippmann, *Public Opinion*.

58. John W. C. Johnstone, Edward J. Slawski, and William W. Bowman, *The News People: A Sociological Portrait of American Journalists and Their Work* (Urbana: University of Illinois Press, 1976), p. 195.

59. Mott, *American Journalism*, p. 863.

60. Johnstone, Slawski, and Bowman, *News People*, p. 188.

61. Ibid., p. 28.

2. Basic Characteristics of U.S. Journalists

1. John W. C. Johnstone, Edward J. Slawski, and William W. Bowman, *The News People* (Urbana: University of Illinois Press, 1976), p. 18.

2. Ibid.

3. American Newspaper Publishers Association, *Facts about Newspapers '84*, April 1984, p. 12. It is possible that some of the increase in the print media editorial workforce is the result of new technology. Some newspapers, for example, have hired young people to handle copy editing, proofreading, and inputting simple material (such as press releases) using electronic editing equipment. These persons may do some reporting, and many are full-time employees, but they are skilled clerks rather than reporters or editors. Personal communication from Richard D. Smyser, president of the American Society of Newspaper Editors for 1985 and editor of the *(Tennessee) Oak Ridger*, January 19, 1985.

4. Siegfried Weischenberg, "Journalismus," in Kurt Koszyk and Karl Hugo Pruys, *Handbuch der Massenkommunikation* (Munich: Deutschertaschenbuch Verlag, 1981).

5. Johnstone, Slawski, and Bowman, *News People*, pp. 7 and 8.

6. Ibid., p. 19.

7. See, for example, David Weaver, Doris Graber, Maxwell McCombs, and Chaim Eyal, *Media Agenda-Setting in a Presidential Election: Issues, Images, and Interest* (New York: Praeger, 1981); Edward Jay Epstein, *News From*

Nowhere: Television and the News (New York: Vintage Books, 1974); and Leo Bogart, "The Public's Use and Perception of Newspapers," *Public Opinion Quarterly* 48 (Winter 1984): 709-719.

8. Johnstone, Slawski, and Bowman, *News People*, p. 20.

9. Ibid.

10. This proportion of women journalists (33.8 percent) is very close to the proportion of women journalists (33 percent) found by the Burgoons in their 1981-82 studies of journalists working for ninety-one U.S. daily newspapers and seven U.S. television stations. But this percentage is well above the 27 percent women working as Washington correspondents in 1978 and the 25 percent women journalists working for daily newspapers in Canada in the late 1970s. See Judee K. Burgoon, Michael Burgoon, and Charles K. Atkin, *The World of the Working Journalist* (New York: Newspaper Advertising Bureau, 1982), p. 122; Michael Burgoon and Judee K. Burgoon, "Summary of Findings from the Gannett Company Study," unpublished report, Michigan State University, East Lansing, Mich., September 1982, p. 24; Stephen Hess, *The Washington Reporters* (Washington, D.C.: Brookings Institution, 1981), p. 141; and Gertrude Joch Robinson, "Women Journalists in Canadian Dailies," *Working Papers in Communications* (Montreal: McGill University, 1981), pp. 3-4.

11. Marvin W. Mindes and Alan C. Adcock, "Trickster, Hero, Helper: A Report on the Lawyer Image," *American Bar Research Journal* 177, no. 1 (Winter 1982): 232.

12. The Burgoons also found that the largest proportion of journalists in their studies was concentrated in the 25-to-34-year-old category (41 percent in the study of 489 journalists in eight daily newspapers, and 51 percent in the study of eighty-three newspapers and seven TV stations owned by the Gannett Company). See Burgoon, Burgoon, and Atkin, *Working Journalist*, p. 122; and Burgoon and Burgoon, "Gannett Company Study," p. 25. In the larger Gannett study, the proportions of journalists 45 years and older were nearly identical to those found in our 1982-83 national study. On the other hand, Washington correspondents in 1978 tended to be older — nearly one-half were 40 years and older. See Hess, *Reporters*, p. 141.

13. When compared to U.S. college and university faculty members, for example, it is striking to see that there are proportionately so few journalists forty-five and older (about 21 percent) and so many faculty members (42 percent). See Everett Carll Ladd, Jr. and Seymour Martin Lipset, *Survey of the Social, Political, and Educational Perspectives of American College and University Faculty* (New York: National Institute for Education, 1976), p. 16. But the percentage of Washington correspondents in their forties and fifties is much higher than for journalists in general. Nearly 28 percent are in their forties, and 11 percent are fifty and older. See Hess, *Reporters*, p. 141.

14. Paul V. Peterson, "Today's Journalism Students: Who They Are and What They Want to Do" (Columbus: School of Journalism, Ohio State University, 1981), p. 15. Also available from the Gannett Foundation, Lincoln Tower, Rochester, NY 14604.

15. Ladd and Lipset, *Survey of Perspectives*, p. 22, report 21 percent U.S. women college and university faculty members in 1975, nearly identical to the proportion of U.S. women journalists in 1971, and considerably below the percentage of women journalists in 1982-83 (33.8 percent).

16. Peterson, "Journalism Students," p. 8-9.

17. Ibid., p. 4.

18. Johnstone, Slawski, and Bowman, *News People*, p. 26.

19. S. Robert Lichter and Stanley Rothman, "Media and Business Elites," *Public Opinion* 4, no. 5 (October/November 1981): 42-46, 59-60.

20. Ibid., p. 43.

21. See, for example, Paul M. Hirsch, "Occupational, Organizational, and Institutional Models in Mass Media Research: Toward an Integrated Framework," in Paul Hirsch, Peter V. Miller, and F. Gerald Kline, eds., *Strategies for Communication Research* (Beverly Hills, Calif.: Sage Publications, 1977); Gaye Tuchman, *Making News* (New York: Free Press, 1978); and Lee Sigelman, "Reporting the News: An Organizational Analysis," *American Journal of Sociology* 79 (July 1973): 132-51.

22. Bob Schulman, "The Liberal Tilt of Our Newsrooms" *Bulletin of the American Society of Newspaper Editors*, no. 654 (October 1982), pp. 3-7; Joseph Kraft, "The Imperial Media," *Commentary*, May 1981, p. 36; Leo Rosten, *The Washington Correspondents* (New York: Harcourt, Brace and Co., 1937), p. 191; William L. Rivers, "The Correspondents After Twenty-five Years," *Columbia Journalism Review* 1 (Spring 1962): 5; and Stephen Hess, *Reporters*, pp. 87-90.

23. Lichter and Rothman, *"Elites,"* pp. 43-44.

24. Ibid., pp. 43.

25. Stanley Rothman and S. Robert Lichter, "Are Journalists a New Class?" *Business Forum*, Spring 1983, p. 15.

26. Our definition of a "prominent" news organization is taken directly from the 1971 Johnstone study. In that study, a prominent news organization was any one mentioned by more than ten journalists in the national sample as either one of the fairest or most reliable news organizations in the country, or as one of the three organizations they relied on most often in their own work. See pp. 89, 90 and 224 of Johnstone, Slawski, and Bowman, *News People*. The prominent organizations included in our study were the three weekly news magazines, the Associated Press, United Press International, and the *Boston Globe*.

27. Rothman and Lichter, "New Class?" p. 15.

28. Ladd and Lipset, *Survey of Perspectives*, p. 284.

29. Lichter and Rothman, "Elites," p. 43.

30. Leo Bogart, *Press and Public: Who Reads What, Where, When, and Why in American Newspapers* (Hillsdale, N.J.: Lawrence Erlbaum Associates, 1981), p. 9, 55. See also Burgoon, Burgoon, and Atkin, *Working Journalist*, p. 83.

31. Burgoon, Burgoon, and Atkin, *Working Journalist*, p. 83.

32. Ibid., pp. 83-84.

33. Johnstone, Slawski, and Bowman, *News People*, p. 224.

34. Ibid., pp. 88-89.

35. Burgoon and Burgoon "Gannett Company Study," p. 16.

36. Bogart, *Press and Public*, p. 180.

37. Ibid.

38. Burgoon, Burgoon, and Atkin, *Working Journalist*, p. 84; Burgoon and Burgoon, "Gannett Company Study," p. 19.

39. Burgoon, Burgoon, and Atkin, *Working Journalist*, p. 84.

40. Burgoon and Burgoon, "Gannett Company Study," p. 19.

41. Burgoon, Burgoon, and Atkin, *Working Journalist*, p. 84.

42. *Magazine Newsletter of Research*, no. 33 (August 1980), pp. 2-3.

43. Bogart, *Press and Public*, p. 4.

44. Burgoon, Burgoon, and Atkin, *Working Journalist*, p. 84; Burgoon and Burgoon, "Gannett Company Study," pp. 16-17.

45. Johnstone, Slawski, and Bowman, *News People*, p. 89.

46. Burgoon, Burgoon, and Atkin, *Working Journalist*, p. 85.

3. Education and Training

1. John Johnstone, Edward Slawski, and William Bowman, *The News People* (Urbana: University of Illinois Press, 1976), pp. 31, 36, and 203.

2. Much of this brief history of journalism education in the United States is taken from David H. Weaver and Richard G. Gray, "Journalism and Mass Communication Research in the United States: Past, Present, and Future," in G. Cleveland Wilhoit and Harold de Bock, eds., *Mass Communication Review Yearbook*, vol. 1 (Beverly Hills, Calif.: Sage Publications, 1980), pp. 124-51. For other, more detailed accounts of the history of journalism education in the United States, see William R. Lindley, *Journalism and Higher Education: The Search for Academic Purpose* (Stillwater, Okla.: Journalistic Services, 1975); and Herbert Douglas Birkhead, "Presenting the Press: Journalism and the Professional Project," doctoral dissertation, University of Iowa, 1982, pp. 235-301.

3. We are grateful to Professor Trevor Brown of Indiana University's School of Journalism for suggesting this "school of life" interpretation of early journalism education.

4. Personal communication from Professor Steven H. Chaffee, School of Journalism and Mass Communication, University of Wisconsin, Madison, April 2, 1979.

5. Lindley, *Journalism*, p. 3.

6. *Journalism Bulletin* 4, no. 3 (November 1927): 9-11 and 25-27.

7. Paul V. Peterson, "Journalism Enrollment Levels Off; Growth Rate Declines Sharply," *Journalism Educator* 31, no. 4 (January 1977): 3.

8. Paul V. Peterson, "Journalism Growth Continues at Hefty 10.8 Per Cent Rate," *Journalism Educator* 26, no. 4 (January 1972): 4.

9. Paul V. Peterson, "J-school Enrollments Hit Record 91,016," *Journalism Educator* 37, no. 4 (Winter 1983): 4.

10. Ibid., p. 3.

11. Lindley, *Journalism*, p. 4.

12. Peterson, "J-school Enrollments," p. 9.

13. Paul V. Peterson, "Today's Journalism Students: Who They Are and What They Want to Do" (Columbus: School of Journalism, Ohio State University, undated).

14. Ben H. Bagdikian, "Woodstein U.: Notes on the Mass Production and Questionable Education of Journalists," *Atlantic* 238, no. 3 (March 1977): 80-92.

15. Peterson, "Today's Journalism Students," p. 5.

16. The Dow Jones Newspaper Fund, Inc., *1984 Journalism Career and Scholarship Guide* (Princeton, N.J.: Dow Jones Newspaper Fund, 1984), p. 14.

17. Ibid.

18. Johnstone, Slawski, and Bowman, *News People*, p. 31.

19. In a 1981 study of 489 newsroom employees at eight U.S. daily newspapers around the country, the Burgoons and Atkin found 64 percent with at least

bachelor's degrees. In a larger study of eighty-three newspapers and seven television stations in the United States owned by the Gannett Company, Inc., the Burgoons found 70 percent of all journalists holding college degrees. (See Judee K. Burgoon, Michael Burgoon, and Charles K. Atkin, *The World of the Working Journalist* [New York: Newspaper Advertising Bureau, 1982], p. 122; and Michael Burgoon and Judee K. Burgoon, "Summary of Findings from the Gannett Company Study," unpublished report, Michigan State University, East Lansing, Mich., September 1982, p. 23.) In contrast, Stephen Hess found 92.8 percent of Washington, D.C. reporters holding college degrees in his 1978 study. (See Stephen Hess, *The Washington Reporters* [Washington, D.C.: Brookings Institution, 1981], p. 165.)

The above figures indicate that U.S. journalists are far more likely to have completed a college degree than are journalists in many other countries of the world. A recent survey of Canadian journalists shows just over 30 percent of those working for French-language newspapers holding a degree, and 51 percent of those working for English-language papers with a college degree. (See Vernon A. Keel and Victor Larouche, "Journalists in the United States, English Canada, and Quebec: Beginning a Comparative Analysis," paper presented at the organizational meeting of the Midwest Canadian Studies Association, Northwestern University, Evanston, Ill., September 1984.) In addition, a 1984 study on the working conditions of journalists in several countries of the world finds that about 22 percent of British journalists held university degrees in 1975, about one-fourth of Austrian journalists did in 1974, about one-fourth of French journalists did in 1971, and only about 10 percent in Sweden held a degree in 1969. (See G. Bohere, *Profession: Journalist* [Geneva, Switzerland: International Labour Office, 1984], pp. 18-21.) A 1981 study of 318 Australian journalists shows 23.1 percent of broadcast journalists and 31.7 percent of print journalists holding degrees. (See Jay Black, "Professionalization of the Australian News Media: Journalists' Education, Training and Job Satisfaction," paper presented at the annual convention of the Association for Education in Journalism, Ohio University, Athens, Ohio, July 1982.)

20. Johnstone, Slawski, and Bowman, *News People*, p. 31 and 200.

21. Ibid., p. 33.

22. Ibid., p. 34.

23. Ibid., p. 36.

24. Ibid.

25. The Dow Jones Newspaper Fund, Inc., *1984 Guide*, p. 14.

26. U.S. Bureau of the Census, *Statistical Abstract of the United States, 1972*, 93d ed. (Washington, D.C.: U.S. Government Printing Office, 1972), p. 133; and *Statistical Abstract of the United States, 1984*, 104th ed., 1984, p. 169.

27. Johnstone, Slawski, and Bowman, *News People*, p. 37.

28. Ibid., p. 40.

29. Ibid., p. 39.

30. Ibid., p. 204.

31. Ibid., p. 44, 207.

32. Ibid., p. 46.

33. Burgoon, Burgoon, and Atkin, *Working Journalist*, p. 112.

34. Some of these predictors were identified with a statistical technique called *discriminant analysis* in a graduate-methods class paper written by Aralynn Abare McMane entitled "The Continuing Education of Journalists: Determin-

ing Who Wants What, If Anything.'' We are grateful for the insights contained in this detailed analysis of the predictors of desire for additional training and type of such training.

35. James W. Carey, dean of the University of Illinois College of Communication, argues that the university must not be captured by any profession wishing to turn its attention to timely and practical matters. He also sees journalism as especially dangerous to the university tradition, because of its preoccupation with the new, the novel, and the immediate. Carey asserts that the history of journalism education is part of the history of the transformation of the American university into a professional school, but that journalism education always has been in an uneasy relationship with this movement toward professionalism, because of the resistance to specialization and special status by many journalists. Carey argues that we would all be better served if journalists were to see themselves as less subject to the demands of their profession and more to the demands of the general moral and intellectual point of view, and he calls for less professionalism rather than more in journalism education. See James W. Carey, ''A Plea for the University Tradition,'' *Journalism Quarterly* 55 (Winter 1978): 846-55.

A related concern about the increasing professionalism of American journalists is expressed in the 1981 study of 489 journalists by Burgoon, Burgoon, and Atkin, *Working Journalist*. In this study, they argue that journalists are becoming more isolated from the public they are supposed to serve because of their preoccupation with their own careers, their specialized education, and their relative lack of regular communication with persons from outside their occupation.

36. For a summary statement of the philosophy and procedures of the accreditation of journalism schools and departments in the United States, see the pamphlet *Accredited Journalism and Mass Communications Education*. This pamphlet is updated each year and is available from the Accrediting Council on Education in Journalism and Mass Communications (ACEJMC), School of Journalism, P.O. Box 838, University of Missouri, Columbia, MO 65205. For a brief history of journalism accreditation and a debate over some of the major issues surrounding it, see *Journalism Educator* 38, no. 4 (Winter 1984): 3-16; and Lindley, *Journalism*, pp. 56-61. For a report on recent revisions in accreditation, see *AEJMC News* 18, no. 3 (December 1984): 1, 3. This newsletter is published by the central office of the Association for Education in Journalism and Mass Communication, College of Journalism, University of South Carolina, 1621 College Street, Columbia, SC 29208-0251.

4. Job Conditions and Satisfactions

1. Mark Fishman, *Manufacturing the News* (Austin: University of Texas Press, 1980), p. 155.

2. Ibid., p. 151.

3. Gene Miller, unpublished remarks at the Roy W. Howard Public Affairs Reporting Seminar, School of Journalism, September 1984, Indiana University, Bloomington.

4. Herbert J. Gans, *Deciding What's News: A Study of CBS Evening News, NBC Nightly News, Newsweek, and Time* (New York: Vintage Books, Random House, 1979), p. 84.

5. Ibid., p. 93.

6. John W. C. Johnstone, Edward J. Slawski, and William W. Bowman, *The News People: A Sociological Portrait of American Journalists and Their Work* (Urbana: University of Illinois Press, 1976), p. 128.

7. Quoted in Eugene C. Patterson, "The Press: A Few Problems to Solve," convocation address to the Indiana University School of Journalism, Bloomington, September 6, 1983.

8. See Vernon A. Stone, "Then and Now: News Directors' Profiles and Problems; Noteworthy Changes in a Decade of RTNDA Surveys," *RTNDA Communicator* 37 (October 1983), pp. 28-30.

9. Johnstone, Slawski, and Bowman, *News People*, pp. 84-85.

10. Bill Green, "The Fake Pulitzer Story: 'How Did It All Happen?' " *Louisville Courier-Journal*, April 26, 1981.

11. Patterson, "The Press."

12. Johnstone, Slawski, and Bowman, *News People*, p. 154.

13. Ibid., p. 147.

14. U.S. Department of Commerce, Bureau of the Census, *Statistical Abstract of the United States, 1984*. The CPI figure for 1970 is 116.3, and for 1981 the figure is 272.3. Dividing the 1970 figure by the 1981 number gives a multiplier of 2.34 (times $11,133), yielding a figure of $26,066.34 needed for the median journalist to have kept up with inflation.

15. The television workforce grew more dramatically than the news workforce as a whole. This increase in the number of low seniority personnel explains partially the decline in TV income estimates.

16. The average salary for public-relations practitioners is for those who are members of the International Association of Business Communicators. Note the shift to *mean* (average) figures. We use the *median* throughout the rest of this chapter so that comparisons can be made with the 1971 data. In the case of public-relations personnel, median salary figures are unavailable. See International Association of Business Communicators, *Profile/83 IABC Special Report*, p. 3. Note: Public-relations personnel tend to be concentrated in larger urban areas than are journalists. That may be a factor in the average salary differences.

17. U.S. Department of Labor, Bureau of Labor Statistics, "Business Occupations," Bulletin 2200-2, p. 3.

18. Ibid.

19. U.S. Department of Labor, Bureau of Labor Statistics, *National Survey of Professional, Administrative, Technical, and Clerical Personnel*, Bulletin 2181, March 1983.

20. Judee K. Burgoon, Michael Burgoon, and Charles K. Atkin, *The World of the Working Journalist* (Newspaper Readership Project, Newspaper Advertising Bureau, New York, September 1982), p. 79.

21. David L. Altheide, *Creating Reality: How TV News Distorts Events* (Beverly Hills, Calif.: Sage Publications, 1974), p. 49.

22. Burgoon, Burgoon, and Atkin, *Working Journalist*.

23. Ibid., p. 5.

24. Ibid., p. 60.

25. See Christine L. Ogan and David H. Weaver, "Job Satisfaction in Selected U.S. Daily Newspapers: A Study of Male and Female Top-Level Managers," *Mass Commmunication Review* 6 (Winter 1978-79): 20-26.

26. The job perception factors were subjected to factor analysis, using Vari-

max rotation. The three emerging factors of economics, autonomy, and personal development were used in multivariate regression analysis. Predictors of an *economic orientation* were these: (1) information transmitter role, beta = .15, r = .14; (2) unionized staff, beta = .12, r = .11; (3) age, beta = .14, r = .09. The predictor of *autonomy values* was: interpreter role, beta = .13, r = .14. Predictors of *personal development* orientation were these: (1) information transmitter role, beta = .13, r = .16; (2) political conservatism, beta = .13, r = .13; (3) age, beta = -.11, r = -.13; and (4) television journalists, beta = .13, r = .16.

27. Johnstone, Slawski, and Bowman, *News People*, p. 152.

28. Ibid., p. 146.

29. Lee B. Becker, Idowa A. Sobowale, and Robin E. Cobbey, "Reporters and Their Professional and Organizational Commitment," *Journalism Quarterly* (Winter 1979), pp. 753-63, as reprinted in G. Cleveland Wilhoit and Harold de Bock, eds., *Mass Communication Review Yearbook*, vol. 2 (Beverly Hills, Calif.: Sage Publications, 1981), pp. 339-50.

30. Johnstone, Slawski, and Bowman, *News People*, p. 239.

31. Discriminant analysis, a complex statistical technique that is sensitive to differences between two discrete groups on a number of independent variables, was used to compare journalists who planned to stay in journalism with those who had decided to leave. Discriminant coefficients were obtained to indicate the specific factors that contributed to differences between committed and uncommitted journalists. A positive coefficient suggests that a particular measure, after controlling for other measures, is positively related to staying in the field.

32. The analysis was restricted to reporters so that we could compare the findings to the reanalysis of the Johnstone data by Becker, Sobowale, and Cobbey, "Reporters."

33. Johnstone, Slawski, and Bowman, *News People*, p. 146.

5. Professionalism: Roles, Values, Ethics

1. Michael W. Singletary, "Commentary: Are Journalists 'Professionals'?" *Newspaper Research Journal* 3 (January 1982): 75-87. This article is a concise review of major work on the professionalization of journalists.

2. Arthur Lawrence, *Journalism as a Profession* (London: Hodder and Stoughton, 1903), p. 170.

3. Ibid., p. 173.

4. Harold L. Wilensky, "The Professionalization of Everyone?" *American Journal of Sociology* 70, no. 2 (September 1964): 138.

5. James Boylan, "News People," *Wilson Quarterly Special Issue* (1982), pp. 71-85.

6. Ibid., p. 79.

7. John W. C. Johnstone, Edward J. Slawski, and William W. Bowman, *The News People: A Sociological Portrait of American Journalists and Their Work* (Urbana: University of Illinois Press, 1976), p. 102.

8. Ibid., p. 111.

9. Ibid., p. 108.

10. Ibid.

11. For example, see *Journalism Ethics Report, 1983*, a tabloid collection of

writings about journalistic practice, published by the National Ethics Committee of the Society of Professional Journalists, Sigma Delta Chi.

12. Keith Buckley, reference librarian, Indiana University Law Library, obtained these data from the American Bar Association, March 19, 1984.

13. Ken Ringle, "Less Than 45 Percent of U.S. Doctors Now Belong to the AMA," *Washington Post*, March 11, 1984, p. A4.

14. John W. Wright, *The American Almanac of Jobs and Salaries* (New York: Avon Books, 1981), p. 349. The American Institute of Certified Public Accountants' Public Relations Division supplied the group's membership data.

15. Barbara E. Nelson, Assistant Director of Research and Information, the Newspaper Guild, helped us verify information about Guild membership.

16. Johnstone, Slawski, and Bowman, *News People*, p. 106.

17. Frances Wilhoit, head of the Weil Journalism Library at Indiana University, obtained the readership data from Rick Fleming of the American Medical Association, Chicago, March 29, 1985.

18. Stanley Rothman and S. Robert Lichter, "Are Journalists a New Class," *Business Forum*, Spring 1983, pp. 12-17. In this article, the authors summarize their popular thesis that journalists are one of the "new elites" that "may have reduced businessmen's confidence in themselves . . . ."

19. *Time*, December 12, 1983, pp. 76-93.

20. Eugene C. Patterson, "The Press: A Few Problems to Solve," convocation address to the Indiana University School of Journalism, Bloomington, September 1983.

21. Louis D. Boccardi, "Press and Public: What to Do?" Address to the Associated Press Membership Meeting, reprinted in *APME News* 149 (August 1984): 16-18.

22. Johnstone, Slawski, and Bowman, *News People*, p. 131.

23. Ibid., p. 132.

24. Michael J. O'Neill, "A Problem for the Republic — A Challenge for Editors," address to the American Society of Newspaper Editors, May 5, 1982. (Reprinted in *The Adversary Press* [St. Petersburg, Fla.: Modern Media Institute, 1983], pp. 2-15.)

25. Johnstone, Slawski, and Bowman, *News People*, pp. 118-32.

26. For a useful discussion of the arguments for and against the notion of neutral, or objective, reporting, see John C. Merrill and Ralph L. Lowenstein, *Media, Messages, and Men,* 2d ed. (New York: Longman, 1979), pp. 204-213.

27. Our analysis uses statistical approaches similar to those used by Johnstone, Slawski, and Bowman. The factor-analytic procedure used principal component solution, Varimax rotation, and 1.00 in the diagonals of the correlation matrix.

28. These role conceptions are similar to those found by Culbertson in his study of 285 editors and writers on seventeen U.S. newspapers. See Hugh M. Culbertson, "Three Perspectives on American Journalism," *Journalism Monographs* 83 (June 1983): 4, 29.

29. Johnstone, Slawski, and Bowman, *News People*, p. 120.

30. Ibid., pp. 124-30.

31. Ibid., p. 233. The researchers reported $R = .35$ for participant values and $R = .34$ for the neutral orientation. Our results are these: adversary, $R = .41$; interpreter, $R = .50$; and disseminator, $R = .44$.

32. Johnstone, Slawski, and Bowman, *News People*, p. 128.

33. Ibid., p. 125.

34. Ibid., p. 129.

35. Ibid., p. 231, table 7.3; the researchers found about 19 percent of their sample subscribing to either extreme neutral or extreme participant roles. Using the same cutting points — but deleting several questions because of their failure to appear in our factor analysis — we find that only about 2 percent of our sample may be classified as extremes. On the other hand, about a third of our sample could be classified as extremes in holding a *dual* interpretive-disseminator role. The earlier research found that about 4 percent could be so classified.

36. The factor-analytic procedure produced strong loadings on all the items mentioned, each in excess of .40 for each of the three factors, explaining 53 percent of the common variance.

37. The items making up each of the factors were treated as scales for application of regression analysis. For media staff, disseminator role (beta = .12, r = .13) and perceived job of informing the public (beta = .15, r = .17) were predictors. For external media, the disseminator role (beta = .18, r = .20) was a correlate. For audience/sources, the disseminator role (beta = .20, r = .29) and staff size (beta = -.17, r = -.25) were predictors.

38. Philip Meyer, *Editors, Publishers, and Newspaper Ethics* (Washington, D.C.: American Society of Newspaper Editors, 1983), p. 71.

39. Lou Cannon, *Reporting: An Inside View* (Sacramento: California Journal Press, 1977), p. 28.

40. Carl Bernstein and Bob Woodward, *All the President's Men* (New York: Simon and Schuster, 1974), p. 224.

41. *U.S.A. Today*, March 21, 1984, p.4.

42. Ibid.

43. Personal interview with David Hawpe, Louisville, Kentucky, September 28, 1984.

44. William Rivers, Wilbur Schramm, and Clifford Christians, *Responsibility in Mass Communication*, 3d ed. (New York: Harper and Row, 1980), p. 197.

45. Michael J. O'Neill, "A Problem," p. 21.

46. Clifford G. Christians, Kim B. Rotzoll, and Mark Fackler, *Media Ethics: Cases and Moral Reasoning* (New York: Longman, 1983), pp. 76-79.

47. Lou Cannon, *Reporting*, p. 29.

48. Personal interview with Lawrence Connor, Indianapolis, Indiana, October 12, 1984.

49. Ibid.

50. Regression analysis was performed using a Guttman scale of three items from the set: (1) Using confidential business or government documents; (2) Using personal letters and photographs; and (3) Getting employed in an organization to gain inside information. These items had a .90 coefficient of reproducibility and a .71 coefficient of scalability. The reporting practices scale was subjected to analysis with thirty-seven independent variables.

51. Nelson Antrim Crawford, *The Ethics of Journalism* (New York: Alfred A. Knopf, 1924), pp. 114 and viii.

52. The ten questions about sources of influence on ethics were subjected to factor analysis. The items loaded on three factors, just as logic would predict: *newsroom content* included senior editor (.72), senior reporter (.72), publisher (.44), peers and coworkers (.42), and newsroom learning (.39); *college teachers* contained university teachers (.85) and journalism school teachers (.55); *family-religion* consisted of religious upbringing (.78) and family upbringing (.54). Each

of these sets was subjected to multiple regression analysis.

53. Thirty-nine items were used in multiple regression analysis on newsroom context. Only ombudsman in the organization (beta = .13, r = .10) and frequency of superior comment (beta = .11, r = .14) were important predictors.

54. In the regression analysis, group-owned medium (beta = -.12, r = -.13) and age (beta = .13, r = .19) were correlates.

55. The college-teacher factor showed these correlates: journalism major (beta = .12, r = .26); number of journalism courses taken if not a major (beta = .29, r = .31); staff size (beta = .12, r = -.15); income (beta = .12, r = -.15), and age (beta = .15, r = -.10).

56. Frank McCulloch, ed., *Drawing The Line: How Thirty-one Editors Solved Their Toughest Ethical Dilemmas* (Washington, D.C.: American Society of Newspaper Editors Foundation, 1984), p. v.

57. Ibid., p. 31.

58. Ibid., p. 95.

59. Philip Meyer, *Editors, Publishers*, p. 54.

60. Jack McLeod and Ramona Rush, "Professionalization of Latin American and U.S. Journalists," *Journalism Quarterly* 46 (Autumn 1969): 583-90.

61. McLeod and Rush, "Professionalism," p. 590.

62. Wolfgang Donsbach, "Legitimacy through Competence Rather Than Value Judgments: The Concept of Journalistic Professionalization Reconsidered," *Gazette* 27 (1981): 47-67.

63. Wolfgang Donsbach, "Journalists' Conceptions of Their Audience," *Gazette* 32 (1983): 19-36.

64. Elisabeth Noelle-Neumann, Renate Kosher, and Wolfgang Donsbach provided data and consultation from the Federal Republic of Germany. James Halloran and Robin McCrone provided data and consultation from Britain. The authors are grateful for their generous assistance.

65. Frank McCulloch, *Drawing the Line*, p. 79.

66. Gunter Wallraff, *Der Aufmacher* (Kiepenheuer and Witsch: Cologne, 1977). See also Gunter Wallraff, *Wallraff, The Undesirable Journalist* (Woodstock, N.Y.: Overlook Press, 1979), pp. 118-35.

67. *The Adversary Press*, p. 104.

68. Sunwoo Nam, "The Government Information Apparatus of the Federal Republic of Germany," *Political Communication and Persuasion* 2, no. 2 (1983): 177-87. See also Karl-Heinz Vaubel, "Seven-hundred Journalists in Search of Information; The Federal Capital Bonn: An Open News Centre," *Scala* 2, no. 1 (January 1985): 12-15.

69. G. Bohere, *Profession: Journalist* (Geneva: International Labour Office, 1984), pp. 18-23.

70. Another possible explanation is that the samples are constructed differently in the three countries. We have investigated that possibility carefully. The three samples appear to have been constructed in similar ways, so that we may regard them as comparable, except in one respect. In England, tabloid journalism has a tradition of what some label "sensationalism" that would be matched in the United States only in such publications as the *National Inquirer*. Journalists from the British tabloids, of course, are sampled because they are an established part of that country's press. We did not, however, include publications such as the *National Inquirer* in our universe of journalists. Had we done so, the data might have been more similar to the British results.

71. *The Adversary Press*, p. 29.

72. This interpretation is based on earlier work by James Carey, "The Communications Revolution and the Professional Communicator," in *Sociological Review Monographs* 13 (January 1969): 32, in which he argues that the contemporary journalist has been "de-intellectualized" to the role of a mere translator in service to the institutions on which he reports.

73. Bernard C. Cohen, *The Press and Foreign Policy* (Princeton, N.J.: Princeton University Press), 1963.

74. *The Adversary Press*, p. 29.

75. Stephen Hess, *The Washington Reporters* (Washington, D.C.: Brookings Institution, 1981), p. 137.

76. Harold Wilensky, "Professionalization of Everyone?" p. 158.

6. New Technology and the Job

1. Richard G. Gray, "Implications of the New Information Technology for Democracy," in John W. Ahlhauser, ed., *Electronic Home News Delivery: Journalistic and Public Policy Implications* (Bloomington: School of Journalism and Center for New Communications, Indiana University, 1981), pp. 69-73.

2. David H. Weaver, *Videotex Journalism: Teletext, Viewdata, and the News* (Hillsdale, N.J.: Lawrence Erlbaum Associates, 1983). See chap. 1, pp. 3-5.

3. Donald L. Shaw, "News Bias and the Telegraph: A Study of Historical Change," *Journalism Quarterly* 44 (Spring 1967): 3-12, 31; and Donald L. Shaw, "Technology: Freedom for What?" in Ronald T. Farrar and John D. Stevens, eds., *Mass Media and the National Experience* (New York: Harper and Row, 1971), pp. 73-79.

4. Ibid.

5. Gray, "Technology for Democracy," p. 71.

6. For a concise review of many of these studies, see David H. Weaver and Judith M. Buddenbaum, "Newspapers and Television: A Review of Research on Uses and Effects," *American Newspaper Publishers Association News Research Report*, no. 19, April 20, 1979. Also published in G. Cleveland Wilhoit and Harold de Bock, eds., *Mass Communication Review Yearbook*, vol. 1 (Beverly Hills, Calif.: Sage Publications, 1980), pp. 371-80. See also Peter Clarke and Eric Fredin, "Newspapers, Television, and Political Reasoning," *Public Opinion Quarterly* 42 (Summer 1978): 143-60; and Donald F. Roberts and Christine M. Bachen, "Mass Communication Effects," *Annual Review of Psychology*, 1981, vol. 32, pp. 307-56.

7. American Newspaper Publishers Association Research Institute, "OCRs and VDTs: Electronic Applications in ANPA-Member Newspaper Departments for 1981" (Easton, Pa.: ANPA Research Institute, 1982).

8. Richard D. Yoakam, "ENG: Electronic News Gathering in Local Television Stations," *Center for New Communications Research Report no. 12* (Bloomington: School of Journalism, Indiana University, 1981).

9. See Bruce Garrison, "Electronic Editing Systems and Their Impact on News Decision Making," *Newspaper Research Journal* 3 (January 1982): 43-53; Larry D. Kurtz, "The Electronic Editor," *Journal of Communication* 30 (Summer 1980): 54-57; William R. Lindley, "Does the VDT Affect News Content?" *Journalism Resource Information*, Fall 1977 (Idaho State University mimeograph), pp. 2-4; Starr D. Randall, "Effect of Electronic Editing on Error Rate of Newspaper," *Journalism Quarterly* 56 (Spring 1979): 161-65; Linda J. Shipley and James K. Gentry, "How Electronic Editing Equipment Affects Editing

Performance," *Journalism Quarterly* 58 (Autumn 1981): 371-74, 387; and Joseph Shoquist, "Coping with the Editorial Load: At *The Milwaukee Journal*," *American Newspaper Publishers Association Research Institute Bulletin*, December 7, 1977, pp. 537-38. For studies showing more errors as a result of VDTs, see Roger Bennett, Randall L. Murray, and Guido H. Stempel III, "Editing Accuracy Drops with VDTs, Ohio Study Shows," *Journalism Educator* 32 (July 1977): 11-12; and James A. Crook, "How the New Technology Affects Student Editing," *Journalism Educator* 31 (January 1977): 12-15, 46. For a study showing that VDT editing is faster than pencil-and-paper editing, see Marty Sutphin, "Plug into a Terminal: Faster, Neater, and More Error-Free," *Quill*, November 1973, p. 25.

10. Stephen Hess, "Adtech and the Washington Reporters," in Gerald Benjamin, ed., *The Communications Revolution in Politics* (New York: Academy of Political Science), vol. 34, no. 4, pp. 102-108.

11. Ibid., p. 107.

12. Telephone conversation between David Weaver and Stephen Hess on August 29, 1984.

13. Ed Lambeth, "Reporting Washington for Main Street," *Washington Journalism Review* 2 (December 1980): 26-28.

14. Yoakam, "ENG."

15. See "VDT Attitude Survey Includes Eighty-two Papers," *Editor and Publisher*, April 24, 1978, p. 33; Roy M. Fisher, "Editing by Pencil Found Slightly Faster Than by VDT," *Publisher's Auxiliary* 130 (March 27, 1978): 2; Warren T. Francke and Douglas A. Anderson, "Expectations and Experience in Conversion to VDTs," *Journalism Quarterly* 57 (Winter 1980): 652-55; Bruce Garrison, "Electronic Editing Systems and Their Impact on News Decision Making," *Newspaper Research Journal* 3 (January 1982): 43-53; Larry D. Kurtz, "Study Examines Impact of Electronic Newsroom," *Editor and Publisher*, September 23, 1978, p. 28; and Jay Rogers, "VDTs, TV Haven't Shocked Editors," and Bob Nordyke, "Opinions Vary on Electronics' Effect," in *Editors in the Electronic Age* (Louisville, Ky.: Associated Press Managing Editors Convention, 1983), pp. 1-7.

16. Garrison, "Electronic Editing Systems."

17. George Killenberg, "Taking the Electronic Plunge? The Questions You Have to Ask," *APME News* 98 (March 1977): 3-5.

18. "VDT Attitude Survey."

19. Fisher, "Editing by Pencil."

20. Larry D. Kurtz, "The Electronic Editor," *Journal of Communication* 30 (Summer 1980): 54-57.

21. Francke and Anderson, "Conversion to VDTs."

22. Linda J. Shipley, James K. Gentry, and John W. Clarke, *VDT vs. Pencil: A Comparison of Speed and Accuracy* (Columbia: University of Missouri School of Journalism Monograph, 1979).

23. Christine Ogan, "Manager Computer Use Survey," unpublished paper, School of Journalism, Indiana University, 1982.

24. Hess, "Adtech." See also Stephen Hess, *The Washington Reporters* (Washington, D.C.: Brookings Institution, 1981).

25. Judee K. Burgoon, Michael Burgoon, and Charles K. Atkin, *The World of the Working Journalist* (New York: Newspaper Advertising Bureau, 1982), p. 100.

26. Conrad Smith, "Newsgathering Technology and the Content of Local

Television News," *Journal of Broadcasting* 28 (Winter 1984): 99-102. The quotes from TV news directors in the next two paragraphs came from material generously sent to David Weaver by Professor Smith, and not from the article in *Journal of Broadcasting*.

27. Hess, "Adtech"; and Lambeth, "Reporting Washington."
28. Yoakam, "ENG."
29. Burgoon, Burgoon, and Atkin, *Working Journalist*.
30. Ibid.
31. Yoakam, "ENG."
32. Conrad Smith, "Newsgathering Technology."

7. Women Journalists

1. Simone de Beauvoir, *The Second Sex*, trans. H. M. Parshley (New York: Bantam Books, 1961), p. 639. Originally published in French, 1949.

2. William Bowman, "Distaff Journalists: Women as a Minority Group in the News Media" (Ph.D. dissertation, University of Illinois at Chicago Circle, 1974).

3. The work in this chapter is based on the author's doctoral dissertation: Sue A. Lafky, "The Women of American Journalism," Ph.D. dissertation, Indiana University, 1990.

4. Victor R. Fuchs, *Women's Quest for Economic Equality* (Cambridge, Mass.: Harvard University Press, 1988).

5. Gilda Berger, *Women, Work and Wages* (New York: Franklin Watts, 1986), p. 2.

6. See Maurine H. Beasley and Kathryn T. Theus, *The New Majority: A Look at What the Preponderance of Women in Journalism Means to the Schools and to the Professions* (Lanham, Md.: University Press of America, 1988).

7. Paul V. Peterson, "Enrollment Surges Again, Increases 7 Per Cent to 70,601," *Journalism Educator* 33 (January 1979), p. 3.

8. See Paul V. Peterson, "Journalism and Mass Comm Enrollment Leveled Off in '87," *Journalism Educator* 42 (Spring 1988), pp. 4–10; and Lee B. Becker, "Enrollment Growth Exceeds National University Averages," *Journalism Educator* (Autumn 1989), pp. 3–15.

9. For a discussion of some of the lawsuits and other strategies used, see Lee Jolliffe, "Liberal Feminism: The Strategies of an Activist Audience," paper presented to the Committee on the Status of Women of the Association for Education in Journalism and Mass Communications annual convention, Minneapolis, Minn., August 1990.

10. Judith S. Griffman, *Women in Television News* (New York: Columbia University Press, 1974), p. 4.

11. U.S. Bureau of the Census, Current Population Reports, Series P-70, No. 10, *Male-Female Differences in Work Experience, Occupation, and Earnings: 1984* (Washington, D.C.: U.S. Government Printing Office, 1987), p. 1.

12. See Beasley and Theus, *The New Majority*; Christine L. Ogan, Charlene J. Brown, and David H. Weaver, "Characteristics of Managers of Selected U.S. Daily Newspapers," *Journalism Quarterly* 56 (Winter 1979), pp. 803–809; and Evelyn Trapp Goodrick, "A Comparison of Women and Men on Editorial Page Staffs," paper presented to the Newspaper Division of the Association for Education in Journalism and Mass Communication, Washington D.C., August 1989.

13. Janet Brand, *ASNE Bulletin* (January 1986), p. 17.

14. Suzanne M. Bianchi and Daphne Spain, *American Women in Transition* (New York: Russell Sage Foundation, 1986), p. 10.

15. Francine D. Blau and Anne E. Winkler, "Women in the Labor Force: An Overview," in Jo Freeman, ed., *Women: A Feminist Perspective*, 4th ed. (Mountain View, Calif.: Mayfield Publishing Co., 1989) pp. 197–216.

16. Unfortunately, the small number of people of color interviewed in 1982–83 did not allow for in-depth statistical analysis by anything other than the white/nonwhite dichotomy.

17. See also Elizabeth M. Almquist, *Minorities, Gender and Work* (Lexington, Mass.: D. C. Heath, 1979); Angela Davis, *Women, Race and Class* (New York: Random House, 1981); and Margaret C. Simms and Julianne M. Malveaux, eds., *Slipping Through the Cracks: The Status of Black Women* (New Brunswick, N.J.: Transaction, 1986).

18. Claudia Goldin, *Understanding the Gender Gap: An Economic History of American Women* (New York: Oxford University Press, 1990), p. 27.

19. Paula Giddings, *When and Where I Enter: The Impact of Black Women on Race and Sex in America* (New York: W. Morrow, 1984), pp. 325–35.

20. Michele Collison, "More Young Black Men Choosing Not to Go to College," *The Chronicle of Higher Education* (Dec. 9, 1987), pp. 1, A26–A27.

21. Giddings, *When and Where I Enter*, p. 329.

22. Ibid., p. 7.

23. "Battling Affirmative Inaction," *Time* (Sept. 12, 1988), p. 64.

24. Christine L. Ogan, "Life at the Top for Men and Women Newspaper Managers: A Five-Year Update of Their Characteristics," a report for the Center for New Communications, Indiana University, May 1983.

25. Lee Stinnett, Linda G. Cunningham, and Barbara A. Henry, *The Changing Face of the Newsroom* (Washington, D.C.: American Society of Newspaper Editors, 1989).

26. Mary Frank Fox, "Women and Higher Education: Gender Differences in the Status of Students and Scholars," in Freeman, ed., *Women: A Feminist Perspective*, pp. 217–35.

27. For a more in-depth analysis of the wage gap among men and women journalists, see Lafky, "The Women of American Journalism," chap. 7; and "Economic Equity and the Journalistic Work Force," in *Women in Mass Communication*, ed. Pamela J. Creedon. Newbury Park, Calif.: Sage Publications, 1989.

28. See Suzanne M. Bianchi and Daphne Spain, *American Women in Transition* (New York: Russell Sage Foundation, 1986), p. 172. In most years, women have earned 60 cents for each $1 earned by men.

29. U.S. Department of Labor, Bureau of Labor Statistics, *Current Population Report*, P-60 series, March 1988.

30. Laura McClure, "Wage Gap Between Sexes Is Unchanged," *New Directions for Women* (January/February 1988), pp. 6, 8.

31. Ibid.

32. Ibid.

33. See, for example, Jane Bayes's article, "Occupational Sex Segregation and Comparable Worth," in *Comparable Worth, Pay Equity and Public Policy*, ed. Rita Mae Kelly and Jane Bayes (New York: Greenwood Press, 1988), pp. 3–47.

34. John J. Sweeney and Karen Nussbaum, *Solutions for the New Work Force*. Cabin John, Md./Washington, D.C.: Seven Locks Press, 1989.

35. Bowman, "Distaff Journalists," p. 113.

36. David H. Weaver, Christine L. Ogan, Charlene J. Brown, and Mary I. Benedict, *Women in Newspaper Management: A Status Report*. Research Report No. 2. Indiana University, Center for New Communications, School of Journalism, July 22, 1977.

37. Susan Holly, "Women in Management of Weeklies," *Journalism Quarterly* 56 (Winter 1979), pp. 810–15. Holly pointed out that weekly newspapers may be a dead-end job for some women and that it might be that men view weeklies as not prestigious enough and move on the daily newspapers, thus leaving more opportunities for women.

38. Jean Gaddy Wilson, "Women in the Newspaper Business," *presstime* (October 1986), pp. 31–37.

39. Vernon A. Stone, "Minority Men Shoot ENG, Women Take Advancement Tracks," *Communicator* (August 1988), pp. 10–14.

40. Ogan, "Life at the Top for Men and Women Newspaper Managers."

41. Bowman, "Distaff Journalists," p. 182.

42. Marion Marzolf, *Up from the Footnote: A History of Women Journalists* (New York: Hastings House, 1977), p. 19.

43. Ibid.

44. William Rivers, *The Opinion Makers* (Boston: Beacon Press, 1965), pp. 31–33.

8. Television, Radio, and Newspaper Journalists

1. Roper Organization Inc., *Trends in Attitudes toward Television and Other Media: A Twenty-four Year Review* (New York: Television Information Office, 1983). Although this report shows increasing percentages of the public saying they rely on television for "most of your news about what's going on in the world today," this measure has been criticized by several scholars as not being a valid indicator of actual frequency of use of TV news. See, for example, Robert L. Stevenson and Kathryn P. White, "The Cumulative Audience of Network Television News," *Journalism Quarterly* 57 (Autumn 1980): 477–81, R. C. Adams, "Newspapers and Television as News Information Media," *Journalism Quarterly* 58 (Winter 1981): 627–29, and John P. Robinson, "Daily News Habits of the American Public," American Newspaper Publishers Association *News Research Report*, no. 15 (September 22, 1978). Adams found that a majority of respondents in three southern California communities named a local newspaper as the source of most information about local events and activities, and Robinson found that on a typical day, more people read a newspaper than watch a television news program. Thus even if more Americans report reliance on television for news, this perception may not be grounded in actual frequency of use of TV news, especially when it comes to local news.

2. Edwin Diamond, *Sign Off: The Last Days of Television* (Cambridge, Mass.: MIT Press, 1982), p. 6.

3. Ibid.

4. Arnold H. Ismach and Everette E. Dennis, "A Profile of Newspaper and Television Reporters in a Metropolitan Setting," *Journalism Quarterly* 55 (Winter 1978): 739–43, 898.

5. John W. C. Johnstone, Edward J. Slawski, and William W. Bowman, *The News People: A Sociological Portrait of American Journalists and Their Work* (Urbana: University of Illinois Press, 1976), pp. 4–11.

6. Lee Becker, "Print or Broadcast: How the Medium Influences the Reporter," in James S. Ettema and D. Charles Whitney, eds., *Individuals in Mass Media Organizations: Creativity and Constraints* (Beverly Hills, Calif.: Sage Publications, 1982).

7. Jack McLeod and Searle E. Hawley, Jr., "Professionalism Among Newsmen," *Journalism Quarterly* 41 (Autumn 1964): 529–38.

8. George Pollard, "Professionalism Among Canadian Newsworkers: A Cross-Media Analysis," *Gazette* 36 (1985): 21–38.

9. Becker, "Print or Broadcast."

10. U.S. Bureau of the Census, *Statistical Abstract of the United States, 1982–1983*, 103rd ed., p. 379.

11. For example, 26.3 percent of the full-time instructional faculty at colleges and universities in 1980–81 were women. These figures are cited in Martin J. Finklestein, *The American Academic Profession* (Columbus: Ohio State University Press, 1984).

12. Johnstone et al., *The News People*.

13. U.S. Bureau of the Census, *Statistical Abstract of the United States*, pp. 32, 33, 54, 55.

14. "Journalism Under Fire," *Time* (December 12, 1983), pp. 76–93.

15. Michael W. Singletary, "Commentary: Are Journalists 'Professionals'?" *Newspaper Research Journal* 3 (January 1982): 75.

16. Ismach and Dennis, "Profile of Newspaper and Television Reporters," and Pollard, "Professionalism Among Canadian Newsworkers."

17. Becker, "Print or Broadcast."

9. Journalists' Best Work

1. Overall intercoder reliability: Holsti's R = .75; Scott's pi = .56.

2. Sixty-seven percent of these respondents sent only one story and 11 percent submitted two. About one-quarter of the sample submitted three or more stories. Most multiple submissions were a series of stories on the same topic or a set of stories covering an on-going news event. (One respondent submitted 20 such stories.) Some respondents sent multiple stories which were unrelated. However, only one story was coded for each respondent. In the case of multiple submissions, the story discussed in the interview was coded for this study. If it was impossible to tell which story had been discussed, a single story was selected by generating a random number to determine which story would be included.

3. The newspaper journalists who submitted stories did not differ significantly from the newspaper journalists included in the original study on several demographic dimensions, including age, years in journalism, political orientation, education, and job satisfaction. Those who sent stories made somewhat less in yearly income (mean of $13,782 versus $19,395), however, and included a greater proportion of women (45 percent versus 37 percent). The greater number of women in the group that sent stories is responsible in part for the discrepancy in incomes, since the average income for women is lower than for men.

In addition, those journalists who sent stories did not differ significantly from the journalists in our larger sample of 1,001. Means for journalists in the larger sample of 1,001 compared to the 131 who submitted stories for this study were: years in journalism, 13.1 to 10.8; job satisfaction (a 7-point scale) 5.4 to 5.5;

political orientation (100-point scale) 47.8 to 50.7; education (6-point scale) 3.9 to 3.7; age 37.3 years to 35.8 years.

4. Judee K. Burgoon, Michael Burgoon, and Charles K. Atkin, *The World of the Working Journalist* (New York: Newspaper Advertising Bureau, 1982).

5. Ibid., p. 69.

6. See for example: Bernard C. Cohen, *The Press and Foreign Policy* (Princeton, N.J.: Princeton University Press, 1963); John W. C. Johnstone, Edward J. Slawski, and William W. Bowman, *The News People: A Sociological Portrait of American Journalists and Their Work* (Urbana: University of Illinois Press, 1976); Hugh M. Culbertson, "Three Perspectives on American Journalism," *Journalism Monographs* 83 (June 1983); and Frederick Fico, "News Coverage of the Indiana State Senate: An Interaction Theory Approach" (Ph.D. dissertation, Indiana University, 1982).

7. To code responses to the open-ended questions and the 131 stories, we measured the seven journalistic roles as follows: Does the respondent mention/ Does the story exhibit:

· adversarial stance or skepticism toward government or a public official?
· adversarial stance or skepticism toward business?
· analysis or interpretation of complex problems?
· investigations of claims made by government?
· discussion of governmental policy as it is developed?
· timeliness (gets story to public quickly)?
· an appeal to the widest possible audience?

We also looked for evidence of the three more general journalistic roles in both responses to open-ended questions about best work and stories submitted by asking questions such as: Can the story be characterized as representing one of the three role concepts? Does anything in the story suggest the:

· Disseminator Role: story tries to convey only the facts. Information is presented in an objective, straightforward way. Story is devoid of interpretation or analysis.

· Interpretive Role: story tries to explain the "why." Story goes beyond the facts to include interpretation, analysis, ramifications, impact or effect.

· Adversarial Role: story displays skepticism toward an individual, an institution of business, or government. Story displays evidence of conflict or confrontation between journalist and a source.

In coding responses to open-ended questions, we looked for evidence in terms of what the journalist actually mentioned about the story.

8. While our intercoder reliability for coding of role concepts was sufficient (Holsti's R = .80; Scott's pi = .50), coders analyzing the responses to open-ended questions based their decisions on the descriptions of stories, not on the actual stories themselves. We believe that some responses about best work were coded as disseminator stories when they may actually have contained interpretation and analysis. Journalists asked to briefly explain what a story was about may not have conveyed to interviewers the interpretive or analytical nature of the story.

This explanation applies equally to the discrepancy found in the individual media role of "analysis and interpretation of complex problems." Of the seven roles, the other two with discrepancies probably occurred because journalists are less likely to mention or discuss the timely nature of their stories or their appeal to a broad audience even when those qualities are evident in their stories. Newspaper stories were coded as getting the story to the public quickly (timely) whenever there was evidence that coverage occurred soon after the event, usually within one or two days. Forty-seven percent of those stories contained that quality. But in the larger sample of question responses, only 15 percent mentioned timeliness as a quality. We assume that more than 15 percent of the stories journalists discussed were timely stories, but timeliness is probably considered a given — part of the definition of news in the first place.

9. To conduct this analysis, we created three variables to indicate whether a journalist had endorsed one of the three role orientations or not, and three variables to indicate whether a journalist had written a story characterized by one of the three role orientations or not. We then did three cross-tabulations using the endorsement variable by the content variable to determine the percent of journalistis who endorsed each role and wrote stories characterized by the same role. After comparing these percentages with the number of stories generally written of each role type, we found that only those who endorsed the interpretive role were more likely to write stories of the interpretive type. The relationship did not stand for endorsers of the disseminator and adversarial roles. (See table 9.4 for details.)

10. Gaye Tuchman, "Objectivity as Strategic Ritual: An Examination of Newsmen's Notions of Objectivity," *American Journal of Sociology*, 77 (January 1972), pp. 660–79.

10. Conclusions

1. David H. Weaver and Richard G. Gray, "Journalism and Mass Communication Research in the United States: Past, Present, and Future," in G. Cleveland Wilhoit and Harold de Bock, eds., *Mass Communication Review Yearbook*, vol. 1 (Beverly Hills, Calif.: Sage Publications, 1980).

2. John Johnstone, Edward Slawski, and William Bowman, *The News People* (Urbana: University of Illinois Press, 1976), p. 181.

3. W. A. Swanberg, *Pulitzer* (New York: Scribner, 1967), pp. 386–87.

4. Personal interview with David Hawpe, Managing Editor, *Courier-Journal*, Louisville, Kentucky, September 28, 1984.

5. Ibid.

6. Johnstone, Slawski, and Bowman, *News People*, p. 188.

7. Ibid., p. 184.

8. Ibid.

9. For arguments in favor of the "total newspaper" approach to management and marketing, see Jon G. Udell, *The Economics of the American Newspaper* (New York: Hastings House Communication Arts Books, 1978), pp. 40–63.

10. Hawpe interview.

11. Michael J. O'Neill, "A Problem for the Republic—a Challenge for Editors," as published in *The Adversary Press* (St. Petersburg, Fla.: Modern Media Institute, 1983), pp. 2–15.

12. Hawpe interview.

13. Ibid.

14. Ibid.

15. Personal interview with Lawrence "Bo" Connor, Managing Editor, *Indianapolis Star*, October 12, 1984.

16. See chap. 1 for a quote from Watterson, as quoted in Tiffany Blake, "The Editorial, Past, Present, and Future," *Colliers's* 48 (September 23, 1911): 35, and chap. 5 for a discussion of professionalism and the U.S. journalist.

Appendix I

1. John Johnstone, Edward Slawski, and William Bowman, *The News People* (Urbana: University of Illinois Press, 1976), pp. 4–11.

2. Judee K. Burgoon, Michael Burgoon, and Charles K. Atkin, *The World of the Working Journalist* (New York: Newspaper Advertising Bureau, 1982).

3. Johnstone, Slawski, and Bowman, *News People*, p. 5.

BIBLIOGRAPHY

"Accredited Journalism and Mass Communications Education." Available from the Accrediting Council on Education in Journalism and Mass Communications (ACEJMC), School of Journalism, P.O. Box 838, University of Missouri, Columbia, MO. 65205.

Adams, R. C. "Newspapers and Television as News Information Media." *Journalism Quarterly* 58 (Winter 1981): 627–29.

Almquist, Elizabeth M. *Minorities, Gender and Work*. Lexington, Mass.: D. C. Heath, 1979.

Altheide, David L. *Creating Reality: How TV News Distorts Events*. Beverly Hills, Calif.: Sage Publications, 1974.

American Newspaper Publishers Association. *Facts about Newspapers '84*, April 1984.

American Newspaper Publishers Association Research Institute. "OCRs and VDTs: Electronic Applications in ANPA-Member Newspaper Departments for 1981." Easton, Pa.: ANPA Research Institute, 1982.

Bagdikian, Ben H. "Woodstein U.: Notes on the Mass Production and Questionable Education of Journalists." *Atlantic* 238, no. 3 (March 1977).

Beasley, Maurine. "Women in Journalism Education: The Formative Period, 1908–1930." *Journalism History* 13 (Spring 1986): 10–18.

Beasley, Maurine H., and Kathryn T. Theus. *The New Majority: A Look at What the Preponderance of Women in Journalism Means to the Schools and to the Professions*. Lanham, Md.: University Press of America, 1988.

de Beauvoir, Simone. *The Second Sex*. Translated by H. M. Parshley. New York: Bantam Books, 1961. Originally published in French, 1949.

Becker, Lee B. "Enrollment Growth Exceeds National University Averages." *Journalism Educator* 43 (Autumn 1989): 3–15.

———. "Print or Broadcast: How the Medium Influences the Reporter." In James S. Ettema and D. Charles Whitney, eds., *Individuals in Mass Media Organizations: Creativity and Constraints*. Beverly Hills, Calif.: Sage Publications, 1982.

Becker, Lee B., Idowa A. Sobowale, and Robin E. Cobbey. "Reporters and Their Professional and Organizational Commitment." In *Journalism Quarterly* (Winter 1979), as reprinted in G. Cleveland Wilhoit and Harold de Bock, eds., *Mass Communication Review Yearbook*, vol. 2, Beverly Hills, Calif.: Sage Publications, 1981.

Bennett, Roger, Randall L. Murray, and Guido H. Stempel III. "Editing Accuracy Drops with VDTs, Ohio Study Shows." *Journalism Educator* 32 (July 1977).

Berger, Gilda. *Women, Work and Wages*. New York: Franklin Watts, 1986.

Bernstein, Carl, and Bob Woodward. *All the President's Men*. New York: Simon and Schuster, 1974.

Bianchi, Suzanne M., and Daphne Spain. *American Women in Transition*. New York: Russell Sage Foundation, 1986.

Birkhead, Douglas. "Presenting the Press: Journalism and the Professional Project." Ph.D. dissertation, University of Iowa, 1982.

Black, Jay. "Professionalization of the Australian News Media: Journalists' Education, Training, and Job Satisfaction." Paper presented at the annual convention of the Association for Education in Journalism, Ohio University, Athens, Ohio, July 1982.

Blake, Tiffany. "The Editorial: Past, Present, and Future." *Collier's* 48 (September 23, 1911).

Blanchard, Margaret A. "The Hutchins Commission, The Press, and the Responsibility Concept." *Journalism Monographs*, May 1977.

Bleyer, Willard G. *Main Currents in the History of American Journalism*. Boston: Houghton Mifflin, 1927.

Boccardi, Louis D. "Press and Public: What to Do?" Address to the Associated Press Membership Meeting, reprinted in *APME News* 149 (August 1984).

Bogart, Leo. "The Public's Use and Perception of Newspapers." *Public Opinion Quarterly* 48 (Winter 1984).

———. *Press and Public: Who Reads What, Where, When, and Why in American Newspapers*. Hillsdale, N.J.: Lawrence Erlbaum Associates, 1981.

Bohere, G. *Profession: Journalist*. Geneva, Switzerland: International Labour Office, 1984.

Bowman, William. "Distaff Journalists: Women as a Minority Group in the News Media." Dissertation, University of Illinois at Chicago Circle, 1974.

Boylan, James. "Journalists' Self-Perceptions in the Wake of Vietnam and Watergate." *Wilson Quarterly Special Issue*, 1982.

Brand, Janet. "You can have it all—if you don't need too much sleep." *American Society of Newspaper Editors Bulletin*, January 1986, p. 17.

Britt, George. *Forty Years—Forty Millions*. New York: Farrar and Rinehart, 1935.

Burgoon, Judee K., Michael Burgoon, and Charles K. Atkin. "The World of the Working Journalist." New York: Newspaper Advertising Bureau, 1982.

Burgoon, Michael, and Judee K. Burgoon. "Summary of Findings from the Gannett Company Study." Unpublished report, Michigan State University, East Lansing, Michigan, September 1982.

Cannon, Lou. *Reporting: An Inside View*. Sacramento: California Journal Press, 1977.

Carey, James W. "A Plea for the University Tradition." *Journalism Quarterly* 55 (Winter 1978).

———. "The Communications Revolution and the Professional Communicator." *Sociological Review Monographs* 13 (January 1969).

Christians, Clifford G., Kim B. Rotzoll, and Mark Fackler. *Media Ethics: Cases and Moral Reasoning*. New York: Longman, 1983.

Clarke, Peter, and Eric Fredin. "Newspapers, Television, and Political Reasoning." *Public Opinion Quarterly* 42 (Summer 1978).

Cohen, Bernard C. *The Press and Foreign Policy*. Princeton: Princeton University Press, 1963.

Collison, Michele. "More Young Black Men Choosing Not to Go to College." *The Chronicle of Higher Education*, December 9, 1987, pp. 1, A26–A27.

Commission on Freedom of the Press. *A Free and Responsible Press*. Chicago: University of Chicago Press, 1947.

Crawford, Nelson Antrim. *The Ethics of Journalism*. New York: Alfred A. Knopf, 1924.

Creedon, Pamela J. *Women in Mass Communication*. Newbury Park, Calif.: Sage Publications, 1989.

Crook, James A. "How the New Technology Affects Student Editing." *Journalism Educator* 31 (January 1977).

Culbertson, Hugh M. "Three Perspectives on American Journalism." *Journalism Monographs* 83 (June 1983).

Davis, Angela. *Women, Race and Class*. New York: Random House, 1981.

Diamond, Edwin. *Sign Off: The Last Days of Television*. Cambridge, Mass.: MIT Press, 1982.

Donsbach, Wolfgang. "Journalists' Conceptions of Their Audience." *Gazette* 32 (1983): 19–36.

———. "Legitimacy through Competence Rather Than Value Judgments: The Concept of Journalistic Professionalization Reconsidered." *Gazette* 27 (1981): 47–67.

The Dow Jones Newspaper Fund, Inc. *1984 Journalism Career and Scholarship Guide*. Princeton, N.J.: Dow Jones Newspaper Fund, 1984.

Emery, Edwin, and Michael Emery. *The Press in America*. 5th ed. Englewood Cliffs, N.J.: Prentice-Hall, 1978, p. 140.

Epstein, Edward Jay. *News from Nowhere: Television and the News*. New York: Vintage Books, 1974.

Fico, Frederick. "News Coverage of the Indiana State Senate: An Interaction Theory Approach." Dissertation, Indiana University, 1982.

Finklestein, Martin J. *The American Academic Profession*. Columbus: Ohio State University Press, 1984.

Fisher, Roy M. "Editing by Pencil Found Slightly Faster Than by VDT." *Publisher's Auxiliary* 130 (March 27, 1978).

Fishman, Mark. *Manufacturing the News*. Austin: University of Texas Press, 1980.

Francke, Warren T., and Douglas A. Anderson. "Expectations and Experience in Conversion to VDTs." *Journalism Quarterly* 57 (Winter 1980).

Franklin, Benjamin. *The Autobiography of Benjamin Franklin*. Edited by Leonard W. Labaree. New Haven: Yale University Press, 1964.

Freeman, Jo, ed. *Women: A Feminist Perspective*. Fourth edition. Mountain View, Calif.: Mayfield Publishing Co., 1989.

Fuchs, Victor R. *Women's Quest for Economic Equality*. Cambridge, Mass.: Harvard University Press, 1988.

Gans, Herbert J. *Deciding What's News: A Study of CBS Evening News, NBC Nightly News, Newsweek, and Time*. New York: Vintage Books, A Division of Random House, 1979.

Garrison, Bruce. "Electronic Editing Systems and Their Impact on News Decision Making." *Newspaper Research Journal* 3 (January 1982).

Giddings, Paula. *When and Where I Enter*. New York: W. Morrow, 1984.

Giffman, Judith S. *Women in Television News*. New York: Columbia University Press, 1974.

Goldin, Claudia. *Understanding the Gender Gap*. New York: Oxford University Press, 1990.

Goodrick, Evelyn Trapp. "A Comparison of Women and Men on Editorial Page Staffs." Paper presented at the annual convention of the Association for Education in Journalism and Mass Communication, Washington, D.C., August 1989.

Gray, Richard G. "Implications of the New Information Technology for Democracy." In John W. Ahlhauser, ed., *Electronic Home News Delivery: Journalistic and Public Policy Implications*. Bloomington: School of Journalism and Center for New Communications, Indiana University, 1981.

Green, Bill. "The Fake Pulitzer Story: 'How Did It All Happen?' " *Louisville Courier-Journal*, April 26, 1981.

Hess, Stephen. "Adtech and the Washington Reporters." In Gerald Benjamin, ed., *The Communications Revolution in Politics*, vol. 34, no. 4. New York: Academy of Political Science, 1982.

———. *The Washington Reporters*. Washington D.C.: Brookings Institution, 1981.

Hirsch, Paul M. "Occupational, Organizational, and Institutional Models in Mass Media Research: Toward an Integrated Framework." In Paul Hirsch, Peter V. Miller, and F. Gerald Kline, eds., *Strategies for Communication Research*. Beverly Hills, Calif.: Sage Publications, 1977.

Holly, Susan. "Women in Management of Weeklies." *Journalism Quarterly* 56 (Winter 1979): 810–15.

Hudson, Frederic. *Journalism in the United States, 1690–1872*. New York: Harper and Brothers, 1873.

International Association of Business Communicators. *Profile/83 IABC Special Report*.

Ismach, Arnold H., and Everette E. Dennis. "A Profile of Newspaper and Television Reporters in a Metropolitan Setting." *Journalism Quarterly* 55 (Winter 1978): 739–43, 898.

Johnstone, John W. C., Edward J. Slawski, and William W. Bowman. *The News People: A Sociological Portrait of American Journalists and Their Work*. Urbana: University of Illinois Press, 1976.

Jolliffe, Lee. "Liberal Feminism: The Strategies of an Activist Audience." Paper presented to the Committee on the Status of Women at the annual convention, Association for Education in Journalism and Mass Communication, Minneapolis, Minn., August 1990.

Journalism Ethics Report, 1983. Published by the National Ethics Committee of the Society of Professional Journalists, Sigma Delta Chi.

Keel, Vernon A., and Victor Larouche. "Journalists in the United States, English Canada, and Quebec: Beginning a Comparative Analysis." Paper presented at the organizational meeting of the Midwest Canadian Studies Association, Northwestern University, Evanston, Illinois, September 1984.

Kelly, Rita Mae, and Jane Bayes. *Comparable Worth, Pay Equity and Public Policy*. New York: Greenwood Press, 1988.

Killenberg, George. "Taking the Electronic Plunge? The Questions You Have to Ask." *APME News* 98 (March 1977).

King, Henry. *American Journalism*. New York: Arno Press, 1970.

———. "The Pay and Rank of Journalists." *Forum* 18 (January 1895).

Kirkhorn, Michael. "The Curious Existence: Journalistic Identity in the Interwar Period." In Catherine L. Covert and John D. Stevens, eds., *Mass Media between the Wars*. Syracuse, N.Y.: Syracuse University Press, 1984.

Kraft, Joseph. "The Imperial Media." *Commentary*, May 1981.

Kurtz, Larry D. "The Electronic Editor." *Journal of Communication* 30 (Summer 1980).

———. "Study Examines Impact of Electronic Newsroom." *Editor & Publisher*, September 23, 1978.

Ladd, Everett Carll Jr., and Seymour Martin Lipset. *Survey of the Social, Political, and Educational Perspectives of American College and University Faculty*. New York: National Institute for Education, 1967.

Lafky, Sue A. "The Women of American Journalism." Dissertation, Indiana University, 1990.

Lambeth, Ed. "Reporting Washington for Main Street." *Washington Journalism Review* 2 (December 1980).

Lane, William Coolidge. "The Printer of the Harvard Theses of 1771." *Publications of the Colonial Society of Massachusetts* 26, Transactions; 1924–1926.

Lawrence, Arthur. *Journalism as a Profession*. London: Hodder and Stoughton, 1903.

Lee, Alfred McClung. *The Daily Newspaper in America*. New York: Macmillan Co., 1937.

Lichter, S. Robert, and Stanley Rothman. "Media and Business Elites." *Public Opinion* 4, no. 5 (October/November 1981).

Lindley, William R. "Does the VDT Affect News Content?" *Journalism Resource Information*, Fall 1977 (Idaho State University mimeograph).

———. *Journalism and Higher Education: The Search for Academic Purpose*. Stillwater, Okla.: Journalistic Services, 1975.

Lippmann, Walter. *Public Opinion*. New York: Harcourt, Brace and Co. 1922.

———. *Liberty and the News*. New York: Harcourt, Brace and Howe, 1920.

Lippman, Walter, and Charles Merz. "A Test of the News." Supplement to the *New Republic*, August 4, 1920.

McClure, Laura. "Wage Gap Between Sexes Is Unchanged." *New Directions for Women*, January/February 1988, pp. 6, 8.

McCulloch, Frank, ed. *Drawing the Line: How Thirty-one Editors Solved Their Toughest Ethical Dilemmas*. Washington D.C.: American Society of Newspaper Editors Foundation, 1984.

McLeod, Jack, and Ramona Rush. "Professionalization of Latin American and U.S. Journalists." *Journalism Quarterly* (Autumn 1969).

McLeod, Jack, and Searle E. Hawley, Jr. "Professionalism Among Newsmen." *Journalism Quarterly* 41 (Autumn 1964): 529–38.

Marzio, Peter. *The Men and Machines of American Journalism*, p. 49. Washington D.C.: Smithsonian Institution, 1973.

Marzolf, Marion. *Up from the Footnote*. New York: Hastings House, 1977.

Merrill, John C., and Ralph L. Lowenstein. *Media, Messages, and Men*. 2d ed. New York: Longman, 1979.

Meyer, Philip. *Editors, Publishers, and Newspaper Ethics*. Washington D.C.: American Society of Newspaper Editors, 1983.

Mindes, Marvin W., and Alan C. Adcock. "Trickster, Hero, Helper: A Report on the Lawyer Image." *American Bar Research Journal* 177, no. 1 (Winter 1982).

Mott, Frank Luther. *American Journalism; A History: 1690–1960*. 3d ed. New York: Macmillan Co., 1962.

Nam, Sunwoo. "The Government Information Apparatus of the Federal Republic of Germany." *Political Communication and Persuasion* 2, no. 2 (1983).

Nord, David Paul. *Newspapers and New Politics: Midwestern Municipal Reform, 1890–1900*. Ann Arbor, Mich.: UMI Research Press, 1981.

Nordyke, Bob. "Opinions Vary on Electronics' Effect." *Editors in the Electronic Age*. Louisville, Ky.: Associated Press Managing Editors Convention, 1983.

Ogan, Christine L. "Life at the Top for Men and Women Newspaper Managers: A Five-Year Update of Their Characteristics." Center for New Communications, School of Journalism, Indiana University, Bloomington, Ind., May 1983.

———. "Manager Computer Use Survey." Unpublished paper, School of Journalism, Indiana University, 1982.

Ogan, Christine L., Charlene J. Brown, and David H. Weaver, "Characteristics of Managers of Selected U.S. Daily Newspapers." *Journalism Quarterly* 56 (Winter 1979): 803–809.

Ogan, Christine L., and David H. Weaver. "Job Satisfaction in Selected U.S. Daily Newspapers: A Study of Male and Female Top-Level Managers." *Mass Communication Review* 6 (Winter 1978–79): 20–26.

O'Neill, Michael J. "A Problem for the Republic—A Challenge for Editors." An address to the American Society of Newspaper Editors, May 5, 1982. Reprinted in *The Adversary Press*. St. Petersburg, Fla.: Modern Media Institute, 1983.

Ott, Louise, and Linda Russman. "The Story of Women in Communications." *The Professional Communicator*, Fall 1989, pp. 7–11, 35.

Parton, James. *The Life of Horace Greeley*. Boston: J. R. Osgood and Co., 1872.

Patterson, Eugene C. "The Press: A Few Problems to Solve." Convocation address to the Indiana University School of Journalism, Bloomington, Indiana, September 6, 1983.

Peterson, Paul V. "Journalism and Mass Comm Enrollment Leveled Off in '87." *Journalism Educator* 42 (Spring 1988).

———. "J-School Enrollments Hit Record 91,016." *Journalism Educator* 37, no. 4 (Winter 1983).

———. "Today's Journalism Students: Who They Are and What They Want to Do." Columbus: School of Journalism, Ohio State University, 1981.

———. "Journalism Enrollment Levels Off; Growth Rate Declines Sharply." *Journalism Educator* 31, no. 4 (January 1977).

———. "Enrollment Surges Again, Increases 7 Per Cent to 70,601." *Journalism Educator* 33 (January 1979).

———. "Journalism Growth Continues at Hefty 10.8 Per Cent Rate." *Journalism Educator* 26, no. 4 (January 1972).

Peterson, Paul V., and Lee B. Becker. "Enrollment Growth Exceeds National University Averages." *Journalism Educator* 43 (Autumn 1989).

Pollard, George. "Professionalism Among Canadian Newsworkers: A Cross-Media Analysis." *Gazette* 36 (1985): 21–38.

Pulitzer, Joseph. "The College of Journalism." *North American Review*, May 1904.

Randall, Starr D. "Effect of Electronic Editing on Error Rate of Newspaper." *Journalism Quarterly* 56 (Spring 1979).

Ringle, Ken. "Less Than 45 Percent of U.S. Doctors Now Belong to the AMA." *Washington Post*, March 11, 1984.

Rivers, William. *The Opinion Makers*. Boston: Beacon Press, 1965.

Rivers, William, Wilbur Schramm, and Clifford Christians. *Responsibility in Mass Communication*. 3d ed. New York: Harper and Row, 1980.

Rivers, William L. "The Correspondents after Twenty-five Years." *Columbia Journalism Review* 1 (Spring 1962).

Roberts, Donald F., and Christine M. Bachen. "Mass Communication Effects." *Annual Review of Psychology* 32, (1981).

Robinson, Joch. "Women Journalists in Canadian Dailies." *Working Papers in Communications*. Montreal: McGill University, 1981.

Robinson, John P. "Daily News Habits of the American Public." American Newspaper Publishers Association *News Research Report*, no. 15, September 22, 1978.

Rogers, Jay. "VDTs, TV Haven't Shocked Editors." *Editors in the Electronic Age*. Louisville, Ky.: Associated Press Managing Editors Convention, 1983.

Roper Organization Inc. *Trends in Attitudes toward Television and Other Media: A Twenty-four Year Review*. New York: Television Information Office, 1983.

Rosten, Leo. *The Washington Correspondents*. New York: Harcourt, Brace and Co., 1927.

Rothman, Stanley, and S. Robert Lichter. "Are Journalists a New Class?" *Business Forum*, Spring 1983.

Salter, L. G. "Edgar Guest Longs for 'Good Old Days.' " *Editor & Publisher* 64, no. 26 (November 14, 1931).

Schlesinger, Arthur. *Prelude to Independence*. New York: Knopf, 1958.

Schudson, Michael. *Discovering the News*. New York: Basic Books, 1978.

Schulman, Bob. "The Liberal Tilt of Our Newsroom." *Bulletin of the American Society of Newspaper Editors*, no. 654 (October 1982).

Shaw, Donald L. "News Bias and the Telegraph: A Study of Historical Change." *Journalism Quarterly* 44 (Spring 1967).

———. "Technology: Freedom for What?" In Ronald T. Farrar and John D. Stevens, eds., *Mass Media and the National Experience*. New York: Harper and Row, 1971.

Shipley, Linda J., and James K. Gentry. "How Electronic Editing Equipment Affects Editing Performance." *Journalism Quarterly* 58 (Autumn 1981).

Shipley, Linda J., James K. Gentry, and John W. Clarke. *VDT vs. Pencil: A Comparison of Speed and Accuracy*. Columbia: University of Missouri School of Journalism Monograph, 1979.

Shoquist, Joseph. "Coping with the Editorial Load: At *The Milwaukee Journal*." *American Newspaper Publishers Association Research Institute Bulletin*, December 7, 1977.

Sigelman, Lee. "Reporting the News: An Organizational Analysis." *American Journal of Sociology* 79 (July 1973).

Simms, Margaret C., and Julianne M. Malveaux, eds. *Slipping Through the Cracks: The Status of Black Women*. New Brunswick, N.J.: Transaction, 1986.

Sinclair, Upton. *The Brass Check*. Pasadena, Calif.: Author, 1920.

Singletary, Michael W. "Commentary: Are Journalists 'Professionals?' " *Newspaper Research Journal* 3 (January 1982): 75–87.

Smith, Anthony. "The Long Road to Objectivity and Back Again." In George Boyce, ed., *Newspaper History from the Seventeenth Century to the Present Day*. Beverly Hills, Calif.: Sage Publications, 1978.

Smith, Conrad. "Newsgathering Technology and the Content of Local Television News." *Journal of Broadcasting* 28 (Winter 1984).

Smythe, Ted Curtis. "The Reporter, 1880–1900." *Journalism History* 7, no. 1 (Spring 1980).

Steel, Ronald. *Walter Lippmann and the American Century*. New York: Vintage Books, A Division of Random House, 1980.

Steffens, Lincoln. "Tweed Days in St. Louis." and "The Shamelessness of St. Louis." In *The Shame of the Cities*. New York: Hill and Wang, 1957.

Stevenson, Robert L., and Kathryn P. White. "The Cumulative Audience of Network Television News." *Journalism Quarterly* 57 (Autumn 1980): 477–81.

Stinnett, Lee, Linda G. Cunningham, and Barbara A. Henry. *The Changing Face of the Newsroom*. Washington D.C.: American Society of Newspaper Editors, May 1989.

Stone, Vernon A. "Women Gaining as News Directors." *RTNDA Communicator*, October 1988, pp. 20–21.

———. "Minority Men Shoot ENG, Women Take Advancement Tracks." *RTNDA Communicator*, August 1988, pp. 10–14.

———. "Then and Now: News Directors' Profiles and Problems; Noteworthy Changes in a Decade of RTNDA Surveys." *RTNDA Communicator*, 1983.

Sutphin, Marty. "Plug into a Terminal: Faster, Neater, and More Error-Free." *Quill*, November 1973.

Sweeney, John J., and Karen Nussbaum. *Solutions for the New Work Force*. Cabin John, Md./Washington D.C.: Seven Locks Press, 1989.

Thomas, Isaiah. *The History of Printing in America*. vol. 1. New York: Burt Franklin, 1874.

de Tocqueville, Alexis. *Democracy in America*. New York: Alfred A. Knopf, 1948.

Tuchman, Gaye. *Making News*. New York: Free Press, 1978.

————. "Objectivity as Strategic Ritual: An Examination of Newsmen's Notions of Objectivity." *American Journal of Sociology* 77 (January 1972): 660–79.

U.S. Bureau of the Census. *Male-Female Differences in Work Experience, Occupation, and Earnings: 1984*. Current Population Reports, Series P-70, No. 10. Washington, D.C.: U.S. Government Printing Office, 1987.

U.S. Bureau of the Census. *Statistical Abstract of the United States 1984*. 104th ed. Washington, D.C.: U.S. Government Printing office, 1984.

U.S. Bureau of the Census. *Statistical Abstract of the United States 1972*. 93d ed. Washington, D.C.: U.S. Government Printing Office, 1972.

U.S. Bureau of the Census. *Statistical Abstract of the United States, 1982–1983*. 103rd ed. Washington, D.C.: U.S. Government Printing Office, 1983.

U.S. Department of Labor, Bureau of Labor Statistics. *Current Population Report*, P-60 series, March 1988.

U.S. Department of Labor, Bureau of Labor Statistics. *National Survey of Professional, Administrative, Technical,and Clerical Personnel*, Bulletin 2181, March 1983.

Vaubel, Karl-Heinz. "Seven-hundred Journalists in Search of Information; The Federal Capital Bonn: An Open News Centre." *Scala* 2, no. 1 (January 1985).

"VDT Attitude Survey Includes Eighty-two Papers." *Editor and Publisher*, April 24, 1978.

Wallraff, Gunter. *The Undesirable Journalist*. Woodstock, N.Y.: Overlook Press, 1979.

————. *Der Aufmacher* (Kiepenheuer and Witsch: Cologne, 1977).

Weaver, David H. *Videotex Journalism: Teletext, Viewdata, and the News*. Hillsdale, N.J.: Lawrence Erlbaum Associates, 1983.

Weaver, David H., Doris Graber, Maxwell McCombs, and Chaim Eyal. *Media Agenda-Setting in a Presidential Election: Issues, Images, and Interest*. New York: Praeger, 1981.

Weaver, David, Dan Drew, and G. Cleveland Wilhoit. "U.S. Television, Radio and Daily Newspaper Journalists." *Journalism Quarterly* 63 (Winter 1986): 683–92.

Weaver, David H., Christine L. Ogan, Charlene J. Brown, and Mary I. Benedict. *Women in Newspaper Management: A Status Report*. Center for New Communications Research Report No. 2. School of Journalism, Indiana University, Bloomington, Ind., July 22, 1977.

Weaver, David H., and Richard G. Gray. "Journalism and Mass Communication Research in the United States: Past, Present, and Future." In G. Cleveland Wilhoit and Harold de Bock, eds., *Mass Communication Review Yearbook*, vol. 1. Beverly Hills, Calif.: Sage Publications, 1980.

Weaver, David H., and Judith M. Buddenbaum. "Newspapers and Television: A Review of Research on Uses and Effects." *American Newspaper Publishers Association News Research Report*, no. 19 (April 20, 1979). Also published in G. Cleveland Wilhoit and Harold de Bock, eds., *Mass Communication Review Yearbook*, vol. 1. Beverly Hills, Calif.: Sage Publications, 1980.

Weischenberg, Siegfried. "Journalismus." In Kurt Koszyk and Karl Hugo Pruys, *Handbuch der Massenkommunikation*. Munich: Deutschertaschenbuch Verlag, 1981.

Wilensky, Harold L. "The Professionalization of Everyone?" *American Journal of Sociology* 70, no. 2 (September 1964).

Williams, Talcott. *The Newspaperman*. New York: Charles Scribner's Sons, 1922.

Wilson, Jean Gaddy. ''Women in the Newspaper Business.'' *presstime*, October 1986, pp. 31–37.

Wright, John W. *The American Almanac of Jobs and Salaries*. New York: Avon Books, 1981.

Wroth, Lawrence C. *The Colonial Printer*. Charlottesville, Va.: Dominion Books, 1964.

Yoakam, Richard D. ''ENG: Electronic News Gathering in Local Television Stations.'' *Center for New Communications Report No. 12*. Bloomington, Ind.: School of Journalism, Indiana University, 1981.

INDEX

.